DIGITAL
LANDSCAPE
ARCHITECTURE
NOW

DIGITAL LANDSCAPE ARCHITECTURE NOW

NADIA AMOROSO

692 illustrations, 620 in color

Thames & Hudson

On the cover: Botanic Bridge Gwangju, South Korea
(© West 8 Urban Design & Landscape Architecture)

Digital Landscape Architecture Now © Thames & Hudson Ltd, London

Text © 2012 Nadia Amoroso

Foreword © 2012 George Hargreaves

Designed by Patrick Morrissey, Unlimited, www.weareunlimited.co.uk

First published in 2012 in hardcover in the United States of America by
Thames & Hudson Inc., 500 Fifth Avenue, New York, New York 10110

thamesandhudsonusa.com

Library of Congress Catalog Card Number 2012931630

ISBN 978-0-500-34282-4

Printed and bound in China by Everbest Printing Co Ltd

CONTENTS

FOREWORD
GEORGE HARGREAVES

The landscape architecture profession has seen a good deal of change in both content and representation tools. We now delve deeper into ecology and sustainability, and more recently into the economics of public landscapes, but it is representation through digital means that has seen the most variety and evolution over the last two decades. Many older practitioners (gasp, I am now one of those) can recall the analogue days – the hours setting up perspectives, trying to master drawings techniques, and the planning and crafting of models. In hindsight, one can see a clear relationship of form and technique.

It was certainly easier to portray a picturesque landscape or a modern straight-line landscape with these simple techniques, but as we tried to pursue, shall we say, more complex formations, we ran into our lack of representational talent or the limitations of analogue. In our case, we began to work with clay as a way to design and model ideas and forms at the same time, and with some degree of complexity. During this period (early to mid-1990s), our construction packages began to use computer-aided design (CAD) as the principal means for drafting. Here, we discovered the ability to study project detailing in three dimensions, rather than in simple plan and section. Both of these instances sprang from the desire to study and evolve design strategies and detailing, rather than mount a purely representational effort.

As we fast-forward to today and the contents of this book, digital representation has exploded and is in the hands of virtually every practitioner, except for the few 'fuzzies' still published by trade periodicals. It seems there are three main areas of work in digital representation. The first is a fairly conventional representation effort to depict in true proportion what the project will look like, but the ability to render real surfaces and plant materials through various techniques, including Photoshop, move these depictions far beyond the watercolour/prismacolour textures, replete with balloons. The second involves the use of collage and some perspectival set-up, used in concert to depict an idea of what the project is about or its feel, as opposed to a measured depiction. The third uses digital means as a way to study the design of the project, and not merely to represent it. This last use is perhaps best shown by the many architects whose projects do not have any corners, otherwise fondly known as 'blob' architecture.

This book is an exploration and survey of many facets of landscape architectural design and representation using digital means; it is an excellent collection of forward-thinking and innovative design and research explorations that use a digital palette to render progressive moves in the field of landscape architecture and design. The use of advanced 3D modelling computer applications has helped us to develop complex formal expressions with more accurate measures of space and earthwork volumes. We tend to work three dimensionally in the early stages of the design process; the wide range of digital tools – including 3D Studio MAX, Rhinoceros, Google SketchUp, 3D Land Desktop (the precursor to 3D Civil), Photoshop, to name a few – has allowed us to quickly dispense more complex designed forms with an understanding of scale, proportion and enclosure or openness. These tools assist us in areas of technology and information, advanced illustration and animation to produce innovative landscapes.

The changes in landscape architecture's digital realm over the last two decades have been tremendous. The adoption by most of the profession is complete, but it is still simply a tool: for designing, studying various aspects of a project, representing the project, and finally creating the legal documents for construction. Though digital tools will never ultimately do the designing for us, the digital realm allows us to expand our thinking and making of a project.

INTRODUCTION
NADIA AMOROSO

Digital Landscape Architecture Now presents a series of profiles of world-renowned landscape architects, researchers, artists and architects who are challenging traditional landscape design through digital means. The professionals in these pages are notable for their concern for radical design, use of fluid forms, and deep commitment to discovering environmentally and socially responsive methods for addressing site-design problems.

   This is a generation of professionals who approach common design issues through the use of new technologies and other digital methods. Their combined practice marks the twenty-first century as a groundbreaking era, informed by 'hybridity' and 'interdisciplinary' practices. This book explores how traditional landscape architectural practices are being pulled forward by innovation in digital tools, from software and mapping systems to interactive displays; what we see is a spirit of active interchange of ideas across disciplines, building on the early work of the environmentally concerned and technologically savvy landscape designers and architects who emerged in the 1960s.

   Through testing and sculpting a wide array of surface modalities, landscape architects actively engage in proposing design solutions, crafting new formal expressions of the land in ways that propose unique visions of possible and future use of space. This can be from individual building projects to participation in the formal reimaging of portions of urban or 'empty' space, or even the complete (re)rendering of city and countryside. As such, landscape design today is a field that is (re)integrating prior historical architectural concern with urban or rural planning. During the twentieth century, architecture often combined, incorporated or juxtaposed such aspects as horticulture, botany and industrial design to reveal possibilities, both philosophical and aesthetic, of the confluences between natural organic forms and technological solutions.

   The Brazilian landscape architect Roberto Burle Marx (1909–94) is one example of a professional who utilized new practices, creating a new aesthetic perspective that revealed how landscape architecture and architecture proper, as disciplines, can be effectively integrated. More recent incorporation of digital rendering with advanced software development, applied to landscape architecture, has expanded the possibilities and potential of combining and imaging interconnections between natural shapes, technological and industrial innovation, sustainability issues, and futurist projection. It is an exciting, expanding, interdisciplinary field.

History

Available methods to express, understand and project the possibilities of our natural and built environments into the future have changed over the years, and methods have grown exponentially in the very recent past. This can be attributed to the numerous opportunities inherent in both science and technology, found in the expanding capabilities of our digital world. Digital landscaping enables a great leap forward in the ability of landscape architects to present visual representations of the ways in which nature and built environments have changed and will continue to change, based upon design decisions and planning possibilities.

   Until recently, however, the majority of architectural ideas developed with digital technologies have been conservative, and orientated to past historical practices. This is evident in the continuing employment or presentation of traditional architectural designs, stemming from or emergent out of classical models and romantic nostalgia, or what is referred to as 'poetic silence' by Arne Saelen, in his introduction to Alex Sanchez Vidiella's *The Sourcebook of Contemporary Landscape Design* (2008). This, of course, is not a description to be discounted; in fact, as Sanchez Vidiella and Saelen maintain, beginning in the 1990s in Spain concern for the future of the planet, from its natural resources to where people live and their quality of life, its built environments and materials, entered the mainstream of concern of landscape architectural discourse.

In architecture, most changes have taken place with reference to drawing, modelling, fabrication, presentation graphics, and the new media in general. But the introduction of computers and even more advanced media technologies have enabled a greater connection between the fine arts, landscape architecture and architecture proper. Numerous formatting techniques have been used to scan and print, with digital technology increasingly relevant to practices of image production (drawing) and use of video for site-location mapping and fabrication. Additionally, the Internet as a resource has enabled landscape architects to interact worldwide, and share creative content regarding an infinite variety of subjects.

Where did these innovations occur, and what encouraged them or fuelled resistance towards the types of experimental projects discussed in this volume? While there may have been initial resistance within landscape architecture to use the new technologies to advance the possibilities and relevance of the field, increasing understanding of the potential of digital technologies to landscape architecture has actually increased the interest in and relevance of it as a specific field. In other words,

traditionalism in landscape architecture stems from the nineteenth century and earlier, from Romanticism and a nostalgia for nature, order and the picturesque. In contrast, contemporary landscape architecture embraces the possibilities of thinking about nature through science and technology; embracing environmental concerns with a growing realization that the twentieth century largely transformed much of the available land use and settlement patterns from rural to urban, as noted by Elizabeth Barlow Rogers in her book, *Landscape Design: A Cultural and Architectural History* (2001).

As Diana Balmori notes in *A Landscape Manifesto* (2010), landscape architecture is poised to become a prominent field in its mix of aesthetic concerns and technological approaches to understanding how we have used nature in the past. Key late twentieth-century designs promote an environmental agenda. These fundamental ideas emerged from the intersection of design firms and earth-artists in California in the 1960s, and later can be found in the work of designers based in the Netherlands. Balmori, drawing from Roberto Burle Marx and others, continues by describing the realization that 'we cannot re-establish ecosystems that have been thoroughly destroyed by human activity, but it is possible to understand scientifically how

they worked, and then to implement that knowledge in the creation of new ecologies' – a movement she calls 'ecogenesis'. This leads to the past decade where globalization, site-specific locality, and concern for community and culture have been incorporated as practical, aesthetic and philosophical concerns, engaging local and vernacular solutions via technology towards methods to address sustainability issues, as noted by Sanchez Vidiella.

One of the earliest practitioners to see the relevance of new technologies to landscape design was Thomas Church (1902–78), an environmental architect based in San Francisco. His studio nurtured the talent of, among others, Lawrence Halprin (1916–2009), an innovative landscape designer who participated in the Donnell Garden project in San Francisco, while part of the Church studio. In his practice, Rogers notes, Halprin promoted the idea of landscape architecture as process-orientated, rather than static. Halprin maintained that landscape architecture had the potential to be a highly creative profession, akin to artists' work, that landscape design could reflect 'celebrating human creativity and community life within the context of nature … using environmental motifs metaphorically in his designs'. Halprin was influenced by landscape architect

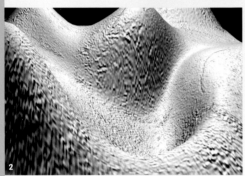

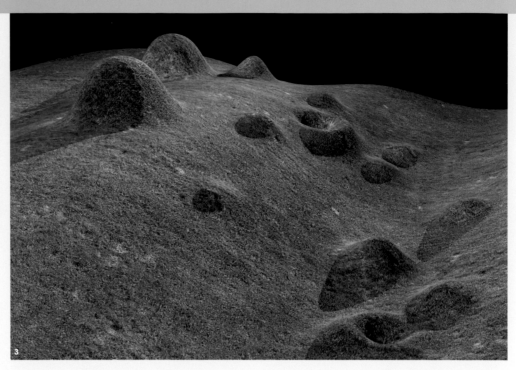

Ian McHarg's views on environmental planning, as was evident in his design for Sea Ranch, California, an eco-coastal housing development that integrated natural topography and landscape with urbanism. McHarg and Halprin were, says Rogers, inspired by the idea of 'seeing city and country as a continuum'.

The work of these innovators in the 1960s, a time of heightened interest in environmentalism that engaged with technological solutions, led to increasing attention to technologically informed, environmentally relevant original design, which often contained spiritual or psychological dimensions – recognized as being of particular concern, noted Rogers, as we began to live in ever-more urbanized environments. And as Diana Balmori observed, with the gap between 'nature' and the city diminishing, forward-thinking landscape architects found ways to enfold the city in nature, rather than replace nature with the city. International awareness of the need for solutions to problems, from avalanches in Iceland to creating ways for people to experience the remaining undisturbed countryside in Norway, Sanchez Vidiella wrote, also revealed the need for minimal intervention to natural environments as a new design paradigm. Digital-mapping techniques, virtual-reality programs, arrays of climate projection, and other new media melded with landscape

architecture to enable the important directions that were emerging. New technology stimulates innovators, and innovators are sensitive to science and to the practices of artists, to the ways that artists today are themselves using new media and technology in their work, envisioning advanced conceptions of land-shaping via virtual, interactive and living, spatial artwork.

Formal Expression, Surface Manipulation and Fabrication

Landscape architecture today can, at its most progressive, be regarded as a mix of practical, functional and visionary impulses. The work of its practitioners may involve, as described by Virginia McLeod in *Detail in Contemporary Landscape Architecture* (2008), everything from conceptualizing and designing parks, cultural centres, civic buildings, waterfronts and private home gardens, to reclaiming industrial wastelands. Developments in computer software have enabled the vast increase in the imaginative possibilities to be found in design and the built environments of the late twentieth and early twenty-first centuries. While in the past visionary architect-engineers may have proposed impossible utopian models, today CAD and other new media tools can provide architects with the capabilities of proposing and rendering drawings that

are abstract in their modalities, but also realizable. This permits more innovative building design, but also engenders improved design development in landscape forms, the visual communication between designers and clients, and opens ways to conceptualize the intersection of technology, form, art and nature, thus allowing landscape architecture to push the boundaries even further with art form. (Ian H. Thompson further discusses the idea of landscape architecture as an art form in *Ecology, Community and Delight: Sources of Values in Landscape Architecture*, 1999.)

Modelling and fabrication through digital means make it possible to pass information in an immaterial realm, as well as to create new forms of architectural designs, aided by the infinite possibilities provided through computer software programs. Architects today also expand their concepts by drawing on ideas and products produced in and disseminated through various mass media. This enables a kind of field work or research-matching design innovation to the client's or the public's desires and demands. Hybridity, or interdisciplinary practices, is therefore a positive future-orientated component of professional exchange, one made possible by the speed of international idea-sharing. Collaborations between visual artists and scientists, or landscape architects and climate specialists, also reveal the

1–3. University of Toronto, student projects in form-making and texturing.
4. Metagardens, Electronic Dreams.
5. Metagardens, Evoterrarium.
6. Kathryn Gustafson, L'Oréal factory.
7. Kathryn Gustafson, Penne-Mirabeau Freeway Exchange.

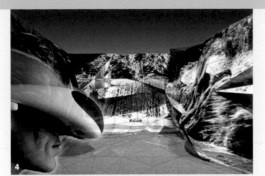

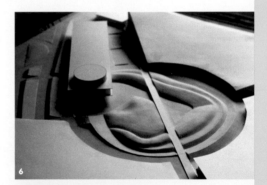

potential and the realization of interdisciplinary practice, made possible through digital technology and new media systems.

Highlighting key digital design experimentations and other technological agents used to conceive creative and radical landscape spaces, *Digital Landscape Architecture Now* documents achievements and explorations in landscape design. It also evaluates the contemporary firms and researchers who are at the forefront of these aesthetic movements, experimenting with alternative form-making and surface manipulation to achieve complex sculptural landscapes. 'Landscape architects are much concerned with beauty,' notes Thompson, as well as with using new media together with traditional values of form, aesthetics, social practices and ecological conscientiousness. Digital application has been the driver behind crafting more dynamic spaces in recent years, especially now with parametric and performative-landscapes, and fabrication of formal expression.

At the University of Toronto, graduate students have explored formal expressions and manipulation of volumetric form using digital processes. Responding to a given action – ripple, flow, bump, carve or pinch – they abstracted their selected action into experimental forms using 3D Studio MAX and Rhinoceros. Once the forms were generated, the students could then apply various groundcovers, which used textures to transform the digital forms into virtual landscapes (figs 1–3). The computer-generated landscapes were fabricated into physical models using 3D-plotting or CNC devices. These projects investigated a three-fold digital formal landscape expression, encompassing the digital model, image-modification materials testing, and physical output. Throughout the process, the students experimented with a range of modelling parameters to creatively engage with the technical and artistic challenges at each stage.

London-based Metagardens (pp. 156–65) is an innovative landscape design firm that is exploring the new possibilities. Through fabrication techniques such as taking rapid-prototyping landscapes from the computer to 1:1-scale creation, they are able to transform creative computer designs into 'real' physical landscapes. Metagardens has also developed a next-generation virtual reality landscape, or immersive environment, as demonstrated in their Electronic Dreams landscapes (fig. 4), as well as augmenting and creating reactive environments, such as their Evoterrarium landscape (fig. 5). Such far-reaching projects expand the possibilities of the field by developing dream-like, easily adaptable landscapes for purposes that range from the artistic to the practical.

8

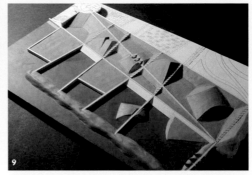

9

Materials, from soil to the most technologically advanced metals, can now be experimented with and employed, joining centuries-old ideas and vernacular processes to computer-modelled usage to create new forms, innovative constructions or new materials, notes Cordula Loidl-Reisch in her introduction to *Constructing Landscape: Materials, Techniques, Structural Components* (2008). Landscape architect Kathryn Gustafson (pp. 94–99) utilizes traditional media, such as clay, to express a poetic visual statement through techniques and methods of production. This is demonstrated in the sculptural clay models for the L'Oréal factory (fig. 6) and Penne-Mirabeau Freeway Exchange (fig. 7), both in France.

Such a commitment to artistry is shared by many landscape architects. The firm Hargreaves Associates (pp. 108–15) has spent more than two decades using clay as a communicative medium to create signature sculptural landscapes and achieve landforms that creatively engage communities, while fulfilling practical requirements (figs 8, 9). In comparison to the landscape architecture of previous generations, today's building designs, gardens, waterways and park projects utilize digital software tools and organic and industrial materials to express complex design solutions, radical forms, realistic renderings and digital production.

Parametric Landscape and Augmented Environments

One of the most influential early practitioners of new digital approaches to architectural design was Ian McHarg. Through his knowledge, he influenced modern geographic information systems, or GIS, which is used today in analysing materials for architecture. With reference to the environment, much concentration was based on topography, hydrology and vegetation. Along with employing GIS and terrain-modelling tools to create and troubleshoot site-related issues and planning design, many contemporary landscape architecture firms also test dynamic landscape designs by using performative measures and digital tools to change the landscape in response to fluctuating site conditions, users, events, and other environmental factors.

The Erie Plaza project (fig. 10), in Milwaukee, Wisconsin, by StossLU (pp. 236–41) employed a variety of digital tools, including software programs Rhinoceros, Flamingo, AutoCAD, Illustrator and Photoshop, to create a flexible landscape design. Digital tools allowed the team to test the ephemeral conditions of the waterfront site prior to construction by creating a flexible 'field' along the river walk, which generated creative forms and spaces through a series of mixed components originally generated in Rhinoceros. A variety of versions were tested in Rhino at this preliminary stage in order to troubleshoot all possible volumetric and topographic assumptions.

Software programs such as Grasshopper and Rhino have allowed landscape designers to push creative boundaries, implementing parametric measures in order to apply certain conditions, parameters and logic to the ever-changing design of the site. Parametric methods are highlighted in many other projects showcased in this publication, including StossLU's Bass River Park (p. 238), in West Dennis, Massachusetts, and Velo Catalyst (p. 85), a bicycle shelter by Chilean design firm GT2P (pp. 80–87); such processes generate complex landscapes quickly. Sometimes these parametric-created landscapes rely on a scripting or algorithm definition, plugged into the generative software, to create undetermined and pleasantly surprising landscape outcomes. This process becomes experimental, allowing added variables and conditions to change the resulting design.

Geomapping, Virtual Reality Landscapes

By profiling research-based projects that experiment with digital landscape design and tools, this publication demonstrates the myriad ways in which professionals in the field are utilizing new technologies. Notable projects include those undertaken

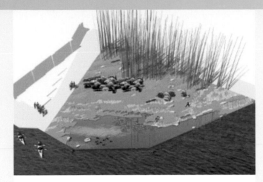

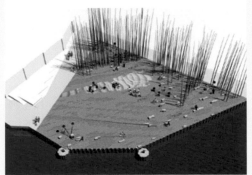

8. Hargreaves Associates, Lisbon Expo 98.
9. Hargreaves Associates, William J. Clinton Presidential Center, Little Rock, Arkansas.
10. StossLU, Erie Plaza, Milwaukee, Wisconsin.
11. Centre for Landscape Research, University of Toronto, immersive lab.

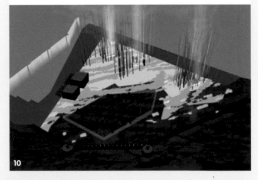

by the University of Toronto's Centre for Landscape Research, including Capital Views (p. 297), which, under the direction of John Danahy and Robert Wright, has developed digital tools designed to explore existing landscape conditions and test proposed designs from a multidimensional perspective. For over twenty-five years, the CLR has experimented with real-time and immersive environments by allowing users to more accurately represent and experience a variety of landscapes.

In the early 1980s, the team pioneered a series of revolutionary tools, including PolyTRIM, a software program that provides a toolkit for the interactive representation and modelling of landscape, synthesizing multiple technologies and digital media types into one complete virtual work environment. PolyTRIM's toolkit includes real-time rendering, ray-tracing export,

paint, CAD, GIS, photogrammetry, parametric modelling, visual assessment, and exhibition interface and network collaboration tools.

The immersive lab at the CLR enables students to fully experience designed landscapes once limited to their imaginations (fig. 11). The lab itself is a room around which large screens are placed to create a panoramic effect. Users can travel through this 4D simulated scene, change the direction of their progress as they 'stroll' or 'drive', look from side to side, and change their viewsheds. Users can interface with the landscape to adjust the time of day, season and climatic conditions. Vegetation can be adapted to correspond with environmental changes; the visualization of a mature tree in full springtime bloom, for example, transforms into one that is now winter-stark and bare of leaves. The CLR lab effectively engages users with the landscape by actively

involving them in choosing the parameters of the scene during their animated journey through the landscape.

The use of digital tools as a means of visualizing and addressing terrain modelling and other landscape issues is demonstrated in the revolutionary work of Philip Paar and Jörg Rekittke (pp. 198–205), who, along with computer scientist Malte Clasen, have developed realistic and compelling graphics that depict plants and landscapes. The team helped to establish Lenné3D, a visualization and software company known for its high level of visual realism and attention to detail in landscape creation. Paar's company also created Biosphere3D (pp. 202–3), a revised interactive visualization system that uses an open-source software platform to support various scales on a virtual globe (Digital Earth). Similar to its predecessor, the Lenné3D Player, Biosphere3D allows for the real-time rendering of vegetation and the export of data formats. While the Lenné3D Player primarily focused on visualizing the landscape from an eye-level perspective, allowing users to walk through planned and directed settings (fig. 12), this second-generation program (fig. 13) accommodates an unlimited topography that 'can be visualized due to the spherical terrain model and the efficient data management', note Paar and Clasen in their paper, 'Earth, Landscape, Biotope, Plant Interactive Visualization

with Biosphere3D' (REAL CORP 007, May 2007). 'Satellite images, raster digital elevation models (DEMs) and aerial views of multiple terabytes can be combined with vegetation plots based on vector shapes and biological sample data to create photorealistic views of planned scenarios,' they continue. 'Since no pre-calculation is required, the data can be edited and reloaded to enable quick development cycles and semi-interactive participation processes. Biosphere3D is compatible to Lenné3D's plant models, permitting access to one of the largest databases of realistic 3D plants.' Paar and his team have recently developed a third-generation version of visualization graphics through Laubwerk, an organization at the forefront of research and development that discovers creative ways to express various landscapes through interactive visualization.

Datascaping

Architecture and landscape architecture have made use of datascaping techniques, in which information from sculpture, arts and code are combined, enabling data to be expressed in a sculptural form. With datascaping techniques, practitioners have been able to come up with improved designs, both in sculpture and architecture. Design solutions have been created through data processing, via various software programs available to architecture. Digital landscape has

played a vital role in shaping the ways in which we examine and incorporate data into form and design. But we must ask: how precisely does one begin to design with data?

In the 1990s, Netherlands-based architecture and urban-design firm MVRDV (pp. 176–83), known for its leadership in shaping spatial solutions through digital means, began to investigate data modelling as it related to visual representation through datascapes. The applications for datascaping are myriad, and include elements of the artistic and the practical. Artist Andreas Fischer, for example, combined information, sculpture and code to create his data-sculpture project, *Fundament*, which mapped the world gross domestic product and world derivatives volume for 2007. By extracting the large amounts of data that emerge during the design processes, a company can apply its automated data-formation software to create new space.

This form of datascaping has assisted in the development of improved design solutions and allowed architects, landscape architects, urban environment planners and public users to achieve a deeper understanding of their specific spaces. MVRDV creates alternative design solutions by using data processing through digital design techniques, and has extensive experience developing

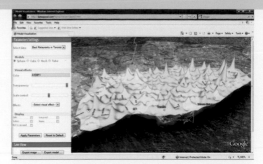

12. Philip Paar, Jörg Rekittke, Lenné3D-Player.
13. Philip Paar, Jörg Rekittke, Biosphere3D.
14, 15. Nadia Amoroso, DataAppeal.
16. MVRDV, Gwanggyo Power Centre, South Korea.

software programs tailored to this concept. With an approach based on experimentation and the extrapolation of data, MVRDV employs an interactive 'planning' device (such as a computer), in which statistical and territorial data are used to generate simplified spaces. Calling this process '3D City' (a datascape of the evolutionary city), MVRDV claims that by utilizing it, 'everyone is a citymaker'.

'The idea of developing user-interactive "planning machinery" becomes more attractive and more necessary,' they noted in *MVRDV: KM3: Excursions on Capacity* (2005). 'Statistical and territorial data are currently filed on the web. Analysis and monitoring systems are progressing … software packages would enable them [planners, development agencies, community centres and political parties] to find data, as well as to communicate, control, discuss, debate, evaluate and protest … This device can select, sort and combine data and illustrate processes.' The citymaker relies on accessing data through huge databanks that are activated by software.

In collaboration with cThrough and others, MVRDV developed two programs that explore issues of datascaping through space parcelization: Climatizer, which analyses the spatial consequences of climate change, and OptiMixer, which consists of spatial envelopes of three-dimensional, orthogonal, homogeneous grids of cubes, or 'voxels'. Each voxel is assigned a single function. Its size and volume constitutes one unit, each of which is then assigned a 'unit-type', such as housing, parks, industries or infrastructure. This application is an updated version of MVRDV principal Winy Maas's ongoing research in datascaping. Maas created software that allows users to type in a certain number of units, uses or sizes in order to create a datascape. It is similar in concept to the popular video game SimCity, but the graphics in OptiMixer are simpler in form and lack artistic detail.

Advanced Image Modification and Animation

Climatizer is a type of datascape software that presents climate statistics, which focus on the effects of economic output and CO_2 emissions. The user inputs values for waste consumption, population growth, the removal of green spaces, energy use of cars, and other types of information that impacts on climate change. Based on the data input, these statistics then produce a new datascape that incorporates the effects of human activity (households, industries, agriculture, forests, and the consumption of energy, goods and food). It is important to remember that this is only a hypothetical simulation; the projections, which look several hundreds of years into the future, have no scientific validity, and the image is merely indicative. In the visualization, coloured three-dimensional bars reveal specific consequences of human activities. As an activity increases, the bars rise to resemble rectangular towers growing from specific geographical points. One such scenario could involve global temperatures; as the designers note, 'due to the changing CO_2 level, the global average temperature is believed to increase and decrease, and the sea level to rise and decline'.

Climatizer's attempts to capture the spatial results of climate changes and the resulting human impact on the Earth is an important component of MVRDV's research into the creation of data-based '3D Cities', particularly with respect to the rising global density and need for future living space. The latest programs created by Maas consist of updated research and interactive versions of the *Metacity/Datatown* concept. MVRDV has taken data to the next level in its most recent designs, as demonstrated in its Almere 2030 project **(p. 180)**. MVRDV's design for Gwanggyo Power Centre **(fig. 16)** resembles a realized datascape in which the green peaks and hills relate to density values. Using advanced technologies and digital means, MVRDV created new landscape mounds as it tested the programme requirements and phasing developments, positions and sizes. These numbers were then turned into an aesthetically engaging, inhabitable landscape –

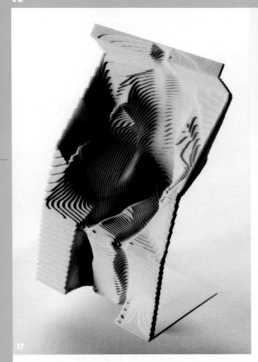

a 3D graph on a digital landscape. This type of research is pivotal in my own topic of study, which was fostered during my PhD studies at the Bartlett School of Graduate Studies, and has numerous applications in both my academic and professional research. Designing with data is a way in which hard data acts as an inspiration for urban form. The difficulty lies in engaging users in information and statistics, which can lean towards dryness. In order to resolve this, my team and I created a means of interacting with data in a simple and visually appealing way through our program, DataAppeal (figs 14, 15). The software uses visual effects, digital applications and the aesthetic principles of design to transform new landscape forms, technical information and data into a stimulating and immersive program that captures users' interest and imaginations.

Practical Applications

Digital landscape technology has applications that extend beyond the merely aesthetic, offering a way for businesses to reduce costs, save on manpower, and troubleshoot projects well before construction begins. At the forefront of landscape visualization and technology is the Calgary-based o2 Planning & Design (pp. 192–97). Utilizing advanced GIS, remote sensing, global positioning devices, 3D modelling and computerized visualization to capture and test the existing landscape conditions, the firm, headed by Douglas Olson, is actively developing accurate, effective designs meant to significantly reduce field costs and allow for projects to be evaluated in virtual detail prior to construction. o2's advanced technology simplifies projects by making them highly visual, engaging and accessible to non-professionals.

Another example of the practical application of digital landscape technology is demonstrated in the work of Nicholas de Monchaux (p. 293), whose project Local Code: Real Estate uses geospatial analysis to recognize thousands of publicly owned abandoned sites in major US cities, and then reimagines these vacant landscapes as a new urban system. Architect and academic Mike Silver (p. 288) utilizes advanced digital applications, including 3D scanners, coordinate measuring machines, computer numerical control (CNC) devices, and light detection and ranging (LIDAR), an optical remote sensing system that measures the distance of light from one point to the target, and is often used to create 3D models of spaces or objects. Combining these technologies to map the space of the human body and elements of architecture results in a registry that represents an unprecedented degree of specificity (fig. 17). Digital applications have also helped to resolve complicated infrastructural landscape and urban design projects, such as those encountered in the Olabeaga and San Mamés masterplans (fig. 18), in Bilbao, Spain, by Zaha Hadid (pp. 100–7); the Aquatic Complex (fig. 19), in Medellín, Colombia, by Paisajes Emergentes (pp. 206–11); and Flowing Gardens (fig. 20), a design by Groundlab (pp. 74–79) for the International Horticultural Expo 2011 in Xi'an, China.

Digital Hybrids:
Art, Imagination, Landscape

Digital Landscape Architecture Now also showcases works that depict digital landscape art – including Orange Power by Land-I Archicolture (pp. 138–43), a design for the Ponte de Lima International Garden Festival 2006; an installation by Fletcher Studio (pp. 58–63) for the Jardins de Métis 2008; and a project by Walter Hood (pp. 116–21) for San Jose Airport, in California – and surveys advanced image modifications and 'digital dynamic simulations', including Fallen Silo by the Freise Brothers (pp. 64–73). It also explores research projects that relate to digitally driven work in addressing landscape architectural designs from some of today's strongest academics and researchers in the field. One such example is Bradley Cantrell (pp. 38–43), of Louisiana State University, who uses digital techniques to represent landscape form and processes.

20

Similarly groundbreaking projects include Rapid Re(f)use (fig. 21), by TerreformONE (pp. 242–47); EcoMachines, by EcoLogicStudio (pp. 44–49); Waterscapes, by students of the landscape architecture programme at the ETH Zürich (p. 296), and the fantastical cyber-projects of R&Sie(n). The latter are varied in scope and purpose, but all aim to combine the fictional and the real, the chaotic and the ordered, the biological and the organic, to create radical landscapes that marry experimentation with contemporary technology (figs 22, 23). 'Each designer must embrace digital media as a tool with analytics, performative, and representational possibilities,' noted Bradley Cantrell and Wes Michael in *Digital Drawing for Landscape Architecture: Contemporary Techniques and Tools for Digital Representation in Site Design* (2010). Focusing on these artistic experiments enables the reader to see the synchronicities that develop, and the technologically driven design solutions that emerge when artists use new media and landscape designers pay attention to the outer boundaries of artistic practice.

'Industrial technology has produced machines that can manipulate landscapes,' noted Elizabeth Barlow Rogers, by crafting them into complex shapes. Today, landscape architects are embracing other technologies and 'smart software' that architects have employed in building construction and design in the digital age. Whether it is parametric programming or CNC fabrication, 3D plotting or 3D scanning, or immersive virtual landscapes, many landscape architects are making these 'tools' a part of their design palette, beyond pencils and trace paper. *Digital Landscape Architecture Now* celebrates this wide variety of work, all of which makes use of digital design application to create new and engaging environments.

21

22

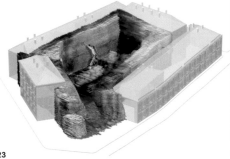

23

PROJECTS

1
BALLISTIC ARCHITECTURE MACHINE

Ballistic Architecture Machine, an architecture, landscape, urban design and art studio based in Beijing, China, focuses on innovative and artistic architectural design moves for urban and landscape settings, and provides a wide variety of creative expressions in their designs. The firm uses an environmental, planning, landscape, architecture and art knowledge-base to arrive at synthetic and dynamic solutions, which are fostered by thinking across multiple disciplines in collaboration with their clients.

BAM's philosophy – 'nature is an idea' – reflects their belief that new developments in technology have reshaped the environment, fostering a gradual decline in how we interact with and value our surroundings. The designers attempt to re-establish 'lost' environmental values, and reposition the future of nature by incorporating ecological processes within their designs, while simultaneously responding to the specific needs of each project. The company uses new technology and digital tools to craft complex and radical designs that challenge nature, artifice and art.

To achieve their synthetic solutions, the designers frequently use advanced modelling software programs, as well as parametric modelling plug-ins, such as Grasshopper for Rhinoceros. Their collective training as artists, architects and landscape architects has allowed them to tackle nature and technology aggressively.

Velopark, London 2012,
London, UK.

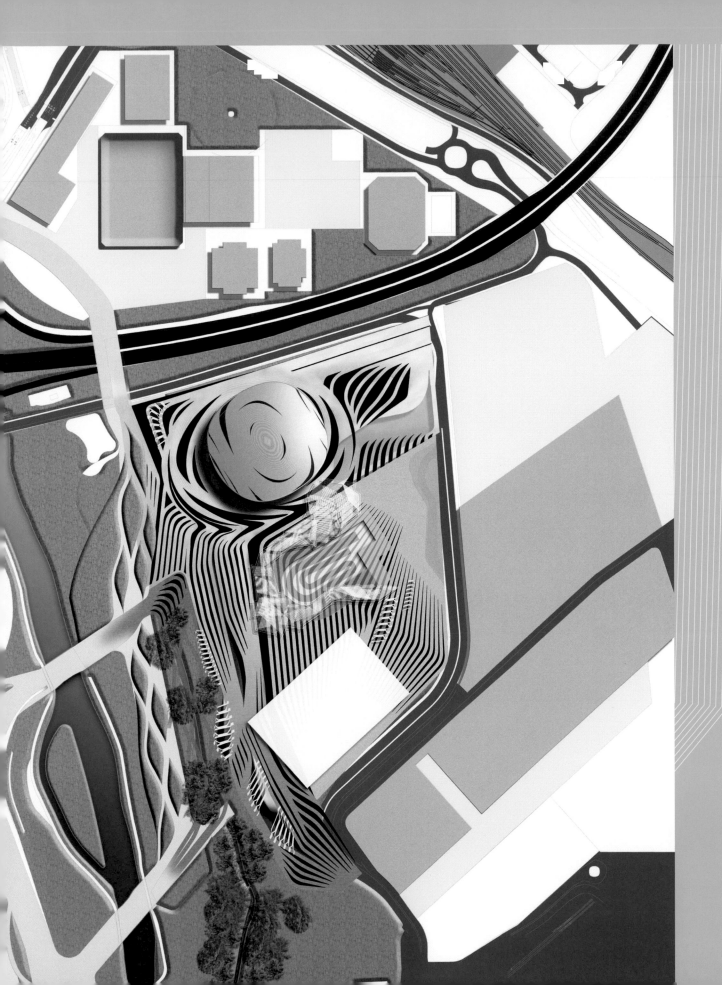

1.1
Velopark, London 2012
London, UK

This competition entry for the London 2012 Olympics – created in collaboration with Thomas Heatherwick Studio, Falkner Browns and Martha Schwartz Landscape Architects – attempts to capture the energy of velo-racing, spinning the wooden architecture of the Velodrome into the park landscape. During the Olympics phase, the park's primary materials would consist of wood pathways, recycled rubber infill zones, and a permeable asphalt material to mitigate the water run-off so often associated with large expanses of hardscape. The asphalt surfaces form curving material sections to facilitate pathway movement, emerging at the Velodrome, and are designed to circulate visitors through such event areas as a BMX course. A 'velo-fountain', situated outside the stadium, creates additional viewing areas and a space for spectators to cool down.

Upon completion of the Olympic Games, the site will be transitioned into a city park, with the park's materials recycled as part of a long-term growth plan. The permeable asphalt is removable in sections, to be reused in the site's northern zone for a new mountain bike course. The recycled rubber areas are also retained to create a BMX 'bikers' heaven'. Surrounded by wooden benches that wind along the pathways, the site will also engage spectators, as well as participants. This dynamic landscape design is carefully woven into the Olympic Park masterplan, with the design modelled upon the spinning energy and the wooden track for races held within the Velodrome. Positioned at the vortex of a swirling landscape, the concept attracts visitors towards the race venues. Folds and hinges in the landscape integrate the programme's different facilities, as well as anticipating a continuous future environment dedicated to bike racing.

1. The site in legacy mode: a post-Olympics city park.
2. Conceptual diagram.
3. Aerial rendering.

1.2
22 Art Plaza
Beijing, China

The Martha Schwartz influence is again in evidence at this energetic and artistic design for 22 Art Plaza, located at the Today Art Museum, a private contemporary museum in Beijing. The landscape design was developed to create a series of spaces for the display of art and to host associated programmes. The firm also created brightly coloured elements, including planters in the form of rubber snails, to make the plaza appear more inviting and to connect the various spaces and provide seating. Their colours and shapes reflect the artwork on display.

Guided by a final conceptual sketch and a series of physical models, the designers developed the concept for the landscape architecture by using a set of digital models that organized the existing architectural conditions in a harmonious manner. They produced specific construction details both two- and three-dimensionally – including for the rubber-snail planters – to enable the fabrication processes to achieve the final, playful forms.

1. Outdoor gallery room no 2.
2. Rendering of the planters.
3. Water feature at the residential entry.
4. Outdoor gallery room no 1.
5. Parking connector zone.

1.3
Biornis-Aesthetope
Manhattan, New York

Created in collaboration with legendary landscape architect Martha Schwartz, this project is a novel design for a green roof, which supports a functioning biotope for birds migrating along the Atlantic Flyway. Sited in Lower Manhattan, the structure sits atop a twelve-storey building and provides visible resting areas, water pools and vegetation to create an attractive destination for the migrating birds.

The proposed roof system offers significant benefits over those of more typically intensive systems. The design team devised a strategic pattern of variables, ranging from the use of organic and inorganic soil substrates, gradients of water retention, insect hibernation patterns and vegetative planting, to the structural loading and construction costs. This matrix allowed the system to function as an active biotope, and to be flexible through its various iterations.

Developed parametrically through advanced modelling software programs, including Grasshopper, the resulting design is a high-performance green roof that is capable of producing the perfect conditions for a biotope. Its sculptural expressiveness is necessary to maintain such quality performance, and to render the beauty of its formal expression.

1. An early concept model for a roof landscape, composed of dune-like forms.
2. Storyboard image of a commuter driving into Manhattan, with Biornis-Aesthetope in the background.
3. Illustrative plan and section.
4. View from the client's sky lobby.

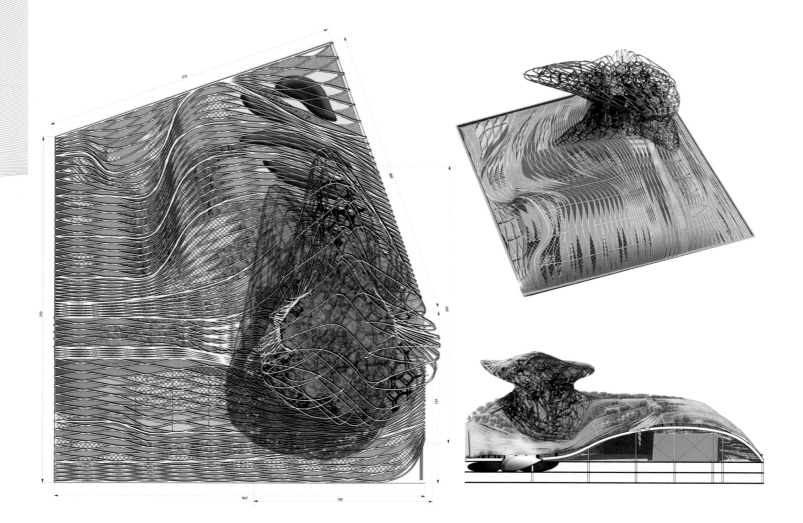

3

4

2

BALMORI

Balmori Associates is a New York-based urban and landscape design firm founded by Diana Balmori in 1990. Known for its creative signature landscapes, the firm has a distinctive functional style, combined with inventive design thinking. Through research, collaboration and innovation, Balmori explores and expands the boundaries between nature, culture, art and structure. Their projects emphasize sustainability through the careful study of the ecological, hydrological and temporal dimensions of their contexts.

Balmori's work includes all scales, and aims to knit larger ecological systems with smaller open spaces. At times, their landscapes are even didactic, revealing otherwise hidden site operations. The firm is technically proficient, using advanced digital applications and explorations in developing creative public spaces and progressive landscape concepts, coupled with an understanding of environmental, social and physical needs. In recent years, Balmori has embraced the digital age, while still retaining some traditional methods. The designers will craft topographical models in clay or cardboard as a testing ground, later developing complex landscapes using a palette of software that includes 3D Studio MAX and Rhinoceros to render complex landscape forms and visualizations.

Shenzhen Cultural Park, Shenzhen, China.

2.1
Shenzhen Cultural Park
Shenzhen, China

1

This competition-winning design for Shenzhen Cultural Park is an active formal expression of the city, woven into the fabric of the metropolis. Its shape and forms are 'extruded surfaces' for pedestrians, cyclists and skaters who commute and connect throughout various parts of the city. The design creates a cultural space that showcases the site's history and cultural functions. A fluid system of green connectors extend to link as many vibrant 'pockets' in the city as possible. It is conceived as an active set of ribbons, weaving through Shenzhen and enlarging at specific moments or nodes of intensified activity and overlapping cultural functions.

The park's signature forms also create a strong intersection of landscape and architecture. The landscape is treated as a continuous surface that sculpts the ground three-dimensionally, according to the city's particular dynamic, and results in layers that weave around and criss-cross each other. Surfaces transform and change into volumes, leading to a three-dimensional reading that is created from the intersection of the landscape with the roads, buildings and programmes at work in the new city. This intersection of landscape with architecture creates a new form of building that the designers term 'parkitecture'.

1. Computer rendering of the proposed design.
2. Aerial view.
3. Vertical landscapes; planting; programme elements.
4. South plan.

2

3

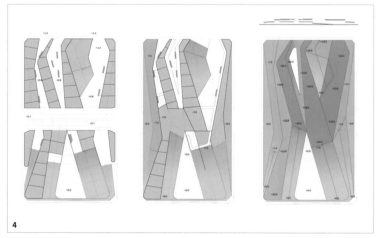

4

2.2
Puerto de la Luz
Gran Canaria, Spain

This 'park of light' is designed as a landscape infrastructural ribbon, one that changes the infrastructure of an ancient port to a 'green one of living systems, producing a beautiful green belt in the middle of the water'. The landscape was defined and modelled through the flow of wind and waves, with the forms extracted from the tidal data and city connections to create a continuous waterfront park and promenade. This living system cleans the water, blocks the wind, and creates an innovative, inviting space.

Green landscape strips link the sea and the land surface, and improve the quality of the water and diminish the environmental impact of the marina. Separate channels at opposite ends of the marina promote flow-through currents, directing the flow of water towards the centre. This design also protects the bulkhead structures from water erosion.

1. Concept diagram.
2. Section.
3. Nighttime view of the park.

2.3
Equestrian venue, NYC 2012
Staten Island, New York

For the NYC 2012 Olympics proposal, the architects designed riding trails and pedestrian paths for an equestrian venue on Staten Island. These trails and pathways connect to existing paths in the green-belt park, creating a large circulation network that further links the park to the various local neighbourhoods. The team created a series of sculptural earth mounds, connected by a winding pathway from which various events can be seen. The ribbon also becomes part of an organizational device that structures the programmes and venues. The mounds enclose the arena, creating a wind buffer and flood shelter; their slopes also double up as public seating.

A large mound and a water channel provides a clever separation between the competitors and spectators by simultaneously offering perceptual integration with unobstructed views into the restricted areas. The facilities, including the grand arena and stables, would remain on the site, and be integrated into the park as permanent equestrian venues, post-Olympic Games. Other facilities would be removed or reprogrammed to fit the community's needs. In this design, the natural landscape formations are extruded to create a horizontal landform that challenges the traditional relationship between spectator and athlete.

1. Aerial view of the main arena.
2. Training field.
3. Show jumping during the three-day event.

2.4
Amman Performing Arts Centre
Amman, Jordan

Located in the centre of the Jordanian capital of Amman, this new venue for the performing arts is an initiative of the Darat King Abdullah II cultural complex. It has been designed to be the major venue for theatre, music and dance in the capital, and will also function as a place for education and as a vital element of cultural life in the area.

In collaboration with Zaha Hadid Architects (pp. 100–7), Balmori developed the spatial flows of the landscape using 3D rendering programs to help with the visualization of 'smooth' transitions from one space to another. The movement of people and location of the plantings were also explored through vector lines that were later translated into extruded three-dimensional models as part of the flowing spaces. Landscaping was used in place of a traditional fence to create a security strip that will both buffer and protect. The use of almond trees and dense leafy plants at varying heights helps to define a space that is soothing and pleasing to the eye.

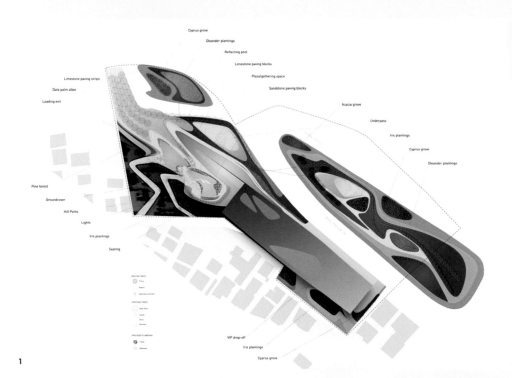

1

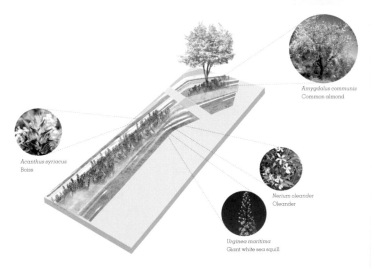

Acanthus syriacus
Boiss

Amygdalus communis
Common almond

Nerium oleander
Oleander

Urginea maritima
Giant white sea squill

2

4

1. Site plan.
2. Security strip.
3. Dense planting, which aids in defining the space.
4. The plaza and ramp.

2.5
University College Dublin
Dublin, Ireland

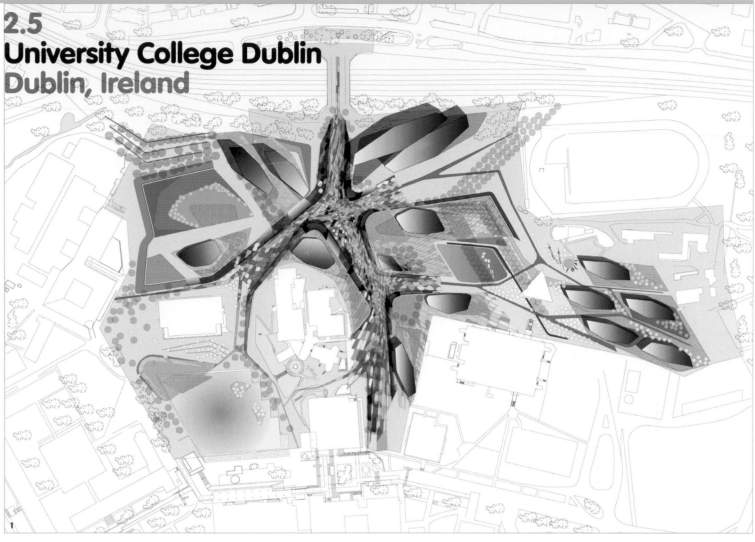

In another collaboration with Zaha Hadid, Balmori proposed a masterplan for the expansion of the University College Dublin competition. This design offers novel hybrid building and landscape typologies as the design strategy, in which landscape and architecture merge to form continuous multilayered public surfaces and green building façades. The slopes that transition between the paths and the building are all interconnected.

The volumetric pathways are layered with plantings and materials and become usable, inhabitable spaces that extend the landscape to the surfaces of the roof gardens and terraces. These surfaces also become a sustainable solution to maximizing the campus's biodiversity by extending the existing green spaces and branching out to form a new hierarchical network. The architecture emerges from the edges of the pathways, creating new spatial relationships between the surfaces where the ground touches the building. The pathways are reinvented as the 'social cores' of the campus. This is further articulated by digitally modelling the relationship and circulation speed of the various users with the building typologies.

1. Plan.
2. Heavily planted paths extend the landscape.
3. Pathway as 'social core'.

2.6
Governors Island
Upper New York Bay, New York

Located at the southern tip of Manhattan, Governors Island is 70 ha (172 acres) in area, half of which is a park with an old military barracks and historic buildings, all of which are designated as remaining; the other half is scheduled for new development. For the latter, Balmori designed three glass structures, or 'biomes'. A user can enter one of these glassed-in landscapes in the middle of winter and experience the warmth and light-saturated atmosphere of a desert under full sun. Another biome contains a tropical lagoon, complete with rainforests. The third biome contains an Ice House, with icebergs and tundra vegetation, for experiencing the arctic climate during the heat of a summer's day in New York.

The project also celebrates the native and cultivated vegetation of the Hudson River Valley by providing a place for research and education. At the centre of the island, Balmori designed a space for agricultural development, which will showcase sustainable technologies and urban agriculture. The public will be able to take courses in organic farming, as well as purchase some of the produce grown on the island. This area could also provide the restaurateurs in the historic district with herbs and fresh vegetables.

These ecological typologies, modelled to create unique spatial experiences, were designed in collaboration with design firm studioMDA. The biomes and green surfaces were modelled and rendered digitally using 3D Studio MAX and V-Ray to capture the atmosphere of the lighting.

1. Montage.
2. Models.
3. Rainforest.
4. Shadow lines form structure.
5. Desert.
6. Agriculture.

2.7
Water (Works)
Seoul, South Korea

resource renewal

waterfront amenities

wildlife refuge

biofiltration

storm water management

1

Water (Works) is a public park and ecological infrastructure that is shaped formally by the flow of water. The park is a sophisticated network of ecological processes, which interweave linear public spaces with natural and experimental technologies. Water (Works) is a working model of the park as an urban regenerator and prototype for future development – a public amenity embedded within a purifying infrastructure. The design is performative and productive.

Water (Works) is the green core of the new research and development zone, an immersive environment of water

remediation, and at the same time a regional playground. Park paths and strips of programme move alongside working wetlands, squash fields are framed by algae tanks, and the convention centre and marina are interlaced with the water system. The marina is interconnected with the Han River, bringing it into the park as a lively recreational port. The marina acts as both social mixing zone and the final cleansing reservoir. It is protected from summer flooding by a levee and gate system that serves as an outlook over the park and river.

Water (Works) is an 'enhanced' natural air- and water-cleaning infrastructure. Wetlands, phyto-remediation, blackwater treatment and air-cleaning trees form the basis of the park's layout and plantings. The living machine provides clean air, water and soil. Water (Works) is also an educational park for children, as well as an experimental think tank and laboratory for ecology and green technology. The water-cleaning process served as the model to generate the spatial form of public spaces and the productive landscape.

2

1. Diagram.
2. Algae.
3. Sanctuary.
4. Axonometric drawing.

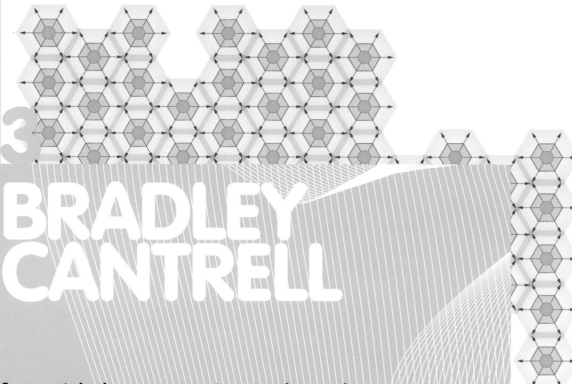

3

BRADLEY CANTRELL

An expert in landscape representation, Bradley Cantrell serves as part of an academic group of researchers dedicated to the development of the landscape architecture profession through the advancement of computation and data visualization. He believes in creative design development through experimentation of visual representation. Cantrell is the director of the Terrain Kinetics (TIKI) Lab, an interdisciplinary research facility for the exploration and testing of new landscape visualization techniques using digital technologies. His recent book with Wes Michaels, *Digital Drawing for Landscape Architecture*, is a manual for educating landscape architects about and training them in contemporary techniques for representing landscape.

Cantrell's research into digital representation techniques vary from those used throughout the design process, including the improvement of workflow through the use of digital media, to landscape representation through compositing and film editing. Using tools such as Photoshop and Illustrator, Cantrell experiments with advanced texture and colour application, shading techniques and lightweights and line-work treatments in order to produce convincing perspective collages. He also experiments with other advanced measures of landscape analysis, including the creation of responsive and ambient landscapes and atmospheric environments. Such 'atmospheric perspectives' deal with layers of 'moisture and particulate matter in the air' causing haze, shift in depth of view in image, and overall air affects, creating a 'veil of atmosphere' onto the picture.

Cantrell also works with advanced 3D modelling using 3D Studio MAX to create virtual landscape space and animated scenes for studio designs. He carries his passion for digital representation in landscape architecture into other works, including reactive spaces such as the Ambient Space project (p. 42).

the Ambient Space project (p. 42).

Abstraction Language:
Digital/Analogue Dialogues.

3.1
Abstraction Language
Digital/Analogue Dialogues

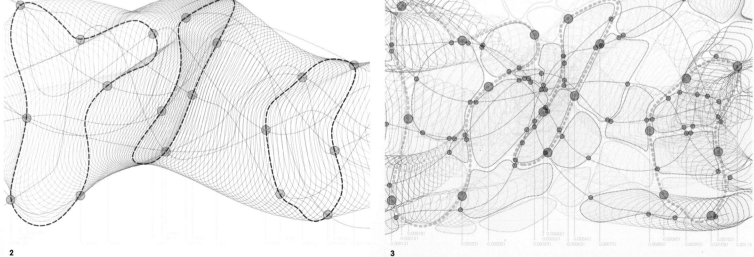

1

2

3

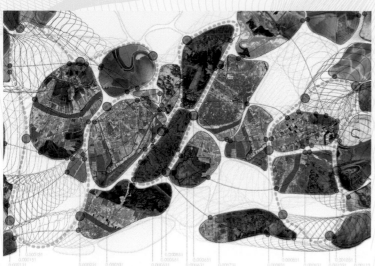

4

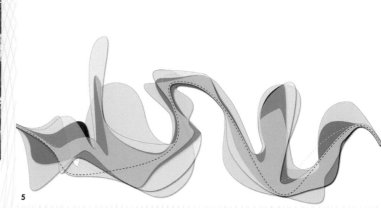

5

The connection between biological systems and machines is becoming an important factor in designing the built environment. As our environment becomes saturated with 'smart' devices that we use every day, sustainable power generation, water management, ecological infrastructures, and other emerging enviro-tech applications require negotiations between digital technologies and analogue systems. These negotiations, however, are often discarded from design, viewed as inaccessible to those designers without specific scientific knowledge or technical skill in electrical or computer engineering.

This project explores the model of abstraction language as a method of creating communications between biological and mechanical systems. Cantrell focuses on integrating language based to the abstraction project, an approach that addresses simultaneous issues in enviro-tech interfaces for sensing, responsiveness, automation and interactivity. According to Cantrell, this language exists in a liminal realm between mechanical or digital devices, and biological or ecological systems. 'Abstraction' addresses simultaneous modes of complexity through a common dialogue. This comes in multiple forms, from a library for design, to a logical interface between chaotic components. The programming of the data and the

control of the abstraction is explored in order to develop linkages between physical systems and digital interfaces.

This examination investigates current methods of data conveyance for the built environment. Cantrell is interested in the ability of abstraction to compress ecological/biological complexity into accessible modules for responsive environments. These modules would be developed to create evolving systems to control, modify, link or explore ecologies, cultures and societies. According to the designer, the processing component of this project provides the greatest range of possibilities for abstraction between data and systems. The output is often the most tangible mode of the sensing, processing, visualizing stream.

1. Single-instance feedback loop.
2. Multi-instance feedback loop.
3. Feedback field, object-orientated loops.
4. Feedback field composite.
5. Composite streams.

3.2
Ambient Space
Manhattan, New York

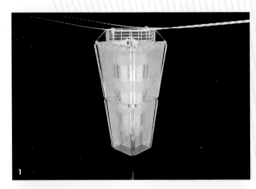

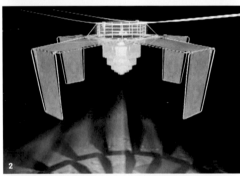

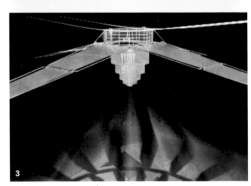

1–3. Animated lamp.
4. Pine Street.

Cantrell focuses on interactive/reactive landscapes, which explore the 'device' or 'infrastructure' that responds to environmental phenomena, using the notion of the landscape folly as a deconstructor that highlights environmental process. Landscape is a complex sensory environment, explored and interpreted by humans through multiple inputs.

This project considers the manipulation of the built landscape through the introduction of landscape devices that create consistent responses to site phenomena, and alter spatial conditions accordingly. This is explored through a hypothetical project on Pine Street, in Lower Manhattan. The project looks at the street-lighting infrastructure as a reactive network that creates evolving spatial conditions through environmental inputs. The device is a responsive lighting structure that opens, closes, contracts, expands, lowers, raises, brightens and dims, according to inputs such as motion, wind speed, ambient light and noise. The device is context-aware, creating new spatial configurations throughout the course of the day, slowly readjusting as environmental inputs change.

Many devices in the landscape use data collection and reactionary systems to perform specific tasks. Street lights turn on at dusk, traffic lights change based on motion or weight sensors, and doors open automatically when sensors are tripped. These are basic binary systems that respond to input through a reaction in the device, a one-to-one mapping of environmental stimuli and device response. Through the mapping of multiple ambient environmental inputs to multiple expressions, the proposed lighting infrastructure develops a complex and ambiguous relationship with the landscape. The proposed street-light system expresses specific site phenomena through the device's ability to transform itself through simple modifications.

These modifications are expressed in the landscape as morphing spatial configurations. The spatial changes rendered by the lighting network are expressed as pragmatic modifications to the physical space. This project explores the boundary between spatial perception and interactive device; specifically, the proposed lighting infrastructure aims to express the ambient environment through recognizable and morphing forms.

3.3
Thresholds
Baton Rouge, Louisiana

1, 2. Installation in situ.
3. Media board.

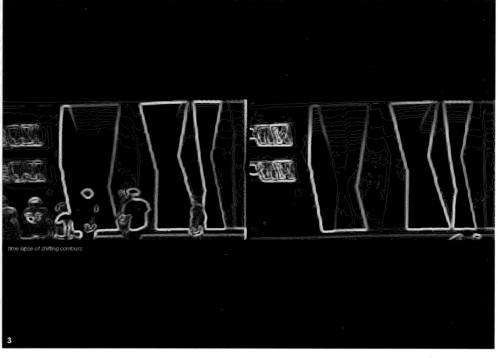

time lapse of shifting contours

This installation explored interactive environments as a means of expressing new landscapes. It was originally installed in the atrium of Louisiana State University's College of Art and Design, and was selected as one of eight projects for ACADIA 2008: Silicon + Skin.

Landscape surface is a dynamic and moving medium, shaped through the natural processes of erosion, deposition, and the interplay of substrate and vegetative matter. This interaction creates complex three-dimensional surfaces that exist on a range of scales, from the structure of soil particles up to the tectonics of mountain ranges. Normal representational methods express the landscape in static modes and limited scales, often disconnecting humans from the environment they occupy. This digital experimentation attempts to use phenomena (light) and human-scale interaction as methods for formulating

and altering representations of landscapes. It explores the limitations and possibilities of conventional representation systems and how they shape our perception of environments. Specifically, Thresholds examines isolines (curves that connect points where the function has the same value) as a means of representing spatial relationships. Landscape surfaces are represented with contours, or isolines, in order to express similar elevations, and in relation to other contours, a clear image of the intricacies of a 3D surface is expressed in a 2D representation.

For this project, isolines define changes in contrast and are generated dynamically to create automated landscapes. Changes in value are calculated in real time and are expressed by isolines – high contrast is represented by closer isolines, and low contrast by wider ones. As pedestrians circulate and lighting conditions change throughout the

day, the isolines are generated in real time, creating new landscape representations. The installation consists of a large wall painted with a simple graphic, used as a datum to generate a baseline representation. This consists of twelve stripes of alternating greys, creating moments of high and low contrast. The wall is monitored by a single camera that is fed through an applet, created in generating a real-time representation of the isolines. The isolines update at a rate of fifteen frames per second in order to create a fluid, real-time representation of the environment.

4 ECOLOGICSTUDIO

EcoLogicStudio is a London-based design and research architectural studio, founded in 2004 by Claudia Pasquero and Marco Poletto. The firm produces innovative work on 'systemic' design, which includes a combination of bio-ecologic, parametric and genetic design, advanced digital application in formal and concept expressions, and rapid prototyping.

The firm believes in a design process based on the development of emerging 'hyper-realities' that constantly play between the realms of the natural and the synthetic, and the 'purposefully designed and the anomaly'. To the designers, paradigmatic ecological thinking plays an important part in their conception of inhabitation and manipulation of the environment in its ability to foster and embed technologic progresses with existing natural phenomena, processes and systems.

Some of their digital design tools include advanced parametric design through the Grasshopper plug-in for Rhino, Arduino/Processing hardware and software, and other digital fabrication technologies. Their projects range from public libraries to private villas, parks to roof gardens, developing landscape and architectural design employing a digital focus.

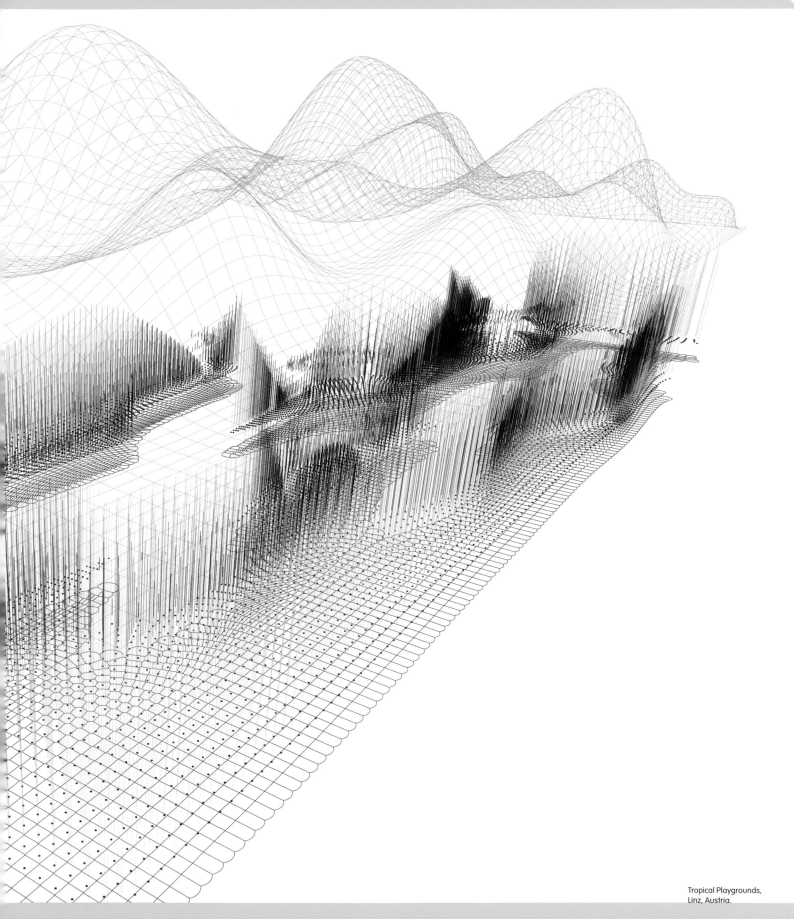

Tropical Playgrounds,
Linz, Austria.

4.1
Tropical Playgrounds
Linz, Austria

For this project, students from the Architectural Association in London created 1:1-scale models of landscape pieces to test how specific 'architectural machines' could generate playfulness. During a three-day workshop at the Kunstuniversität Linz, they were challenged to design a 'landscape' based on the notion of playfulness. Using complex digital process, including parametric modelling, the students explored the concept of muscular systems as found in heliotropism or insectivorous plants. They extracted three possible structural organizational systems that could be translated into their design:

— Kinetic modelling the geometric logics of the fibrous filaments that constitute muscular systems, and that support kinetic response;
— Cybernetic diagramming the flows of information that regulate cybernetic feedback in muscular response to environmental stimuli; and
— Molecular/material experimenting with the hybrid material composites that characterizes muscular assemblages.

The students used these parameters of artificial muscles as fibrous systems in which the systems respond, react to and interact with environmental changes and human touch. The process was engineered by developing specific mechanisms of production and fabrication, including the sensing and computational components. At the end, a 'playful landscape' of bright-red, tall fibrous grasses was created, which responded to movement through the space and changed with the different environmental conditions.

This project investigated design as an iterative process, responding to changing environmental pressures, and it is an attempt to develop behavioural pattern in relation to its context, which includes sensual and atmospheric changes that are provided and adapted to varying surrounding conditions. Some of the materials used for this project included wax, wool fibres, high-density cardboard, and so on. Students used laser-cutting and wax heating, along with software programs such as Rhinoceros and Grasshopper for parametric modelling.

1. Fibrous filaments (detail).
2. Prototype, fibrous filaments.

4.2
EcoMachines
Venice, Italy

This project challenges the notion of the 'interaction between the natural and the artificial realms through the making of artificial ecologies' for the 2008 Venice Biennale. Here, nature is hybridized, equipped with the adaptive mechanisms of management and direct evaluation of the effects of human transformation of natural ecosystems. The designers call these mechanisms 'eco-machines'.

EcoMachines is designed to capture a response to flows of energy and information. The machines are able to respond and react to changes in the environment and human feedback (touch and senses), creating a new understanding of urban ecology. In a larger sense, these eco-machines are meant to support interaction between various systems, including social, infrastructural, architectural and environmental. They allow us to sense, register and manipulate these 'artificial eco-spaces', and to redefine our cities and artificial environments.

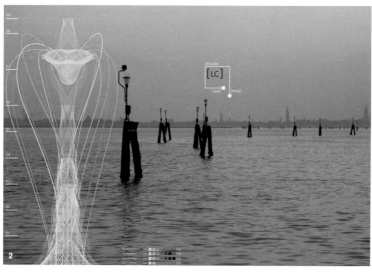

1. Site map.
2. Digital collage.
3. Prototypes.

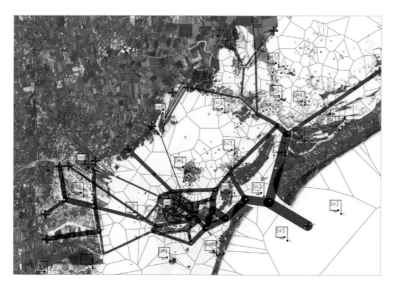

4.3
CyberGardens
London, UK

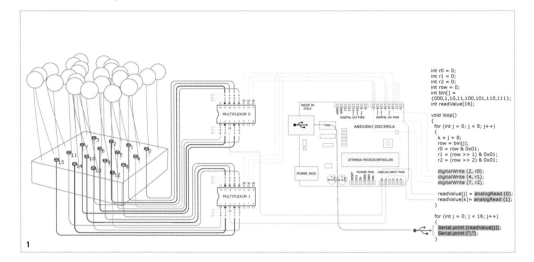

```
int r0 = 0;
int r1 = 0;
int r2 = 0;
int row = 0;
int bin[] =
{000,1,10,11,100,101,110,111};
int readValue[16];

void loop()
{
  for (int j = 0; j < 8; j++)
  {
  k = j + 8;
  row = bin[j];
  r0 = row & 0x01;
  r1 = (row >> 1) & 0x01;
  r2 = (row >> 2) & 0x01;

  digitalWrite (2, r0);
  digitalWrite (4, r1);
  digitalWrite (7, r2);

  readValue[j] = analogRead (0);
  readValue[k] = analogRead (1);
  }

  for (int j = 0; j < 16; j++)
  {
  Serial.print (readValue[j]);
  Serial.print (",");
  }
}
```

1

CyberGardens is part of the coral gardens project developed by students at the Architectural Association in London under the supervision of Claudia Pasquero and Marco Poletto. The students investigated the design process as a 'cultivation' of artificial gardens and engaged with the material and growth of these mini-cyber gardens, allowing them to understand the flows of light and nutrients, maintenance, and the overall ecologic systems required to cultivate and promote growth in the digital abstract garden. The students developed the physical interfaces, equipped by sensors, which captured and outputted information in real time in order to 'feed their own virtual/digital images'. Emergent digital patterns of the garden allowed them to alter their physical interface, changing the 'digital sedimentation'. In this project, ecology and cybernetics merged to develop a new way of gardening.

During the three-day workshop, the students initially investigated the cyber garden's physical interface and its ability to sense and react to the surrounding environment and to human interaction. Following this, they developed the design and created scripts in Grasshopper before testing the growing process and patterns through the interactions of the cyber garden's gardeners; taking stimulus from the physical into the digital through a series of feedback loops, 'from the human, to the machine, to the computer, to the environment, to the human, to the machine and back again'. Some of the materials used for the project included flex and light sensors, LEDs, foam, plywood, Arduino Duemilanove boards, fishes, acrylic sheeting, water and lights. Software programs used included Processing, Rhinoceros and Grasshopper.

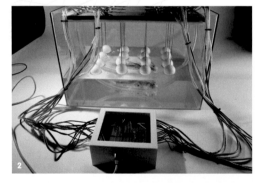

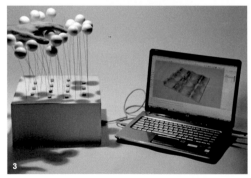

1–3. Capturing information from environmental stimulus, the machine becomes a means of sampling, concentrating and modifying the variability of its surroundings.
4. Digital sedimentation patterns.

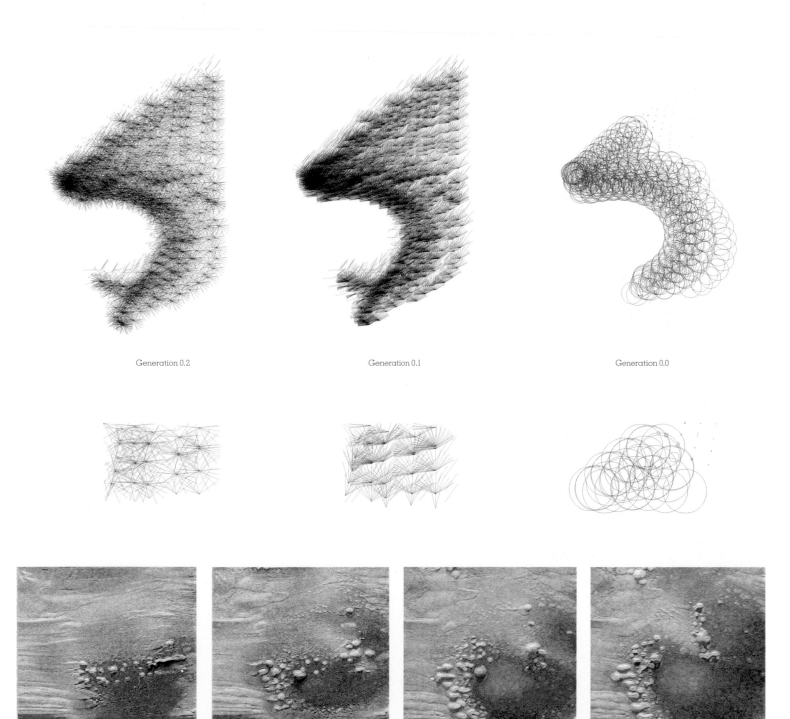

Generation 0.2   Generation 0.1   Generation 0.0

4

5
EMERGENT

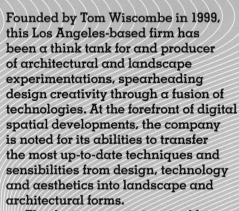

Founded by Tom Wiscombe in 1999, this Los Angeles-based firm has been a think tank for and producer of architectural and landscape experimentations, spearheading design creativity through a fusion of technologies. At the forefront of digital spatial developments, the company is noted for its abilities to transfer the most up-to-date techniques and sensibilities from design, technology and aesthetics into landscape and architectural forms.

The design team is inspired by natural biological processes that function according to a cyclical progressive logic. These systems include structures of evolutionary ecological selection and patterns of transformation in atmospheric conditions. To enhance efficiency in their designs, the firm replicates these organic feedback loops in the design process by using digital computation technologies, including parametric software such as Rhinoceros. Through custom-designed workflows, digital engineering tools and analysis programs, the team enables a heterogeneous design methodology that incorporates variances and allows for performance adaptations over time.

Advanced digital tools are used to craft sophisticated, inventive and, on occasion, sci-fi spaces and landscapes.

Digital tools, including parametric modelling, digital fabrication, 3D and 4D programs (such as Finite Element) and vector-based and computer fluid dynamic softwares, have helped the firm to produce quick yet complex designs that have aided their attempts to advance creative expression.

Garak Fish Market, Seoul, South Korea.

5.1
Garak Fish Market
Seoul, South Korea

At over 54 ha (133.4 acres) of land and 1 km (0.6 miles) long, the Garak Fish Market, located in the Garak-dong neighbourhood of Seoul, is the largest wholesale market in South Korea. In collaboration with Changjo Architects, the designers developed proposals that examined future outcomes of the market and its connection to and integration with the city and surrounding neighbourhoods. In addition to having to contend with the unpleasant odours and visual clutter associated with markets in general, the team also had to strategize the market's level of openness and enclosure.

The designers' aim was to urbanize and intensify the fish market by 'stemming its organic sprawl and creating sectional properties'. Their concept proposed two zones: natural and urban. The western part of the site, adjacent to the Tan Stream, was designed as a wetland preserve and recreational area, while the eastern side, where the production and market areas are located, is stacked with multiple programmes, creating a hyper-dense, two-level spatial organization.

A signature large roof provides both a semi-enclosed space and a robust community roof-garden landscape. The structure of the roof is designed in a well-ordered, grid-like pattern, due to the constraints of the arrangement of the columns for structural and programme support. The design of the roof unfolds into a series of loose, spiralling patterns as it approaches the wetland areas. The roof gardens were designed as a network of various-sized plots, stemming from the roof's structural pattern. Strong colour variations in the flower and vegetable fields provide a vibrant and dynamic mosaic, and create a balance between the natural and synthetic landscape.

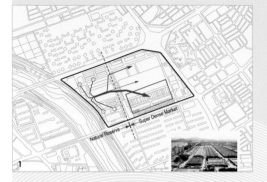

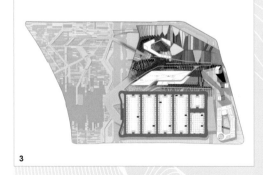

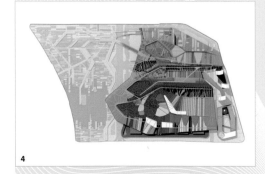

1. Densification and wetlands.
2. Plan of the community gardens.
3, 4. Plans.
5. Community gardens.
6. Vegetation patterns.

5

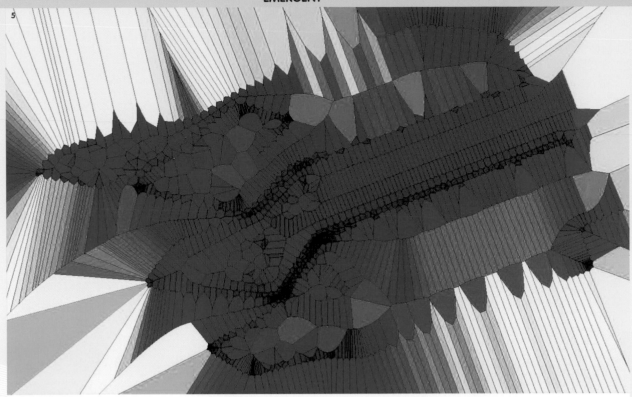

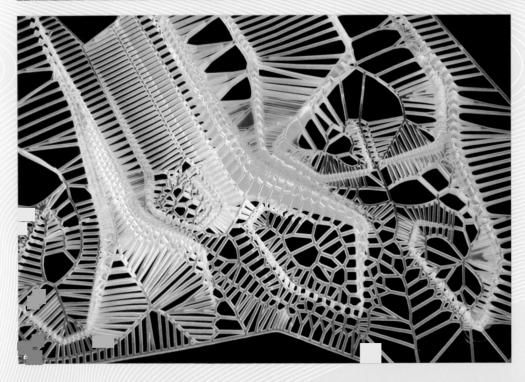

6

5.1
Garak Fish Market
Seoul, South Korea

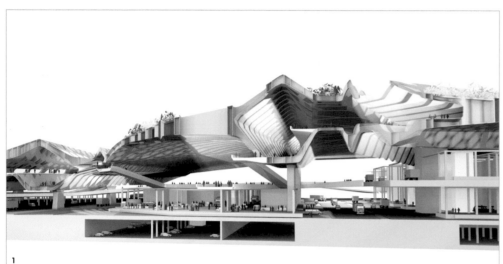

1. Section.
2. Aerial perspective.

5.2
Prototypes I–III
Los Angeles, California

Tracery Glass, Thermo-Strut and Lizard Panel are three interconnected prototypes that form part of Emergent's research into the unpacking of the spatial and ornamental potential of airflow, fluid flow and glow. Based on chunk logic, rather than layer logic, these prototypes are manufactured and delivered as fully integrated, three-dimensional assemblies, embedded with all internal infrastructural systems. They are constructed of moulded fibre-composite and polycarbonate materials, embedded with socket connections and structural adhesive, as well as more normative materials, such as plate steel. They feature embedded solar thermal and photovoltaic systems, algae photobioreactor cells, radiant cooling systems and grey-water capture systems.

Tracery Glass reconsiders stained glass in contemporary architecture. Rather than dematerializing glass, this polycarbonate is characterized by embedded technology that does both ornamental and physical work. Thermo-Strut combines welded plate-steel beams with fibre-composite shells, embedded with solar thermal tracery, while Lizard Panel, or Grey Water Panel, is a puzzle-piece system with socketed structural and mechanical members for continuity.

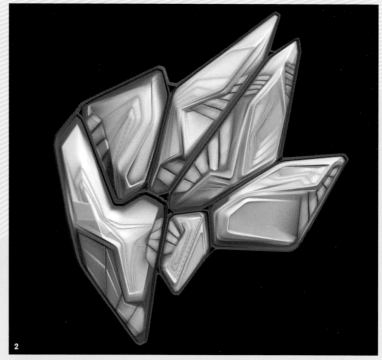

1, 4. Lizard Panel.
2. Tracery Glass.
3. Thermo-Strut.

5.3
Perth Photobioreactor
Perth, Australia

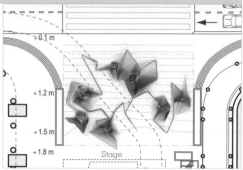

2

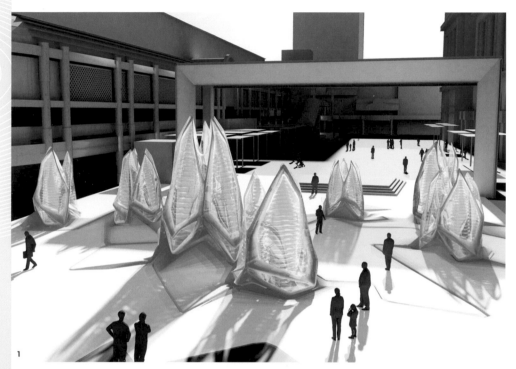

1

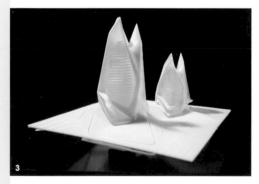

3

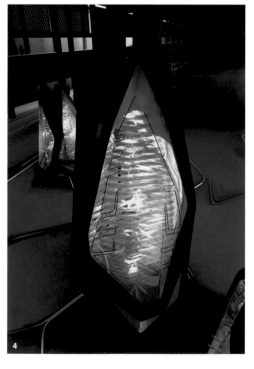

4

1, 2. Models.
3. Installation.
4. Plan.

The Perth Photobioreactor is an attempt to avoid the trappings of conventional public art, which is often associated with large, modern expressions of form. The nine photobioreactors gather energy via several interwoven high- and low-tech systems, including a luminous, photosynthetic helix invented by OriginOil, and thin-film solar transistors that are woven into ornamental electronic tracery.

The outer shells of the photobioreactors are fibre-composite monocoque construction, pleated for stiffness. These structures support transparent polycarbonate apertures to allow in sunlight, while also protecting internal moving parts. Inside are coils of transparent acrylic that contain green or red algae colonies. The algae's photosynthetic processes require carbon dioxide on the front end, to produce biodiesel or hydrogen at the back end. The devices simultaneously remove carbon dioxide from the atmosphere, and generate fuel in a closed-loop, off-the-grid system.

The benefit is that it allows for continued operation in shade and complete darkness through the use of a helix of lights inside each algae coil. These lights are triggered by low sunlight, so that at dusk the cells will begin to turn on, one by one, generating a kaleidoscope of coloured light and glowing algae. The result is a technologically ambient urban space, which also conveniently provides ground lighting for passers-by. Electricity required for this lighting is provided by the thin-film solar transistor system embedded in the transparent polycarbonate apertures, which charge during the day.

6
FLETCHER STUDIO

San Francisco-based Fletcher Studio, founded by David Fletcher in 2004, pushes the boundary of complex landscape design by using advanced digital experimentation. Fletcher, who is also a professor and lecturer in landscape architecture at the University of Southern California, undertakes research that looks at time and process in design, urban ecology, alternative transportation networks, green infrastructure, phenomenology and post-industrial urbanism.

The firm's designers are not afraid to design their landscapes parametrically, using Rhinoceros, Grasshopper and RhinoScript software. They test complex form, layout, functionality and overall design through computer rendering, simulation and careful calculation across a range of scales. This is also supported by a collaborative and contextual approach to spatial design practice and to the planning of unique and sustainable landscapes, urban spaces and living infrastructures. Design and planning solutions stem from interaction with the users, processes, histories, policies, economies and ecologies that are specific to a place.

At the studio, digital experimentations are conducted to provide deeper insights into spatial form and ecological performance. Software including 3D Studio MAX, Google SketchUp and Rhinoceros is used to generate experimental form and to test design concepts, while Maya software is used for generating Voronoi shapes, and Adobe Illustrator and Photoshop for image modifications.

6.1
Horseshoe Cove
Marin Headlands, California

Over the last hundred years, Horseshoe Cove, located in the Marin Headlands, California, has undergone immense spatial, programmatic and ecological change, evolving as one of the area's most significant cultural, educational and recreational sites. The project brief called for the redevelopment and restoration of the water's edge. The design concept, therefore, began with the creation of a dynamic, mixed-use site, accomplished through the construction of an interwoven landscape.

The scheme 'stitches together' the larger landscape into San Francisco Bay, like the fingers of two interlocking hands. Using advanced digital explorations, the designers, in collaboration with design studio Matsys, tested various forms that link between land and sea, which would most suit the concept. Land is pushed out into the water, and water is pulled back into the land, creating a harmonious blend of the two. Although the overall 'horseshoe' shape of the cove is retained, a dynamic and diverse waterfront is created.

Using complex geometries and form-testing in Rhino software, the designers were able to increase the overall surface area by 'folding' the water's edge, with the folded join between land and sea acting as the central circulation route across the site. Through digital design experimentation, the meandering geometry extends the promenade, connecting it to site features. The interior of each fold contains the main functions of the site. The bermed area creates new fishing piers and an amphitheatre; this spine connects and redistributes the activities of the site. The inland landscape folds contain programmes that include a National Park Service visitor centre and shop, as well as bike and boat rental/repair facilities.

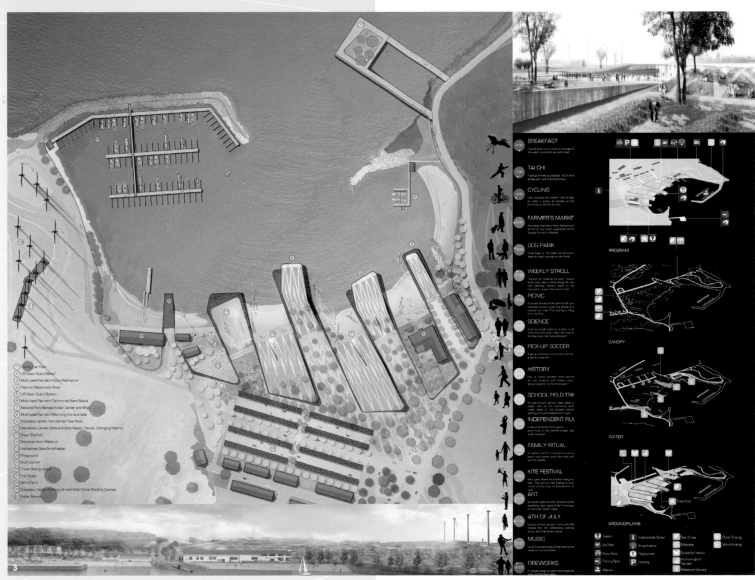

1. Long section.
2. Computer rendering
of the finished project.
3. Plan.

6.2
Polish History Museum
Warsaw, Poland

This proposal for a new Polish History Museum encompasses a covered public space over an existing motorway, which bisects the castle grounds and the botanic gardens. The new public space would replace the agricultural and community gardens that once occupied the site. The proposal also includes an integrated water-management system that captures, stores and reuses water, as well as cleaning water that would otherwise flow into the adjacent river untreated. The architects examined the overall geometries, form, functionality and integrations of the surface through digital applications. Stretching, pulling, reshaping and connecting spaces can be easily achieved through advanced modelling software, including Rhino.

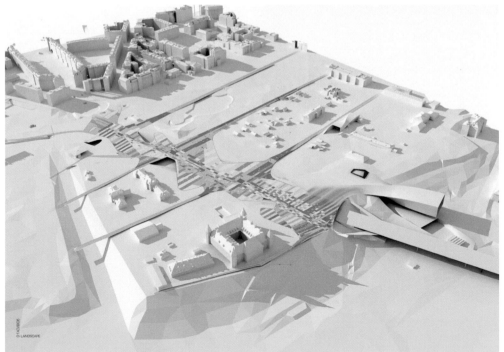

4

7 FREISE BROTHERS

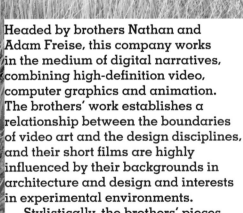

Headed by brothers Nathan and Adam Freise, this company works in the medium of digital narratives, combining high-definition video, computer graphics and animation. The brothers' work establishes a relationship between the boundaries of video art and the design disciplines, and their short films are highly influenced by their backgrounds in architecture and design and interests in experimental environments.

Stylistically, the brothers' pieces range from possessing a flat, two-dimensional graphic quality to a more photorealistic and cinematic aesthetic, and explore themes of technology and design through moving images. Their working processes incorporate composite rendering that combines the use of digital software, including 3D Studio MAX rendered with Mental Ray. Three-dimensional models are often textured two-dimensionally in post-production software (such as Photoshop), or with scanned images that have been drawn by hand.

In 2007, Nathan and Adam Freise were recognized as two of Chicago's Visionary Young Architects. Having previously trained with 'starchitect' Jean Nouvel, in Paris, the brothers have also worked in several architecture offices in Chicago as designers and digital illustrators. In both current and future projects, the brothers intend to continue their exploration into the relationships between digital design, narrative and cinema.

7.1
Unseen Realities

1

Unseen Realities is a visual narrative about a community of artists who inhabit an abandoned industrial landscape. Rather than redrawing and redesigning the landscape from scratch, the brothers retrofitted the space. The 'inhabitants' piece together and reclaim old buildings, establish a marketplace within the junkyard, and create a new community completely fabricated from the recycled materials. The landscape thus maintains the industrial character that attracted the citizens here in the first place.

The renderings are crafted as a combination of digital media and traditional hand-media to reflect the dual aesthetic of reclaimed structures. A greyscale model was illuminated and rendered as a background matte, then textured two-dimensionally, digitally and by hand. Software used for this exploration included 3D Studio MAX rendered with V-Ray and Photoshop.

1. This project explores utopic (and dystopic) possibilities for the future of infrastructure.

7.2
Fallen Silo

Fallen Silo is a concept based on a community's inhabitation of abandoned grain silos, and nostalgia for the pastoral. The digital images propose scenarios of 'green-washing trends' in sustainable-design lifestyles. Overall, the project portrays a poetic vision of refitting old structures in order to create new typologies and landscapes.

The multilayered rendering style is achieved through a combination of 3D software (including 3D Studio MAX rendered with Mental Ray), 2D painting software (Photoshop) and hand-drawing. The collapsing silos were created through a digital dynamic collision simulation, while the grass was generated through a digital spline system.

1. Poetic visions of refitting old structures, night scene.
2. Digital prototype plan, green render.

7.3
Virtual Reality
Topology

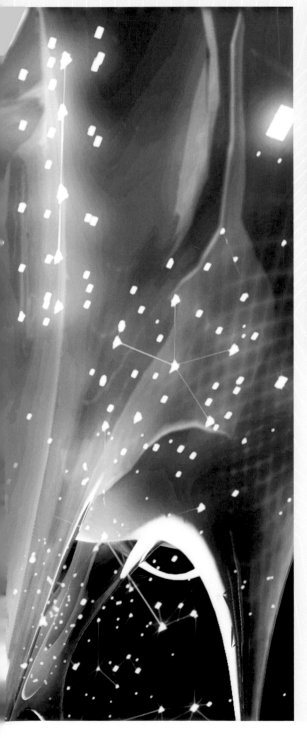

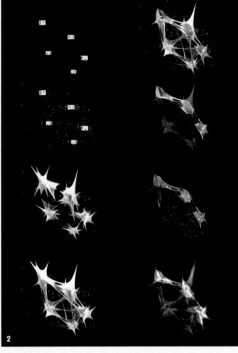

Virtual Reality Topology attempts to redefine the way people experience virtual environments; the idea is to replace the stationary physical elements with a multiuser interactive surface, which evolves from the simplest to the most complex environment. Environments are created when the surface makes many connections with 'image-generators'. Within this virtual landscape, connections are formed between environments when many of the same user 'energies' are shared, thereby creating a topology of virtual reality.

The diagrams depict how the user's energies are translated into generators, and the three-dimensional images show the final topology that is formed when these generators connect and expand. The images were created with a combination of software; an 'L-system generation program' was used to produce the framework of the growing surface, and then a three-dimensional model of the surface was created by connecting the points of the branching L-system.

1. Virtual topology.
2. Connecting generators.

7.4
Megatourism
Saemangeum, South Korea

1

Megatourism poses an alternative to a proposed government masterplan. Saemangeum, an estuarine tidal flat on the coast of the Yellow Sea, is one of the world's largest mudflat sites, about 200 km (124 miles) south of Seoul. Around it, the South Korean government constructed the world's longest seawall (33 km, or 21 miles) along the perimeter, and intends to landfill the site for future commercial development – a situation that will destroy the mudflat ecology by drying up the marshlands and devastating the habitat of the native birds.

The government's primary objective with this scheme is to bring 100 million tourists per year to the newly created area. Freise Brothers' proposal aims to achieve this goal, while developing at most 50 per cent of the site, leaving the rest for land reclamation. The mega-structure proposal is only a fraction of the size of the current scheme, and accommodates twice the population density. The design's porous structure allows for a variety of programmes, including train stations, recreational parks, elevated boardwalks, hotels and apartment units.

The illustrations seen here focus on the two different design proposals: a habitable mega-structure to be built along an existing sea dyke, and a hydroelectric city that pairs contrasting programmes to form symbiotic relationships. This strategic pairing aims to meet the land-usage requirements, while at the same time balancing the site's ecology. Three-dimensional models were illuminated and rendered as background mattes, then textured two-dimensionally. Software used for this digital landscape exploration included 3D Studio MAX rendered with Mental Ray and Photoshop.

1. Dike structure.
2. Hollow gardens.
3. Hydro-electric city.

7.5
Scapegote

Scapegote is a virtual-reality visitor centre, where data posts and information meshes take the place of physical manipulation, with the intention of developing an ever-growing catalogue of visitor experiences, while at the same time preserving a site's delicate ecology. The aim of the centre is to provide users with a deeper knowledge of the site's history, its evolving ecology, and its uncertain future, due to complex siting and contamination.

The park is overlaid with a mesh network of large-scale 'helio-displays' (images of the history and ecology of the site), which reconfigure their position over time, based on users' input and the changing ecology. Visitors wear a lens that displays information specific to data inputted to collection posts on the park perimeter. Each experience is then stored in a database, with the recorded video and audio material accessible to future visitors. The idea is that different moments in time, different stages of the site's development, and other people's visual experiences and knowledge will be catalogued and showcased, to be experienced again by others at a later date. In fact, this becomes part of an augmented and reactive environment using advanced digital means. The 'exaggerated atmospheres' aim to highlight the surreal visitor experience during different times of day and seasons. They are purely digital in their creation.

berm patch west
spartina alterniflora
smooth cordgrass

footage: 03.14.06
berm patch west
northern bobwhites flocking
colinus virginianus

footage: 01.02.0
berm patch west
grey birch cluster
callus ridge from frost
cracks developed between
01.05 - present.

3

1. Feedback station.
2. Input-scape.
3. Output-scape.

8
GROUNDLAB

London-based Groundlab is an emerging practice led by four partners: Eva Castro, Holger Kehne, Alfredo Ramirez and Eduardo Rico. In addition, Castro is the director of the landscape urbanism programme at the Architectural Association (p. 294) in London, where Ramirez and Rico also conduct research and teach. Groundlab explores landscape urbanism as a new mode of practice, capable of responding to contemporary social, economic and environmental conditions, beyond landscape and towards urbanism. Their research is interdisciplinary, and the group collaborates with professionals across a range of fields.

The partnership believes in process, changeability, flexibility and resilience, so that their designs have the potential to adapt themselves within their greater environments over time. The design process involves a balance between a critical understanding of existing site conditions, and projections as to how the site might evolve in the future. Using parametric modelling, sophisticated diagramming and CNC fabrication, the group's visionary landscapes become plausible solutions for new ways of examining urbanism in the future. These parametric tools allow for a fluidity within the design process that enables the firm to test variable options with minimal effort, almost in real time.

Flowing Gardens,
Xi'an, China.

8.1
Flowing Gardens
Xi'an, China

In association with architects Plasma Studio, Groundlab was invited to design the landscaping for the International Horticultural Expo 2011, in Xi'an, China. The design was generated as a synthesis of ecology and technology, in which landscape and architecture fused together into a progressive, sustainable vision. The proposal included an exhibition hall (5,000 m^2; 53,820 sq ft), a greenhouse (4,000 m^2; 43,056 sq ft), and a gatehouse (3,500 m^2; 37,674 sq ft), all situated in 37 ha (91 acres) of landscape.

The masterplan achieved a balance of functionality between water, vegetation, circulation, programme and architecture to create a working system. The three buildings are located at the major intersections of the pathways, providing strong nodal focus. Connected to the landscape surface through pathways and emerging vegetation, the buildings anchor strong connecting strands throughout the site. The gatehouse provides a threshold for a framed view of the gardens, while at the same time offering areas for public meetings. The building and landscape are part of a fluid form, interconnecting various spaces, surfaces and materials into a collective unity.

1. Digital render: aerial view.
2. Aerial view, with the Creative Pavilion in the foreground.
3. Aerial view of the greenhouse.
4. Digital render: greenhouse.
5. Overall masterplan.
6. Aerial view from the lake.

4

5

6

8.2
Deep Ground:
Longgang Masterplan
Shenzhen, China

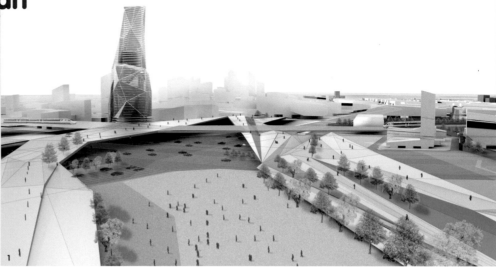

Groundlab, together with Plasma Studio, won the international design competition for the regeneration of the centre of the Longgang district of Shenzhen, including Longcheng Square. The project covers 11.8 km² (4.6 sq miles) of urban fabric, with an estimated population of 350,000 and 9,000,000 m² (96,875,194 sq ft) of new development. For the design, the firm used a landscape urbanism approach, and proposed a 'thickening' of the ground by implementing underground development, in combination with designs for public spaces and a river crossing.

The team also applied the notion of the ground as an attempt to 'understand and design the space as a surface, which acquires thickness and spatial complexity as the different programmes and land uses start to combine'. The new, thickened ground provides a mixed-use programme that is open-ended and adaptable to change, based on future infrastructural development and population growth. Despite the fact that Longgang River is located at the centre of the district, there was no substantial connection between the city and the river. Groundlab's proposal includes an infrastructural landscape project that uses and connects the river to the city, revitalizing both through a large-scale green system that is interactive and interconnected. According to the designers, this new infrastructure 'will serve as an anchor point to deploy

cleansing strategies, rainwater collection and flooding defenses, while creating green areas, ecological corridors, public open spaces, sports fields and leisure areas'. The design provides the perfect blend between ecology and the city, using creative infrastructural solutions to connect the two.

The team used parametric modelling to test and control built mass quantities, as well as a 3D model of the built fabric, simultaneously. The model is based in sets of urban relationships, which connect to one another. One of the advantages in working parametrically, say the designers, is that doing so 'enables the generation of different options with relatively minor effort, as most of the drawing gets automatically produced, while there is potentially the chance to evaluate the overall built volume before the volume is even generated'. This digital process offers the combination of variables related to density with variables related to typology. This parametric combination could be used to generate and test diverse urban patterns with simple controls. The 'volume' of the proposed built fabric shown in the final drawing and renderings has been modelled to fit the quantity of land use calculated for the site.

Working parametrically and through this digital process has provided Groundlab with a series of design options that allow the team to examine the effects

of different massing forms simultaneously. The images depict various iterations of the landscape and model. Through the parametric process, new designs are quickly generated, based on a number of building changes, including density, urban reconfiguration, and so on. When making these changes, the parametric software also offers evaluation options to aid the team in making wiser design moves. Longgang masterplan offers adaptable design, where changes to different variables can be introduced to the design almost in real time.

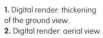

1. Digital render: thickening
of the ground view.
2. Digital render: aerial view.

9
GT2P

GT2P (Great Things to People) is a young, Chilean-based design firm that focuses on parametric architecture and design. Their main area of interest is in the design process, assisted by computer-aided design and manufacture (CAD/CAM). They have developed parametric design rules and conditions that apply this digital knowledge for the scalability, adaptability and connectivity between architecture, landscape, art and furniture design. Through this digital process, the firm has developed various DNA scripting groups, which are related but programmed to different ends to achieve unique mass customization in the design of their landscapes and architectural pieces.

Important to the firm's research is the inclusion of fabrication techniques and materiality in their design process.

By involving advanced digital fabrication technologies, they achieve a new level of experimentation, while optimizing time and cost management by utilizing scripting and defined parameters in current production methods. By incorporating materiality, the designers can create algorithms that specifically tailor the material properties to the design question at hand. To do this, they use advanced digital parametric modelling software, including Grasshopper for Rhino, and digital fabrication systems such as CNC machining and thermoforming. The significance of this digital process can be found in increased efficiency and productivity in design, as well as in the beautifully intricate forms it creates.

Furrow Fields.

9.1
Furrow Fields

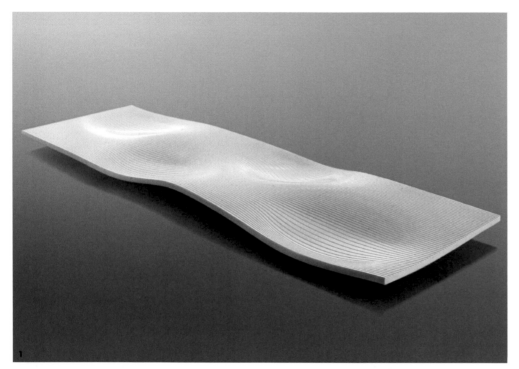

1

This project investigates new 'rules and definitions' that modify to a previously defined parametric surface, in the directions X, Y and Z through points of attraction and/or repulsion. The operation creates a new surface defined by the isocurves (the curves that follow the U and V directions of the surface of an object). Furrow Fields deals with parametric generation, using 'Corian stripes' surfaces (a solid surface made from polymer and alumina trihydrate), the result of the interaction between PN points and the SO original surface, which are derived from PO points that are part of curves systems. These points and definitions are programmed into the Grasshopper plug-in for Rhinoceros, which also allows for changes in form and shape to occur automatically based on these new inputs.

Furrow Fields is made of Corian, which has been thermocreated and routed. It is created by routing a piece in a low surface of 12-mm (½-in) Corian. Two moulds are made in a low-density MDF block – a positive and a negative one – and the piece is finally thermoshaped (in the shape of a sandwich, using the Corian piece). Both processes have been parametrically designed for CNC construction routines.

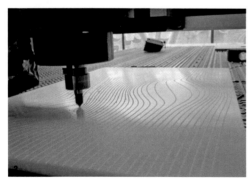

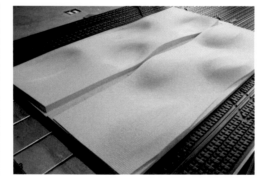

1. 'Corian stripe' model.
2, 3. Fabrication.
4. Digital model.

9.2
Wave Interference

Wave Interference is a project of thermoformed backlit acrylic coatings, which resemble the shape of a vertical flowing landscape or waterfall. By using advanced digital design processes, the surface is generated by six curves that are defined from mathematical equations, based on a range of points.

Each curve is generated through a numerical range from 0 to N, and by factor X distance. Within this range, a mathematical equation of sine, cosine, tangent or wave is applied to the surface interference. The two upper curves, together with the two lower curves, generate part of the c1 (curve 1) applications, which are crafted through this parametric process. The second central curve (c2) is derived from the central 'spline'. The construction of the outer surface is connected by six corners, with opening and closures of the spaces. These openings also allow light to penetrate through the vertical landscape surface.

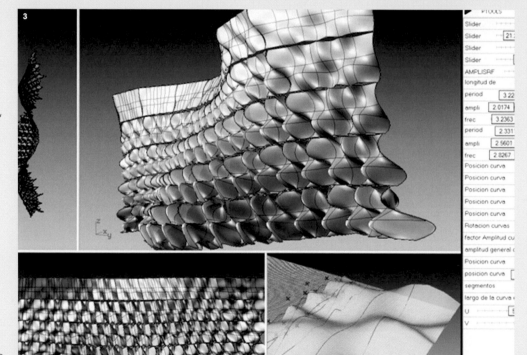

1, 2. Vertical landscape.
3. Digital-design processes; curve experiment.
4. Colour testing.

9.3
Velo Catalyst
Santiago, Chile

GT2P was commissioned to create bicycle parking shelters, or *bicicleteros*, for the city of Santiago. By exploring adaptive infrastructural solutions, the designers defined three situations: first, they considered the users' short commuting time by car; secondly, they examined data from a study by the National Corporation for a second transit site in the selected areas; and finally, they considered the shape of each *bicicletero*, depending on the number of users per site.

The designers utilized a contextual strategy, analysing and identifying the main roads used for cycling, the infrastructure relating to the *bicicleteros* (for the metro, buses or public spaces) and the plans for building cycle lanes. Through this analysis, two main sites were selected to test and develop the adaptive shelters: Plaza Egaña, and a small site near the Mapocho River. Within these sites, the designers identified the optimal location

for their adaptive bicycle shelters, taking into consideration visibility, the distance between the entrances to the space (such as metro entrances), the existing capacity of the growing infrastructure to support bicycle shelters for short or long-term stay, and the overall enhancement of the public space. Once these factors were identified, various configurations of the *bicicleteros* were created at each site to respond to these local conditions.

The basic structure and the roof were configured to support new and changing programmes, including circulation, trade events, meeting spaces and parking, allowing for the creation of dynamic public spaces. The structure is adjustable, changing and responding to the number of bicycles and their possible parking stations. The final form is derived from the creation of an adaptive shaded shelter that resembles a massive 'tree', situated in an urban landscape.

1. Nighttime scene.
2–5. Various daytime scenes.
6. Aerial overview.
7. Section.

9.4
Grapevine
Vibrational
Rancagua, Chile

1. Model.
2. Night scene.
3. Ceiling detail.
4. Entrance.
5, 6. Branching system.
7. Branching system, parametric
generation.

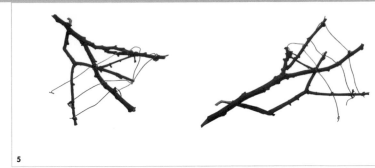

5

6

4

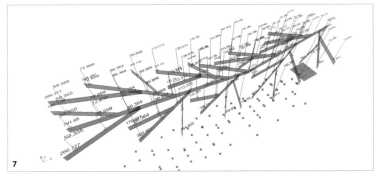

7

The winner of a competition for the incorporation of works of art into buildings and public spaces, Grapevine Vibrational is an installation for the entryway of a health-care centre in Rancagua, Chile, located in the western part of the city. The concept incorporates the designers' analysis of the site, which was then 'parameterized' through Grasshopper to engage the location's 'forces' into a physical output. The digital design was then fabricated into an elegant, interactive trellis system, providing two distinct spatial experiences: that of the organic growth pattern, created by a series of dangling structures in various positions; and of the wind vibrations resulting from these delicate structures.

A series of models defining the existing growth of the vine were articulated as part of the structural trellis system. The effect of leaves moving in the wind was cleverly realized through faceted crystal balls, which reflect an array of colours from the surrounding sunlight and create a serene 'passage' through the space. The colours also symbolize the hues of the various leaves on the site. The designers created a 'definition' in Grasshopper that would parameterize the growth of the structure, defining trunks, branches and leaves, and taking into consideration access to the building. The definitions modelled a structure that mimics the branching patterns of the vines. For the leaves, the designers created another definition in Grasshopper that regulated the density of elements, spacing, distance from hook and orientation of the grid sheet over a previously modelled surface.

The numbering of each branch of the vine, the trellis joint types and each crystal pendant, including the length of the cables, were all crafted parametrically, significantly reducing waste and enabling the project to keep to a low budget.

10
PAULO GUERREIRO

Specializing in advanced digital modelling, Paulo Guerreiro is currently coordinator of the digital concept lab for CLCS Architects, in Lisbon, where he looks into new ways of understanding and generating architectural and landscape spaces under the digital paradigm. His work is inspired by nature, ecology, living organisms and the environment, and is based on generative and parametric design models, with an emphasis on morphogenetic strategies and biomimetic logic.

Guerreiro's research also includes references to artificial intelligence, augmented reality and meta-universe relations. Through a dynamic digital design process, he develops generative algorithms and reactive environments that evolve relationships between existing atmospheres and proposed structural conditions. When beginning a project, Guerreiro collects site information, including images, statistics, history, cultural, geology and climate data. Images are tagged with numeric data through OpenOffice Calc, before climate data is analysed in Autodesk Ecotect. All information collected is merged into an OpenOffice database, to be processed digitally by 3D modelling engines.

Guerreiro uses advanced computation processes and software, including Cinema 4D, Rhinoceros, the generative engine in Grasshopper for Rhino, Blender, Python and Qhull. Surfaces and polysurfaces are modelled as NURBS surfaces, before being edited and sculpted using a HyperNURBS modifier. Physical outputs of digital models are then created by means of subtraction and section, using CNC machining processes.

Biotope: Open possibilities on a symbiotic shelter.

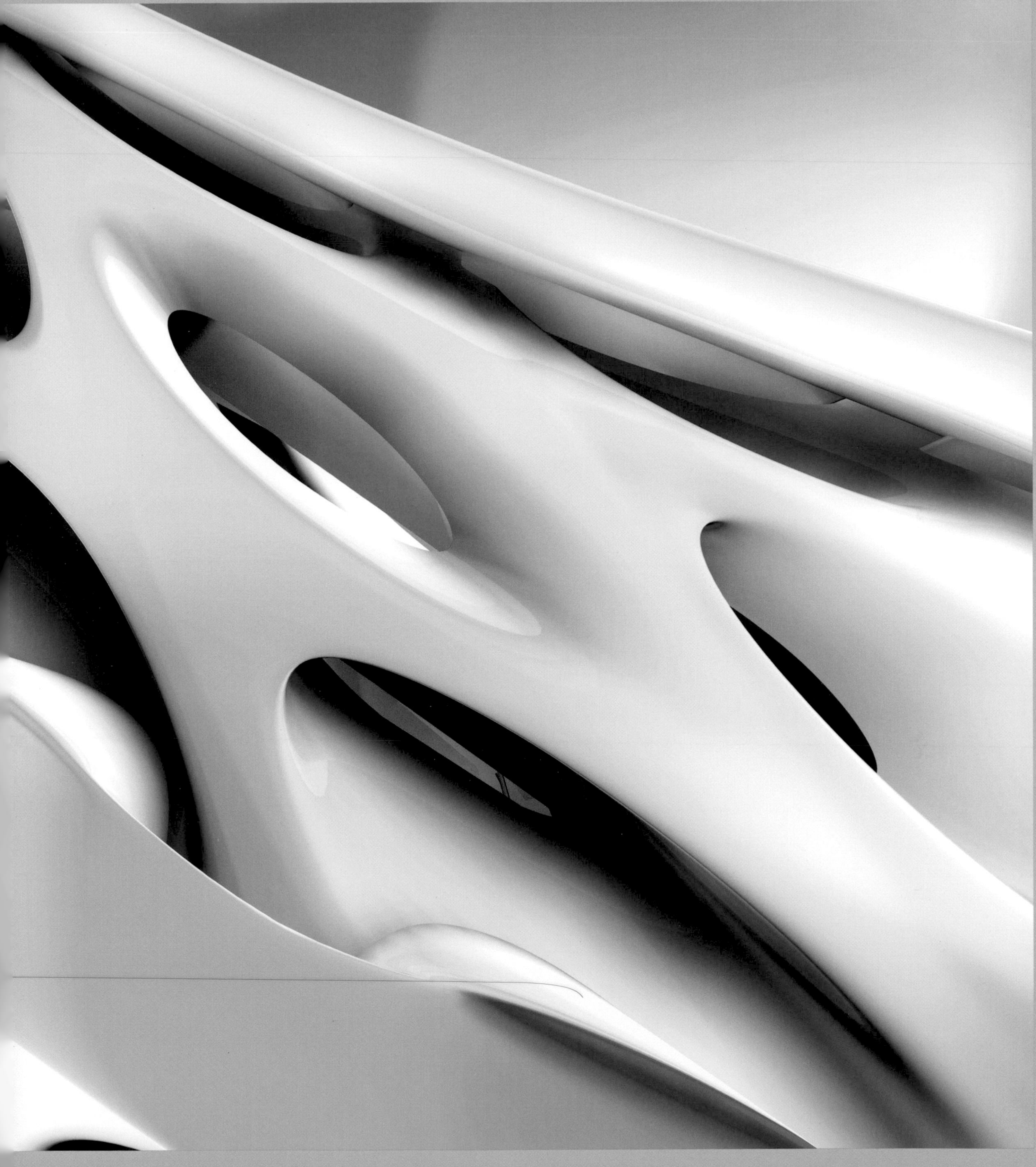

10.1
Biotope
Open possibilities on a symbiotic shelter

1. Assumed porous façade.
2. The structural shell generates interior spaces.
3. Façade openings for light and ventilation.
4. The coral-like shell of the building.

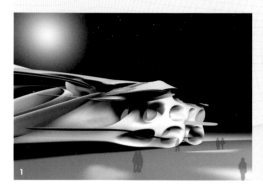

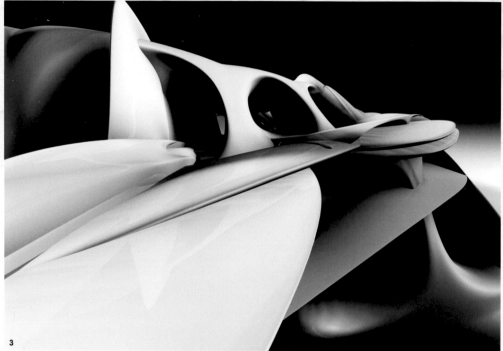

Inspired by nature, the basic concept of the Biotope project derives from an examination of small, porous rocks and coral, which provide habitats for living micro-organisms and small animals. The building, or shelter, would control shade, light, temperature and humidity levels, similar to that of living organisms; this is part of a reactive environment between the atmospheric forces with the structure. Based on advanced generative algorithms, the biotope would be able to negotiate and manage the relationship between the inside space and the outside environment. Guerreiro used advanced technologies and software, including Cinema 4D, Rhinoceros and CNC output.

The main structure was modelled as a NURBS-type polysurface, with the interior spaces and porous-like openings sculpted by a HyperNURBS modifier. The function combines and merges the interior spaces with the exterior polysurface, creating a unified, porous biotope shape. A physical model was created by sectioning the biotope in Rhinoceros, and produced through several sections of the model in a CNC machine by means of subtraction.

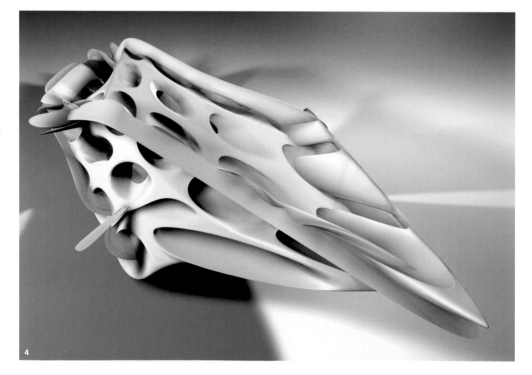

10.2
Fractal Grid
From the topological model to the fractal field

Fractal Grid is a metaproject that investigates the conceptual explorations of a non-topological model, based on generative and parametric approaches. It is founded on mathematical principles, and evolved using 3D digital-design tools, including Rhinoceros, Blender, Python and Qhull. It explores concepts relating to fractal development and crystal structures imposed onto urban and non-urban landscapes, and attempts to bridge the gap between traditional topological models and abstract mathematical models in a dynamic relationship of interactions. This is achieved by generating a 'fractalization layer', with the option of reprogramming space through the structure, layers and densities.

The landscape is the medium that connects the urban, highly populated areas with the non-urban, less populated areas, creating a field of distortion and continual topographical changes. Within the urban layer, the fractal systems are generated through a mathematical form in the city's empty spaces. This process creates a new infrastructure, which generates a 'non-empty' place above, between, even underneath the urban topography. The infrastructure continues to change between the cage and the topological urban scene. This constant transformation creates a new layer-system in the city. The fractalization layer is part of a parametric development that

bridges both landscape models, one of urban topological origin and the other of pure mathematical abstraction. Within the non-urban landscape, the fractal relationship is derived by the landscape morphology. The fractalization layer is still assumed as a self-driven infrastructure by means of its generative process. Due to the closer relationship with the terrain's morphology, the layer becomes part of the nature of the place, merging with landscape or becoming an extension of it.

The main geometrical form is modelled as a NURBS-type polysurface. Guerreiro defines key control points, and establishes generative limits to grow the fractalized volume into a cloud of points, which are then transformed into a cage. The mathematical process is applied in an unusual research context, and can be obtained via code (Python), through Qhull or Blender software.

1. Experimental output grid.
2. Grid propagation in the natural environment.

10.3
Skinning Steel
Skinning the 'in-between'

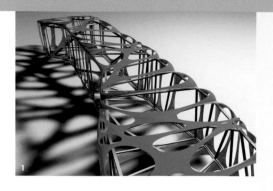

Skinning Steel is part of a parametric landscape, based on logical functions and equations. Derived from a reflection about the urban environment, the project explores the evolutionary cityscape, focusing on the primary approach of fragmented thoughts about the city. To help generate the project, Guerreiro explores such questions as: 'How do new spaces interact with the old? How do the spaces between become mediate? How do they craft our urban fabric?'

The residual voids above, beneath and between large structures somehow become incongruous spaces that tend to assume a novel hybrid nature. Skinning Steel is a small experiment that reuses steel structures in urban niches, exploring the possibility of reframing those that grow around existing urban spaces. The landscape structure is 'skinned' with a polymeric membrane that acts as a roof, façade and floor simultaneously,

subverting the notion of interior and exterior. This hybrid environment offers the possibility of an independent support system for various programmatic purposes. The possibility of generating a support structure for an augmented reality layer is also assumed for this project, enforcing the notion of a hybrid space (an urban reality and an augmented space).

The structure is generated through a palette of computational tools, including Google Earth, Adobe Photoshop, Rhinoceros, Grasshopper and Cinema 4D. The urban fabric is analysed in Google Earth and processed in Photoshop, and the urban elements separated into layers. The space between the mass elements is presumed as growing space; within this layer, key points are selected in the x, y and z axes, which will be assumed as coordinates for the frame nodes. Structures between these nodes are

generated in Rhinoceros, using the Grasshopper generative engine. Through this process, there is a level of control in terms of the position of the nodes, and also of aspects relating to the frame structure in a parametric method. A bounding box is then extracted and later transformed into a polymeric skin in Cinema 4D, achieved by a HyperNURBS modifier. Both pieces are composed together to form the main support structure.

1. Assumed hybrid and mediating nature.
2. Stretched membrane, generating dynamic hybrid space.
3. Polymeric compound membrane, evolving the skin structure.

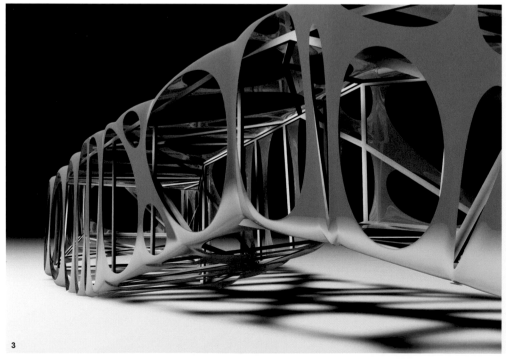

10.4
Digital Waterfront
(Gen)erative scapes

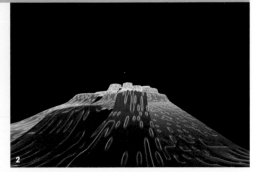

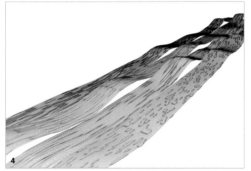

1. Nighttime simulation: integrating light into water niches.
2. Morphology essay.
3. Tides output study.
4. Layering stripes, each integrating different levels of interaction.

With this project, Guerreiro explores the dynamic relationships between land and water, thus creating a new understanding of the waterfront as a unified, dynamic and flowing system. Changing water flow and other relational information are stored into a data bank, with the data merged with other elements from various origins to form a 'meta-concept' of the new waterfront. This new digital model is designed as a generative base model, making it parametric, which allows the structure to change shape, based on the metadata between the basic elements and the relationship between the sequence of events, tidal fluctuation, and other water and land conditions.

The first part of the digital process is concerned with developing the site's data bank with regards to the waterfront. This includes collecting images, statistics, morphology, geological data, weather data, sun charts, walking paths and landmarks of the area. The images are tagged with meta-content in Adobe Lightroom and numeric data in OpenOffice Calc, and weather and climatic changes are analysed in Autodesk Ecotect, with particle simulations rendered in Cinema 4D. All possible data is merged in OpenOffice database. A possible conceptual approach is modelled with Rhinoceros, using the generative engine in Grasshopper, which can merge directly in the model definition data from other sources.

11
KATHRYN GUSTAFSON

Gardens by the Bay,
Marina East, Singapore.

Kathryn Gustafson has over twenty-five years of distinguished landscape design practice. Her two firms – Gustafson Porter in London and Gustafson Guthrie Nichol in Seattle – have developed award-winning work, including a widely recognized series of projects throughout Europe, North America and the Middle East. Her projects, primarily for civic, institutional and corporate clients, range from parks and gardens to community spaces. Gustafson's output continues to evolve with a design approach that combines contexts of time, culture and nature, and she believes in site-specific work that is conscious of its surroundings, revealing to its users characteristics that are already embedded within the site.

Gustafson works with both analogue and digital processes, and is particularly known for her poetically sculptural clay models and sensuous topography and landforms. Her models are often scanned three-dimensionally or through reverse engineering. She also uses 3D-modelling software programs, including Rhinoceros and 3D Studio MAX, to position, form and test the dimensions and openings in a design. The resulting digital model can then be used for a variety of other design explorations or for presentational purposes, such as perspective drawings or plans.

11.1
Gardens by the Bay
Marina East, Singapore

This multilayered series of gardens in Singapore aims to become a vital part of the city by offering cultural, educational, urban and leisure activities within a tropical environment. Comprising three distinctive waterfront gardens – south, east and central – the project will occupy a total of 101 ha (250 acres) in the new downtown area at Marina Bay.

The design proposes to create a landscape vocabulary that is three-dimensional in form and experience. The spatial interpretation of the city is recorded through sensuous landforms, variations of which were explored by the design team using advanced 3D modelling software, which allude to the lush leaf shapes found in the tropics. These leaf forms open up to embrace water 'inlets' that appear to flow from the site's eastern boundary to the bay's edge.

Water underpins the design aesthetic of the gardens, from the scale of the bay and its boating activities to the reed-bed cleansing system, the aquatic gardens and terraces, fountains and wave pools. Throughout the site, restaurants and bars are set within the landforms that cluster around the water features. They contribute to a seamless landscape experience, where eating and planting can be themed to coincide with the gardens, and where sweeping views across the bay to the city skyline can be enjoyed.

1. Detail of the leaf-like landform.
2–4. Collage perspectives of various experiential walkways.

11.2
Lurie Garden
Chicago, Illinois

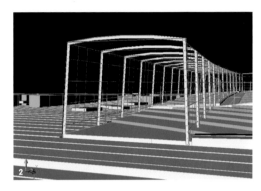

This proposal brings a new public botanic garden to downtown Chicago. Sited in Lakefront Millennium Park, it is located between a bandshell by Frank Gehry and a new wing of the Chicago Art Institute by Renzo Piano, and is constructed over the roof deck of the Lakefront Millennium parking garage. When it matures, a large, muscular hedge will enclose the garden from the north and west. From the Art Institute, the 'shoulders' of the Shoulder Hedge – a living wall that protects the garden's interior from the pedestrian traffic moving through the park – appear to support the luminous headdress of Gehry's bandshell to the north.

The Shoulder Hedge organizes circulation patterns through the perennial garden, both inside and out, to develop a legible hierarchy of pedestrian movement. Like a distant ridge in an open Midwestern landscape, the Shoulder Hedge is a horizon that defines the bright foreground of the garden interior. It is structured by a metal framework, or armature, that shapes several varieties of plants into one monumental hedge feature. The structure is generated using sophisticated three-dimensional software, including 3D Studio MAX, to test the design, position and form, dimensions and openings. The armature provides a simple and permanent clipping guide to maintain the precise sculpted profile of the mature Shoulder Hedge. As the hedge plants grow, visitors can watch them develop into their full form, filling the armature.

Within the Shoulder Hedge, the garden has two interior 'plates' that are planted with perennials and trees. The plates appear to be punched up from the surface of the plaza, like a muscular torso. Dark Plate, which references the poorly drained, flat landscape of the site before settlement, offers an experience of dream-like immersion in a volume of robust perennial compositions. Light Plate,

which references the city's modern and artistic controlling of nature, provides an exhilarating experience of surveying a bright, clean, controlled landscape. The Seam Boardwalk is where the past and future exist face to face, on either side of pedestrians travelling along the boardwalk. The boardwalk is the special corridor, or 'break', between the two plates. The orientation of the boardwalk expresses the angle of the various historic retaining walls beneath the site, which created boundaries between its moist past and dry future. Water fills the Seam Boardwalk between the vertical stone faces of the two plates.

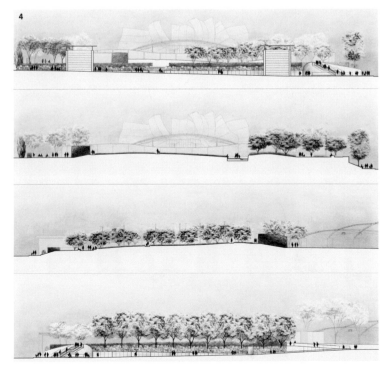

1. Concept sketch.
2. Shoulder Hedge armature.
3. Model.
4. Section.

11.3
Diana, Princess of Wales Memorial Fountain
London, UK

The proposal for this memorial fountain in London's Hyde Park expresses the concept of 'Reaching Out and Letting In'. It is also based on the late princess's most admired qualities – her inclusiveness and accessibility – which are reflected in the different water effects of the finished scheme. The fountain was integrated into the natural slope of the land in the park, using as a starting point the existing ground level around the canopies of the mature trees that encircle the site.

The memorial stands out as a light-coloured ring in the landscape, which contrasts with the surrounding meadow and planting, and has an energy that radiates outwards, while at the same time drawing people near. The fountain has specific features to create the different water effects, including 'Chadar Cascade', 'Swoosh', 'Stepped Cascade' and 'Rock and Roll', as well as a still basin at the bottom, all of which reflect various qualities of the princess's life.

The project was generated using advanced computer modelling programs, including the creation of a 1:1-scale digital model of the fountain in 3D Studio MAX. The digital model was then processed using CNC machinery, and the fountain was fabricated in sections at 1:1-scale, and assembled on site.

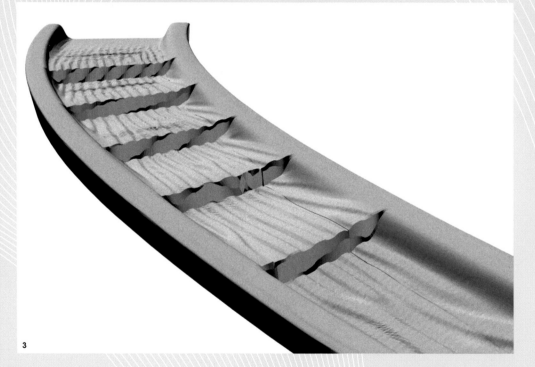

1, 2. The oval structure surrounds and is surrounded by a lush, grassy field.
3. 545 pieces of Cornish granite were cut using computer-guided cutting machines.
4. Digital model.

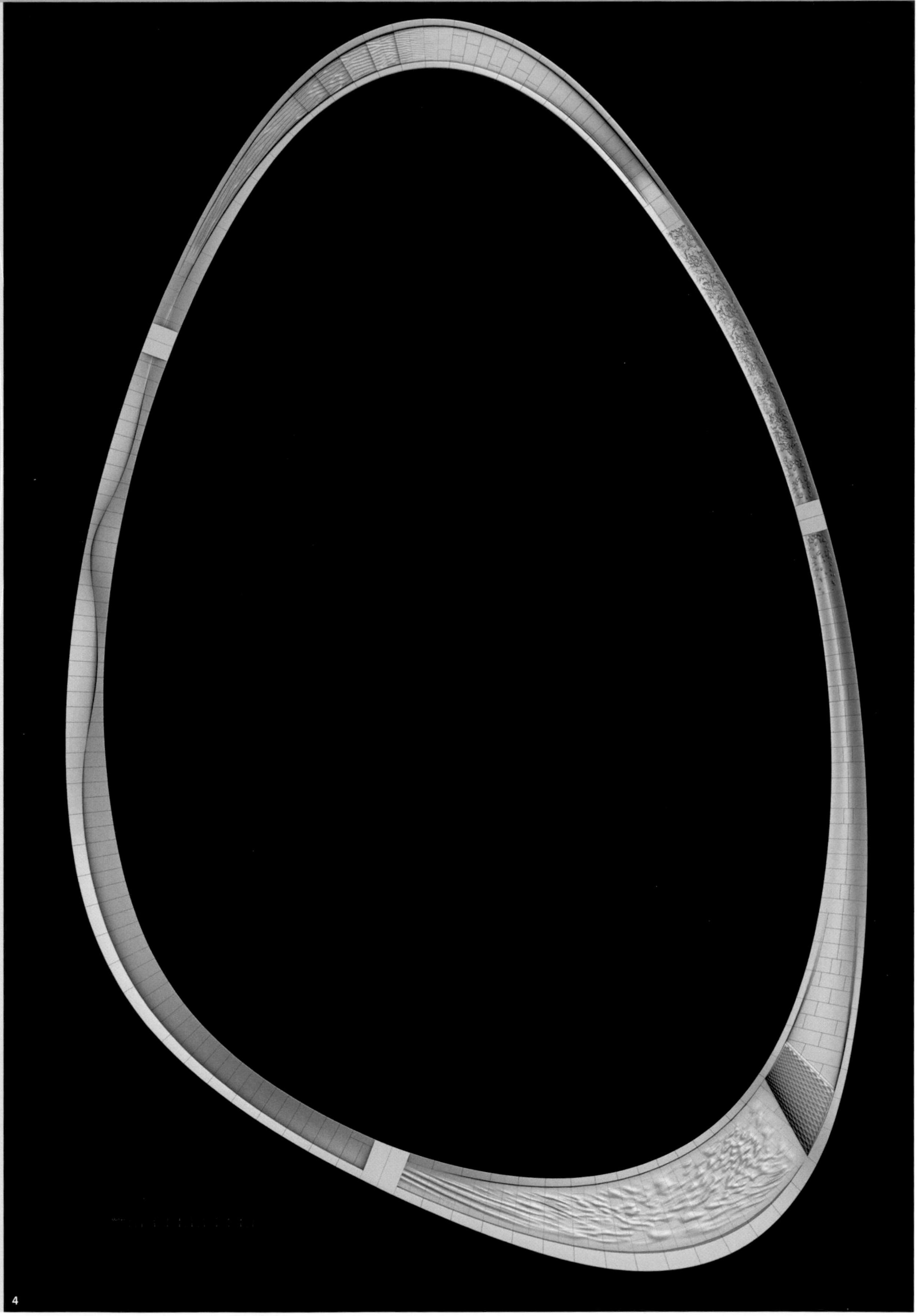

4

12
ZAHA HADID

Zaha Hadid, founding partner of Zaha Hadid Architects, was awarded the Pritzker Prize in 2004 and is known throughout the world for her built, theoretical and academic work. Having studied architecture at the Architectural Association in London, her London-based office now has over 350 employees. Over the last thirty or so years, Hadid has had a profound influence on the shape and direction of contemporary architecture.

Her practice and research challenges traditional notions of architectural and urban design practices. The firm is particularly known for its unique formal language, which strives to integrate existing natural topographic site conditions with cutting-edge and geometrically complex surface experimentations. With the aid of various digital design technologies, Hadid produces distinctive fluid, dynamic forms that sit between the boundaries of architectonic and geologic formations. The office particularly relies on advanced 3D design visualization software tools to accomplish this. In collaboration with Gehry Technologies and Dassault Systèmes, Hadid and her team have developed a digital information modelling system to increase productivity and accelerate the design process. The landscape forms have a particular signature quality that reflects Hadid's philosophy about innovative design that fuses with geometrically progressive surface experimentations.

Abu Dhabi Performing Arts Centre, Abu Dhabi, United Arab Emirates.

12.1
Abu Dhabi
Performing Arts Centre
Abu Dhabi,
United Arab Emirates

A series of analytical studies based on organizational systems and urban growth became the basis for the set of topologies that are the framework of the Abu Dhabi Performing Arts Centre's unique formal signature. These concepts were derived by 'energy being supplied to enclosed systems', and the subsequent 'decrease in energy caused by the development of organized structures'.

The 'energy' of the performing arts centre is symbolized by the intersection of predominant flows in the urban fabric along the pedestrian corridor and the seafront promenade. Defined rhizome-like algorithms and growth-simulation processes were used to develop spatial representations into a set of basic geometries, and then superimposed with programmatic diagrams and built-form interpretations in a series of iterations. The primary components of this biological analogy (branches, stems, fruits and leaves) were transformed from abstract diagrams into formal design.

The sculptural form of the performing arts centre emerges from this linear movement, evolving into a growing organism that stems a network of successive branches, like a new landscape. As it winds through the site, the architecture increases in complexity, building up in height and depth, achieving multiple summits in the bodies that house the performance spaces, which spring from the structure like fruit on a vine and face westward, towards the water.

1. Bird's-eye view from the northwest.
2. North elevation.
3. Bird's-eye view from the east.

12.2
Dubai Opera House
Dubai, United Arab Emirates

This proposal is for an exciting new cultural centre in the Seven Pearls district of Dubai. The landmark development will accommodate an opera house, playhouse, arts gallery, performing arts school and themed hotel on an island in Dubai Creek, just off the mainland part of the district. The opera house and playhouse will have a seating capacity of 2,500 and 800, respectively, while the arts gallery will have 5,000 m² (53,820 sq ft) of exhibition space. The development will be connected to the greater metropolitan area by a road to the mainland.

The design houses all of the facilities within a single evocative structure, whose gentle, winding form recalls images of mountains or sand dunes. Rising out of the ground, this form is both a part of the landscape, as well as a distinctive element in the skyline. Surrounding the site are open park spaces and ancillary functions such as parking facilities and a monorail station, which are tucked underneath or integrated into the landscape forms. From the two peaks of the opera house and playhouse, the building form gradually swoops down to touch the earth. The form is scalloped away where the three major entrances to the complex are sited. The main foyer is a gentle, multi-tiered landscape, set one storey above the ground floor. It serves both the opera house and playhouse, and has an interior connection to the arts gallery.

1. Digital model, aerial view, capturing the flowing forms.
2. Digital model, nighttime view, with cityscape background.

12.3
Olabeaga and San Mamés Masterplans
Bilbao, Spain

The masterplanning of the Olabeaga and San Mamés neighbourhoods presented a unique challenge for the Spanish city of Bilbao and the surrounding region of Bizkaia. While the area's steep topography once made it the natural border for the city's nineteenth-century grid, the expansion of the city has been such that the neighbourhoods now occupy a key left-bank position for the expanding core of the metropolitan centre.

A series of compelling, three-dimensional approaches towards a new urban morphology was identified. Existing patterns within the urban fabric of the waterfront community on the lower slope of the hillside could be pulled into a mesh network of streets and paths to negotiate between the steep terrain and city above. Natural crevices in the fabric connect local paths to distinct plateaus. A sweeping yet elegant downslope of built forms depicts a landscape mass that reflects the existing topography, while accommodating both circulation and a sequence of pocket-sized open spaces. The sweeping curve of the hillside and river offer dramatic potential for promoting a range of panoramic views.

In addition, this fabric could be shown to accommodate major infrastructural change, facilitate large-scale redevelopment and promote the effective inclusion of the area's major institutions and structures into a continuous local pattern. The Olabeaga and San Mamés masterplanning has highlighted what formal three-dimensional investigation offers to urbanism.

1. Overview of the masterplan, capturing sinuous forms.
2. Perspective.
3, 4. Mass modelling forms.

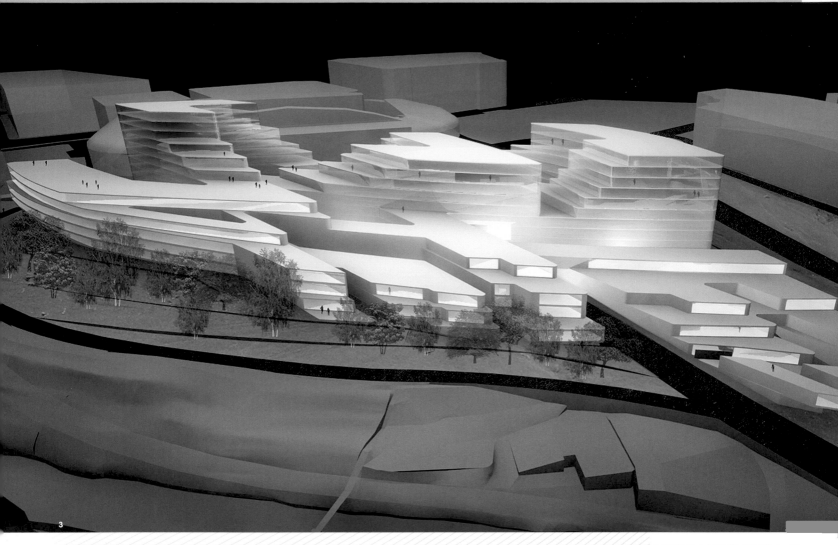

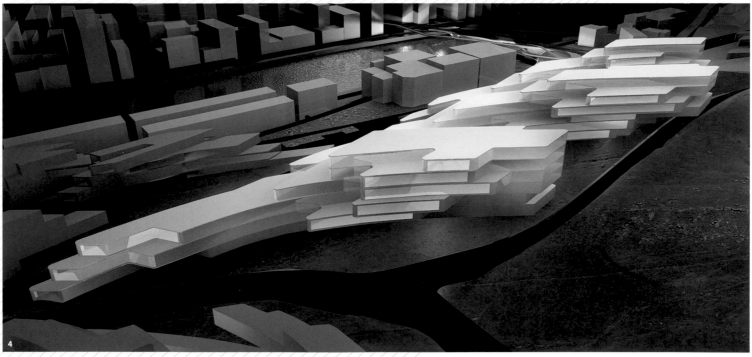

13

HARGREAVES ASSOCIATES

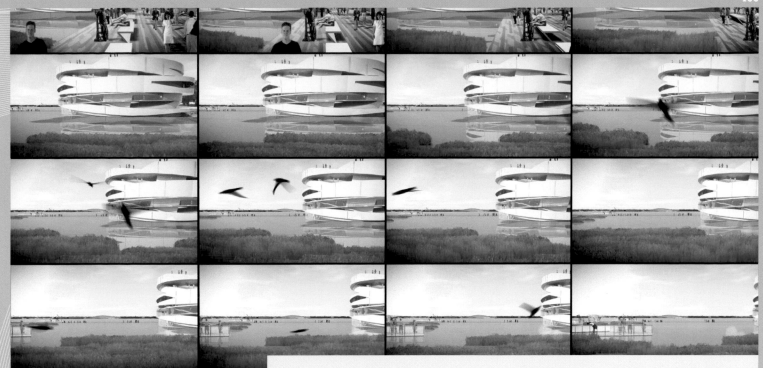

Having been at the forefront of landscape architecture for over twenty years, the San Francisco-based firm Hargreaves Associates continues to create memorable and innovative landscapes through a progressive design process. Recognized for their distinctive and poetically sculptural landform works, the designers have successfully integrated such traditional methods as making clay models of a landscape's new topography, together with the new advanced digital techniques, into their design process.

The marriage between analogue and digital has strengthened the company's experimental and visual approach to their landscape designs. The development of digital design from 3D models and rendered illustrations into moving, detailed animations has enabled both designers and clients alike to better convey the experiential potential of projects. Three-dimensional modelling programs are also used to move beyond design study tools to provide rough but accurate frameworks for more refined presentation materials. The use of advanced collaged methods have helped in visualizing several iterations of changing conditions of day to evening, the different seasons, or over longer durations.

The final animation for the London 2012 Olympic Park proposal (p. 114) integrated panned aerial views that were generated from aerial photographs, 3D Studio MAX models and Photoshop. 3D Land Desktop (the precursor to 3D Civil) is often used to develop sculptural forms with accurate cut and fill information, such as those used in the design for the American Indian Cultural Center (p. 113), in Oklahoma City. The designers use a palette of software packages including 3D Studio MAX, Google SketchUp and Rhinoceros during the design process. These tools offer, at times, quick changes to the firm's signature 'formscaping' and designs in general.

Governors Island,
Upper New York Bay, New York.

13.1
Governors Island
Upper New York Bay, New York

For a competition to design a landscape for an island in Upper New York Bay (see also Balmori; p. 34), a combination of 3D Studio MAX, Photoshop and Maya software programs was used to develop a series of 2D renderings, which were then unfolded into layers to create a three-dimensional environment, through which a camera was tracked to produce a cinematic sequence.

The designers' proposal maintains and enhances the inherent attractions of the island, while introducing new qualities of circulation, distinct landscape typologies and unique programmatic potentials. The landscape plan integrates the 33-ha (82-acre) proposed park and development parcels at the south end of the island, with the 36-ha (90-acre) historic National Monument site at the north end. A central feature of the new proposal is the promenade 'Necklace', a multi-circuit, three-dimensional system of movement that encircles the island at its perimeter and offers a dynamic sequence of views and interaction with the water. The island's interior is characterized by six landscape typologies that provide distinct scales and kinds of space, light and enclosure. From 'Pine Barrens' and 'Dunescapes' to existing orchards and athletic fields, the landscape typologies accommodate a diverse range of programmes, events and park users. Animation effects, including an 'entourage in motion' (pedestrians, bikers, wildlife, and so on), were integrated throughout the fly-through, reinforcing the sensory immersion for this particular project.

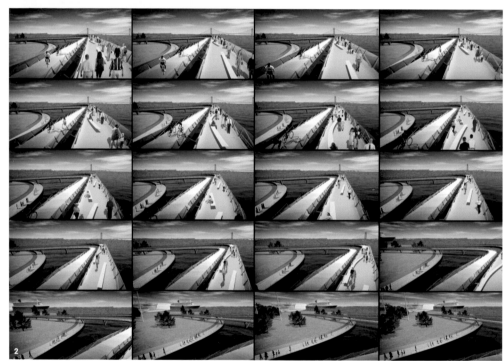

1. Digital model, overview.
2. Animation frame.
3. Panoramic view by night.

13.2
One Island East
Hong Kong, China

The development of digital design from 3D models and rendered illustrations into moving, detailed animations has allowed both designers and clients to better communicate the experiential potential of their projects. As the technologies, in-house skills and project requirements have expanded, the firm has incorporated animations into its design and presentation approach. During the design process, and in particular as a means of evaluating kinetic aspects of the plaza fountain at One Island East in Hong Kong, 3D Studio MAX and Rhinoceros were used to develop a true environment for the animation of sequencing options for the water trajectories of the jets, together with depictions of the expected wind and gravity forces.

This urban design features three civic spaces that converge at the base of a new seventy-storey office tower designed by Hong Kong-based architects, Wong & Ouyang. Three great lawn panels subtly step up to the tower podium of the plaza by means of a unique geometry of water stairs and terraces, vegetated with tropical plants, from a lower-level garden that features calming water basins. To differentiate each lawn, key native tree species, each with its own unique character, were planted. To demonstrate the transition from space to space, the designers created an animation to communicate the appropriate 'feel' of the design.

1, 2. Digital perspectives, night view of plaza.
3. Animation frame.

13.3
Allergan
Headquarters
Irvine, California

The use of 3D Studio MAX, Google SketchUp and Rhinoceros during the design process enables new modes of study, evaluation and representation, not least for this design for a corporate headquarters in California. The ability to interchange viable design options in 3D views is instrumental for both the design team and in terms of discussions with the client.

For this project, the firm utilized these digital ways of working to explore a variety of aspects of the design, including formal and spatial conditions, natural and artificial lighting, and the effects of differing and altering plant types, along with material colours, textures and layouts. These become important digital design tools while complementing the repertoire of analogue methods.

1–3. Digital perspectives, highlighting the vibrant colours of the various tree species.

13.4
American Indian Cultural Center
Oklahoma City, Oklahoma

For this cultural centre in Oklahoma, the designers created a series of large topographic elements with a circular, arcing landform that elevates to over 30.5 m (100 ft) as it rises from the interpretive centre entry to its apex overlooking Oklahoma River and the surrounding prairie. In order to accurately depict and study the different iterations of this element during the design process, 3D Land Desktop was used to generate the overall massing.

During its formal refinement and as technical realities were tested and incorporated, a digital model was employed to describe and coordinate the facets of the design. Ultimately, the construction documents incorporated volumetric drawings to communicate the metrics of rough and finished grades, cut and fill calculations, soil stabilization, run-off and erosion control. These were essential both during the latter portions of interdisciplinary design coordination, and for the contractor.

1

Site plan

Northern promontory
+102,000 cu yds

River-edge setback
-145,000 cu yds

Village parking
+22,000 cu yds

River-edge setback
-381,000 cu yds

Eastern promontory
+150,000 cu yds

Great promontory
+220,000 cu yds

Playa Lakes
-4,375 cu yds

Collection pond
-8,300 cu yds

Southern promontory
+331,000 cu yds

Collection pond
-13,800 cu yds

2

1. Site construction overview, capturing the landform.
2. Construction CAD drawing.

13.5
Olympic Park, London 2012
London, UK

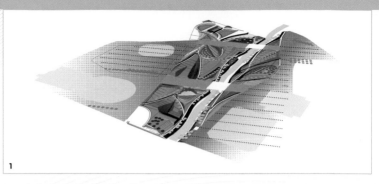

1

For this proposal for the London 2012 Olympic Park, the parametric modelling software Rhinoceros was utilized to develop a 3D model of the entire park, and to study the site and programmatic conditions within the generated topography. The model offered critical insights into exploring the park's design, including the generation of systems diagrams that pulled apart the topography, planting, circulation and water components, as well as the framework, which led to captured views that were later rendered and animated.

In order to emphasize the park's two modes – one during the Olympic Games, and in a second manifestation as the Legacy Park – two renderings for each view were developed to illustrate how the different spaces could handle the sheer volume of visitors during the Olympic Games, and later become a large park to serve the surrounding communities and neighbourhoods of East London.

2

3

1. 3D digital model.
2, 3. Digital collage perspectives.

13.6
Mission Rock Seawall 337
San Francisco, California

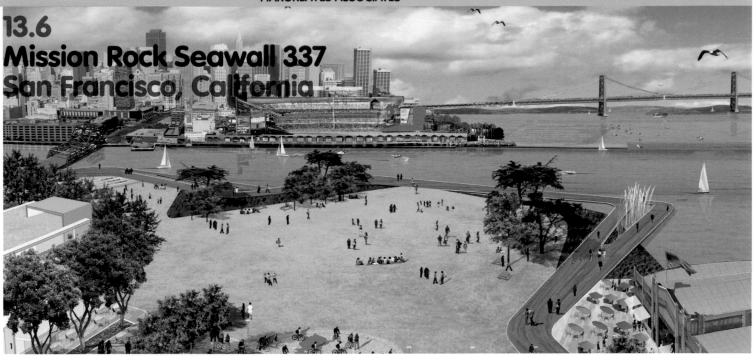

1–4. Digital collage perspectives, various views along the waterfront.

For this proposal, 3D modelling programs were used to move beyond design study tools to offer quick but accurate frameworks for more refined presentation materials. By laying out much of the vector-based information prior to executing the rendering in Photoshop, the regulation of the spatial coordinates maintained true perspective data, and allowed for the manipulation of forms, topographies, pattern layouts and tree and lighting cadence. This degree of precision also contributed to a realistic legibility, in which rendered components could be placed at the appropriate size to reinforce the viewer's perception of distance, leading the eye away from the picture plane into the depiction of the three-dimensional space.

This kind of legibility is well illustrated in the Mission Rock Seawall 337 project for San Francisco's Pier 48, located across the street from the baseball park. The design,

created in conjunction with architectural design firms Perkins & Will and Atelier Ten, captures the rich history of the site by creating expansive open spaces that interact with and celebrate the water, and by preserving and creating dramatic views out to the bay. The design expands upon Pier 48's heritage, highlighting its maritime history and the uncommon beauty of the San Francisco waterfront.

14
HOOD DESIGN

Walter Hood, principal of Hood Design in Oakland, California, is also professor and former chair of the landscape architecture department at the University of California, Berkeley. Hood has worked in a variety of situations and settings, including architecture, urban design, community planning, environmental art and research, and his work is focused on reinforcing the role of landscape within the city. Hood's philosophy is based on a fundamental awareness of place, context and community.

The firm provides reconstructions of urban environments, which use various landscape strategies that are rooted in the needs and wants of both clients and the public, and reflect a sense of familiarity with existing surrounding contexts. The company's landscape expressions are progressive, liberating and poetic. In recent years, the designers have begun to use animation in the design process to suggest a more dynamic landscape experience. Animation as a tool for representation has provided a fluid understanding of the landscape, offering a string of continuous vantage points that alter in elevation, speed and subtle differences of light throughout the day and night, and has allowed the designers to fully conceptualize the design of their

spaces. Animation also offers an experiential sequencing of spaces for clients.

Of particular interest is the concept of montaging and linking the constant unfolding of space through the manipulation of foreground, middle ground and background, as demonstrated in the firm's Airport Gateway renderings for the San Jose airport in California (p. 120), which take the viewer on a virtual drive. An experiential quality is captured, allowing the viewer to see the field of dotted sculptural steel barrels of hay through the threshold of the airport gate. Digital applications have further propelled the company's other design work to employ a didactic approach to the design of urban landscapes.

Garden Passage,
Pittsburgh, Pennsylvania.

14.1
Garden Passage
Pittsburgh, Pennsylvania

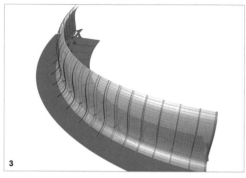

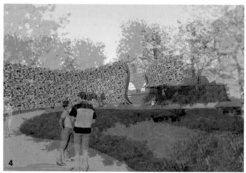

Garden Passage is an artistic pedestrian-friendly park in Pittsburgh, Pennsylvania, comprised of a twisting path that links Fifth Avenue in Uptown and Centre Avenue in the Hill District. This landscape-connector is framed by a weaving steel-mesh wall, covered in a mosaic of photographs – donated by local residents – that are set into resin tiles. The design was inspired by the full-stage panorama of the Hill District neighbourhood by artist David Gallo Walter, which served as a backdrop for all ten plays in August Wilson's *Pittsburgh Cycle*, as performed at the Kennedy Center in Washington, DC.

Four terraced rain gardens on the west elevation of the new Pittsburgh Arena take advantage of the site's topography. The patterning of the 'curtain wall' evolves over time. As more images and photographs are added to the framework (up to 27,000 tiles), a continuous backdrop of the art and culture of the site is formed as people walk through the space. During the design process, Hood used image-sequencing and animation to showcase the user's experience and the passage's cultural and artistic identity to his clients.

1, 3, 4. Perspective views.
2. Curtain structure.

14.2
Timber Crossing: Damming I-5
Vancouver, Washington

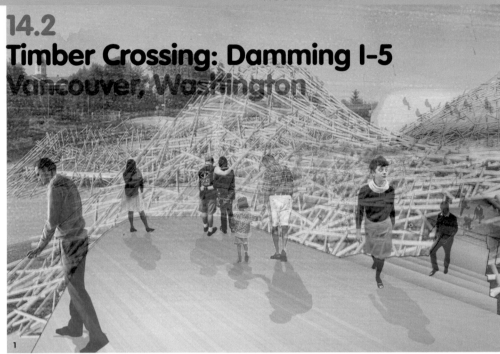

This proposal was for a pedestrian-friendly landscape-connector that links to Interstate-5 in Vancouver, Washington, just across the Columbia River from Portland, Oregon. The design concept for this linkage was inspired by investigations into the characteristics and ecological outcomes showcased in the activity of beavers, who create new habitable spaces by increasing river or stream biodiversity through the damming and reconfiguration of streams, and in particular by the layering of tree branches to create an elegant and strong structure.

The design reinterprets the typology of the freeway, conceiving it as 'lid' with a 'porous' framework that allows for light to penetrate to the street below, and to act as a buffer against noise and pollutants. The programmatic spaces and pathways are comprised of locally grown, sustainably harvested wood, which is very much part of the identity of the place. In this case, the designers used animation to capture multiple vantage points to highlight the complexity of the structure and the overall passage throughout the crossing.

1–4. Digital collage perspectives, various views along pathway.

14.3
Airport Gateway
San Jose, California

1. Window view from vehicle approach to airport (frame from animation).
2. Aerial view (frame from animation).
3. Plan.

Airport Gateway is an environmental artwork, designed to be viewed from a car on the freeway or from an aeroplane landing on the runways at the adjacent San Jose Airport. A series of polished, perforated aluminium barrels appear to roll down the site, leaving behind trails of contrasting groundcover in the gleaming grasses of the landscape.

Reflecting the bales of hay that once rolled across the agricultural fields that formerly occupied the site, the large, sculptural barrels are illuminated at night, providing a surreal atmosphere. The designers used animation as a key marketing and immersive experience tool; this fly-through allowed the user (or client) to experience the design's fantastical approach to the airport.

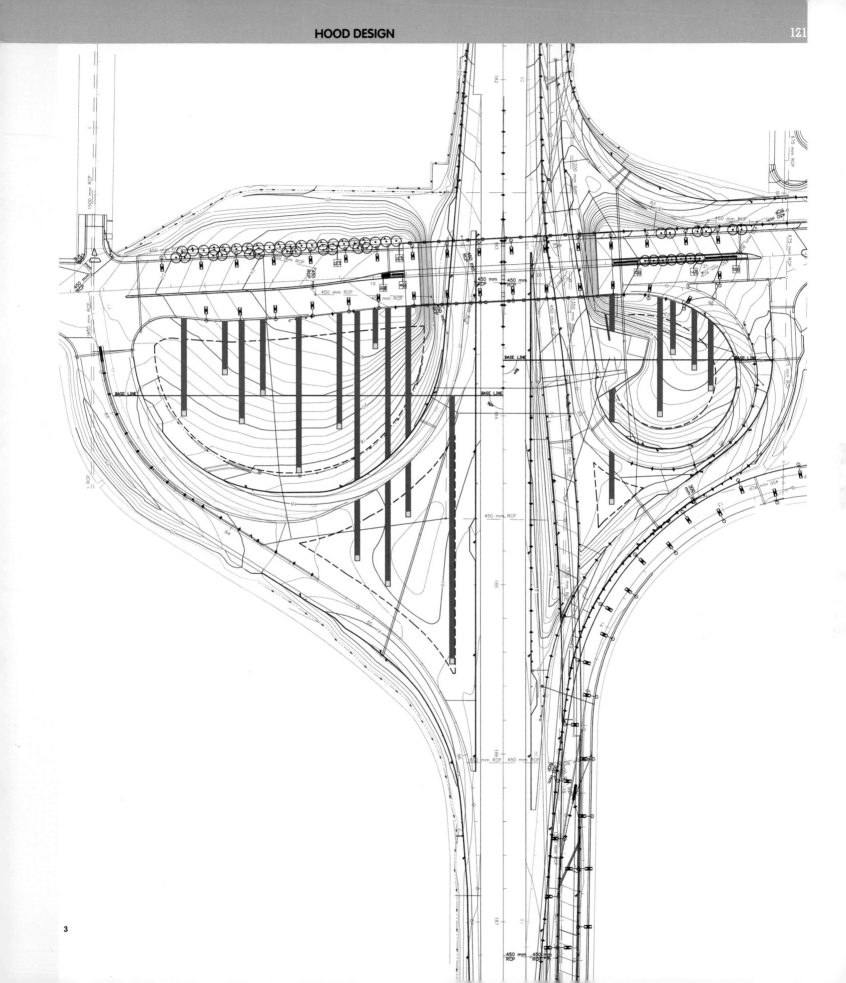

15
ANDRÉS
JAQUE
ARQUITECTOS

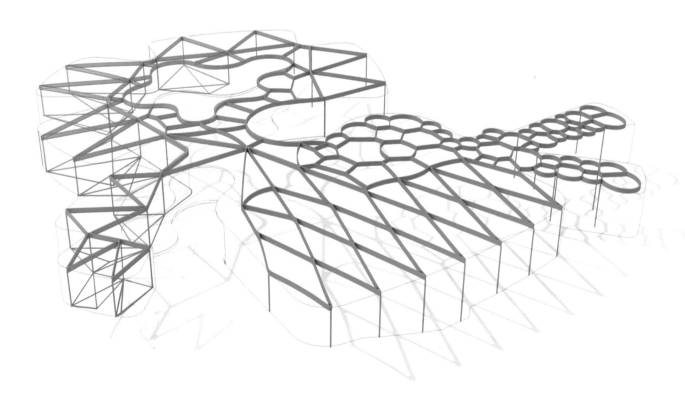

Andrés Jaque is principal of a small eponymous firm and think-tank studio – the Office for Political Innovation – both located in Madrid. Jaque characterizes himself through networking and fieldwork research, and his work offers inspiring visions of alternative landscape interventions in socially viable spaces.

As a political activist, Jaque is more interested in the people that use the architecture than in the architecture itself. He does not have a specific style or formal basis, but instead aims for public democracy, inclusivity and participation through his design process and methodology. This process is thus informed by a 'qualitative sociology' that allows the user to participate through the aid of digital platforms and Web 2.0 networking systems. Jaque's landscape design projects are concerned with ecology and technology, as evidenced in Landscape Condenser (p. 124), a building for the city of Yecla, Spain. Another project, the unconventional and political Fray Foam Home, was showcased at the 2010 Venice Biennale.

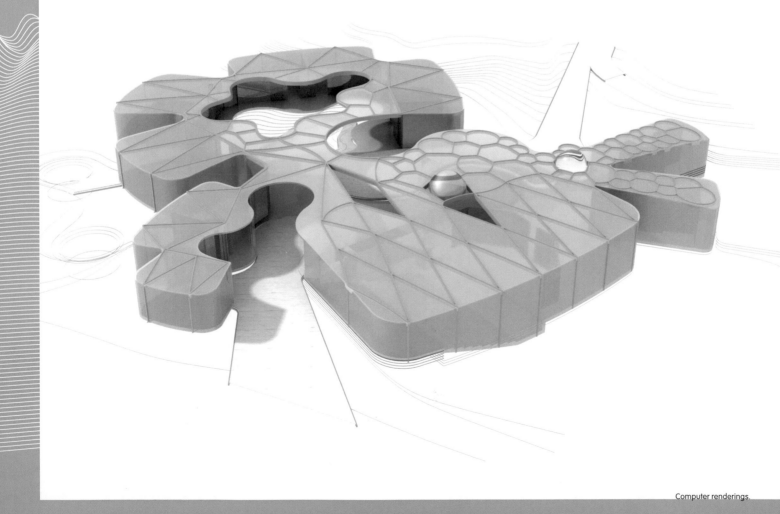

Computer renderings.

15.1
Landscape Condenser
Yecla, Spain

The Spanish city of Yecla has expanded within a significant undeveloped natural area that contains a variety of landscape typologies. Landscape Condenser is a unique kind of building, which attracts the programme development needed to socially reintegrate the land as a natural device that promotes a variety of programmatic activity from the neighbouring urban population. The 'condenser' then turns the landscape into a device that promotes its natural richness and fragility.

The building is organized into three layers of artificial landscape. The bottom layer is treated as a shaded meeting place, where water is stored and naturally cools its surroundings – it is a place that attracts those waiting to enter the natural infrastructure. A second level, slightly raised from the ground, contains a number of spaces able to maintain a continuous programme of workshops, lectures and meetings with landscape, environment and sustainability as a central theme. The upper level is designed as a condenser of all the different landscape units presented in the surrounding area, making the taxonomy of natural diversity transparent, easy to identify and easy to recognize – a system that allows the citizens to appreciate their natural environment.

1

1. Schemic plan.
2. Planting scheme.
3. Axonometric drawing.

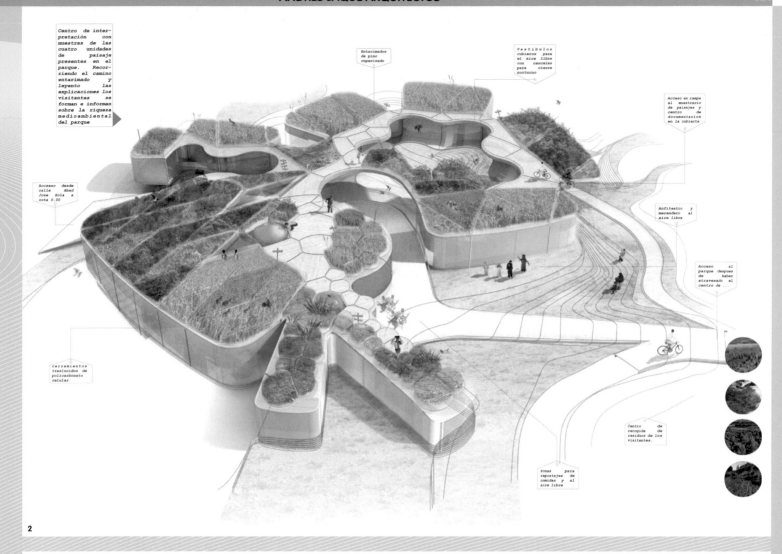

Centro de interpretación con muestras de las cuatro unidades de paisaje presentes en el parque. Recorriendo el camino entarimado y leyento las explicaciones los visitantes se forman e informan sobre la riqueza medioambiental del parque

Entarimados de pino cuperizado

Vestibulos cubieros para el aire libre con canceles para cierre nocturno

Acceso en rampa al muestrario de paisajes y centro de documentacion en la cubierta

Accceso desde calle Abad Jose Sola a cota 0.00

Anfiteatro y merendero al aire libre

cerramientos traslucidos de policarbonato celular

Acceso al parque despoes de haber atravessado el centro de ...

Centro de recogida de residuos de los visitantes.

Zonas para repostajes de comidas y al aire libre

2

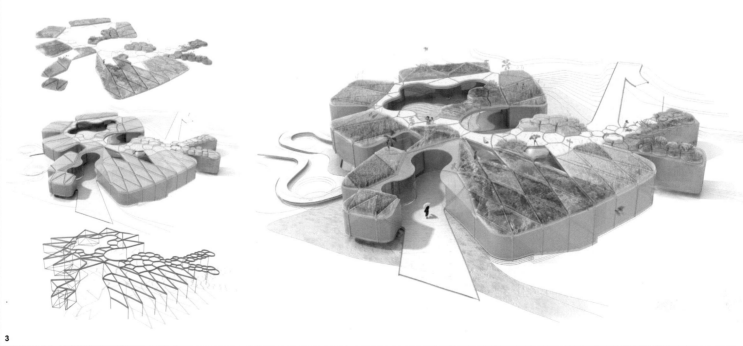

3

16
LABORATORY FOR VISIONARY ARCHITECTURE

Founded by Chris Bosse and Tobias Wallisser in 2007, with offices in both Sydney and Stuttgart, Laboratory for Visionary Architecture is a leader in digital design experimentation and innovation, and is behind a collection of projects in Germany, Austria, the United Arab Emirates, China and Japan. The firm believes that architecture is a reflection of the society in which it is based, and that it needs to embed the latest principles of technology and culture within its development. To do this, LAVA's design process includes the latest advances in computing digital technology.

The firm looks to nature and the environment in its creation of artificial systems with working natural ecological principles. The designers experiment with formal, cladding, structural, spatial, ventilation, material and climate systems. Some of their projects include the use of CNC fabrication technologies, embedding even the production phases into the design process. Their work is also research-based, examining complex spatial concepts, parametric design and virtual-reality environments.

Municipal Office District, Hanoi, Vietnam.

16.1
Municipal Office District
Hanoi, Vietnam

1. Digital collage perspective, capturing horizontal and vertical green skin.
2. Green ribbons.
3. Overview of site.
4. Green skin, profile.
5. Plan.

For this project in Hanoi, Vietnam, the design team examined novel concepts of connecting the horizontal landscape with the vertical by creating a 'green skin' that attaches itself to its surroundings. The landscape draws upon the traditional 'allotment' pattern, which generates 'strips' of programme and activities that are used in turn to generate horizontal landscape elements and built forms. The entire landscape reflects the local cultural elements, and provides dynamic interaction between social, cultural and environmental conditions within the green strips. Government, commercial and recreational programmes are combined together to present an image of a new Vietnam.

The sloping strip façades are a key signature of the buildings, and are able to carry various services and functions. The strips retain water for the natural passive cooling systems and the planting systems. The organization of the horizontal landscape allows for a variety of programmes and interactions to be incorporated and given a distinct identity, while the strong, orthogonal gesture of the landscape provides clear movement and access paths across the site. A bold, central axis unites the ceremonial plaza to the north of the site and the park at the south. The digital design process experimented with the potential of these flexible green strips, using parametric measures to create a network that would react and inform the site spaces and facilities, including parking, entries, access and loading. The series of systems allows the design to unfold as a result of its own necessities: light, air, views, structure, shading and leisure.

4

5

16.2
Oasis of the Future
Masdar, United Arab Emirates

Masdar is a futuristic eco-city, one that integrates sustainable technology into modern architectural and landscape design. The firm designed a plaza for the city centre as an 'oasis of the future' – a living, breathing, active and adaptive environment, stimulated by the social interaction of people. The design proposal focused on three key issues:

— Performance, demonstrating the use and benefits of sustainable technology in a modern, dynamic, iconic architectural environment.
— Activation, operating sustainable technology in accordance with the environment's functional needs, twenty-four hours a day, 365 days of the year.
— Interaction, encouraging and stimulating a social dynamic in which the life, values, ideals and vision of the population of Masdar evolve.

This oasis of the future demonstrates sustainable technology in a user-friendly architectural environment, presenting a flexible use of space, outdoor and indoor comfort, and optimum performance. This includes radiant surfaces, air movement that supplements natural wind patterns, evaporating cooling mist, thermal mass and pulse-code modulation, slab cooling and Luna ClimaPlus acoustical panels, and shading of external façades that surround the plaza. The goal was to provide the Abu Dhabi Energy Company with the lowest possible carbon footprint, while maintaining the highest level of user experience within the practicalities of affordable architecture.

Interactive umbrellas (the architects' 'petals of the future') also open to provide shade and capture energy during daylight hours, folding at night to release stored heat from the day. Solar analysis provides insight into the rotating of the façades to respond to varying sun angles and levels of solar intensity.

1–3. Digital collage perspectives.
4. Interactive umbrellas (detail).
5. Interactive umbrellas, closed.
6. Interactive umbrellas, opened, providing shelter.

17
LAND

LAND is an environmental and landscape architectural practice, based in Italy and Germany, which realizes projects for both private and public clients that favour well-balanced management of all environmental resources, with a focus on sustainable development. The firm operates through an interdisciplinary and collaborative design philosophy, sharing values and ideas from various fields, including environmental and ecological science and planning, architecture and urbanism.

The firm's design work and research experiments are concerned with strategic planning, primarily on a large regional scale. LAND's scope includes the development of parks and gardens, both private and public. The company's design methodology is supported by the use of various digital technologies, including AutoCAD, GIS for site analytics, Photoshop for image modifications, and Illustrator for mapping and diagramming and the development of masterplans. LAND is comprised of architects, landscapers, foresters, agronomists, naturalists, environmental engineers, and other design professionals. New associates bring continual methodological, technical and digital innovation to the firm's diverse practice.

Duisburg Bahnhofsvorplatz, Duisburg, Germany.

17.1
Duisburg Bahnhofsvorplatz
Duisburg, Germany

This new city square is in the heart of Duisburg, a location that reflects the site's industrial history. The city of Duisburg has proposed covering over the main street to create a new square in front of the central train station. LAND's award-winning design proposes an innovative pedestrian infrastructural scheme, derived by first examining the changing programmes – the users' movements and overall 'flux' of the square.

This movement is analysed through access points, people traces, main exits and meeting points. Travellers arriving or departing from the station use the square primarily as a place of transition, and occasionally as a place of rest. According to the architects, the design of the square is shaped by these pathways of movement into natural islands, which represent the natural changes of the seasons over time. The team used AutoCAD, Adobe Illustrator and Photoshop to craft the eye-catching illustrations that capture the spatial feel of the design.

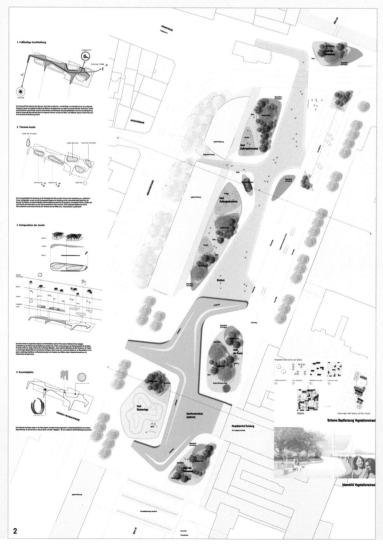

1. Key map.
2. Plan.
3, 4. Digital collage perspectives.

17.2
Econovello Cesena
Cesena, Italy

This proposal for a park – another competition-winning design by the team at LAND – examined a series of landscape strategies that connects to the 'lines of the landscape', and re-establishes a relationship between the two halves of a city, divided by the railway.

The project proposed a new image of the city of Cesena, Italy, one that is contextual, poetic and reflective. This is achieved by smooth, undulating earthwork designs, reflecting the presence of water and its connection to surrounding parks. The rendering of the main park, which faces the railways, is described by a plot of pathways that conform to a series of islands, made of trees, grasses, flowers and functions, which suggest a domestic connotation to the public space.

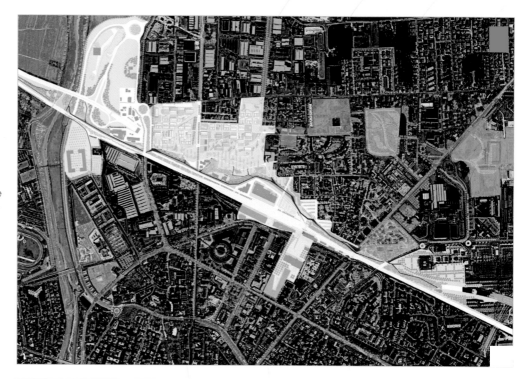

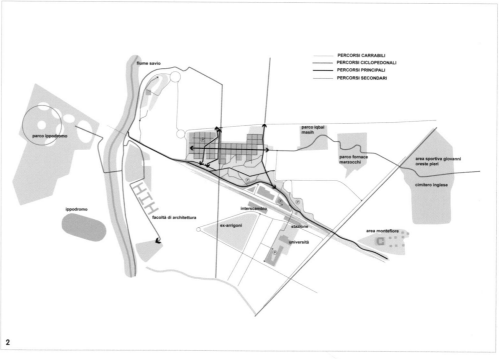

1, 2. Masterplan of
landscape strategies.
3. Perspective view.
4. 3D digital model of
masterplan.

18
LAND-I ARCHICOLTURE

Italian-based landscape practice Land-I Archicolture has produced a number of projects concerned with landscape planning and environmental design, with a particular focus on contemporary garden design, both for public and private clients and for exhibition at international competitions. The designers approach the landscape with an artistic vision that is achieved, they say, when the combination of function and creative formal expression is in harmony.

The use of the digital has allowed the designers to test sinuous formal expressions and artistic interventions through modelling and image modification. Using such programs as 3D Studio MAX and V-Ray rendering techniques, along with the more traditional imaging software, including Photoshop digital collage, the firm is able to generate artistic visual interpretations of their projects.

Ombre, Montreal, Quebec, Canada

18.1
Ombre
Montreal, Quebec, Canada

According to the designers, shadow is a key element of both architecture and garden design, defining space and distance and giving perspective. In gardens, shadows refer to a darker, emotional level of perception. The firm's design for the Jardins de Métis festival in 2002 treats the site as an archaeological excavation field. The viewer is confronted with an array of seemingly identical but freely placed openings in a bare ground, and then, upon entering the garden, discovers that the ground inside the openings is unexpectedly covered with shallow, dense vegetation. When walking through the site, visitors pass through a seemingly endless repetition of 'excavations' – sunken beds containing micro-gardens – which provide a sense of a playful yet eerie setting.

Using 3D modelling software, the designers were able to test the size, depth and perception of random 'ground openings' in the surface of the landscape. This digital testing allowed the designers to try out various shadow projections and atmospheres in the garden. The rendered images and the realized project are comparable because of the predominant geometry of the excavations.

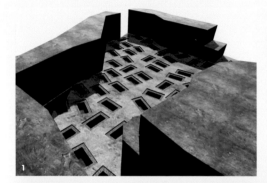

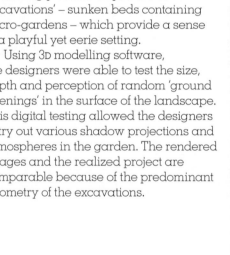

1. Repetition of 'excavations'.
2, 3. Demonstrating the use of shadows.
4. Garden entrance.
5. Overview of the site.

18.2
Orange Power
Ponte de Lima, Portugal

1. Bird's-eye view of the plastic balls around the single tree.
2. Children at play, interacting with the garden.

At the International Garden Festival 2006 in Ponte de Lima, Portugal, an orange tree (*Citrus x sinensis*) was placed at the centre of the team's design, with fifty thousand orange plastic balls at its foot – representing the harvest of a single orange tree over the course of one hundred years. The firm took the festival's theme, 'Energy in the Garden', as an opportunity to reflect on gratitude for the wonders of nature, and chose the orange tree as a symbolic gesture because it has been cultivated for over four thousand years, and because it is a plant that has connected East and West throughout history. Citrus fruits are evocative of Southern Europe, and also have symbolic importance in China and the Far East.

The visual impact of a sea of oranges was achieved by the contrast of the natural element in the centre (the orange tree) and the artifice of the plastic balls that cover the soil. It is a playful garden that also hides an ominous ecological message: new generations of plants are forced to produce fruits that never decay, eventually becoming genetically altered in the quest to achieve 'perfection'. Using advanced modelling software, the designers tested the sea of oranges in the site, examining the contrasting of colours. Four orange trees were placed symmetrically, with each carefully and geometrically surrounded by oranges on the ground, aligned and on a single level, making it theoretically possible for them to be counted. The digital image illustrates the concept behind the design in a more accurate way than the built work could ever achieve.

18.3
Tracce
Lucca, Italy

For the 2001 Festival di Arte Topiaria, held at the Villa Grabau, the designers reinterpreted the idea of topiary – the human controlling of nature by shaping its vegetation. Here, it is not the vertical vegetation that is shaped, but rather the lawn surface that becomes the sculpted material. The team imagined a huge hand scratching the soil, tearing ribbons of grass and leaving the earth bare.

According to the architects, this reshaping of the ground surface is not destructive, but instead presents a deeper reading. It is meant to celebrate this historic site through careful measures, and a playful, artistic manner. The untangling of nature through artificial shapes and coloured sands, paradigmatic elements of topiary art, reappear to redefine topiary. The designers used advanced photomontaging methods and techniques to produce a realistic and synthetic vision of the landscape.

1. 'Scratches' in the soil.
2, 3. Collage perspective, ribbons of grass.
4. Ribbons of grass, within the context of the space.

19
LANDWORKS STUDIO

Founded in 1996 by Michael Blier, Landworks Studio is a landscape architectural practice based in Boston, Massachusetts, with an artistic, ecological and technological focus. Since 1999, Blier has been leading design studios and representation courses at both the Harvard and Rhode Island schools of design, and the progressive digital-design approach he employs in his teaching is carried through in his practice. Prior to setting up Landworks Studio, Blier worked at the office of Martha Schwartz, and this Schwartzian background is evident in many of the firm's artistic and creative landscape projects.

Landworks Studio maintains a sustainable and innovative position in design that varies across a range of project types and scales. The firm believes in a collaborative and interdisciplinary methodology that takes advantage of different disciplines to solve the design problems at hand. Important to its work is the integration of context and regional environmental systems. Whenever possible, the company aims to incorporate the use of local, indigenous vegetative and ecological systems to better adapt its designs within the surrounding environments.

As part of their design process, the designers thoroughly test the formal, technical and environmental suitability of each design, in order to provide the best proposal that responds to its context and scale, and the users of the space. To do this, they use a variety of digital design software, including 3D Studio MAX, Google SketchUp, Autodesk Revit, AutoCAD and BIM (building information modelling).

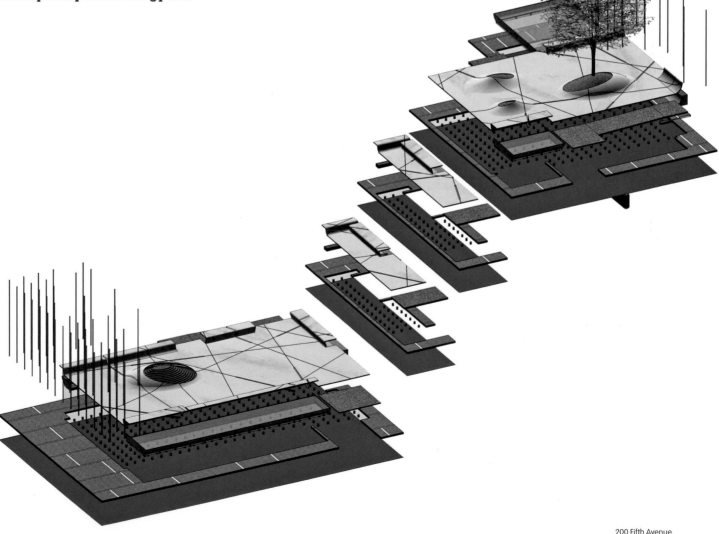

200 Fifth Avenue,
Manhattan, New York.

19.1
200 Fifth Avenue
Manhattan, New York

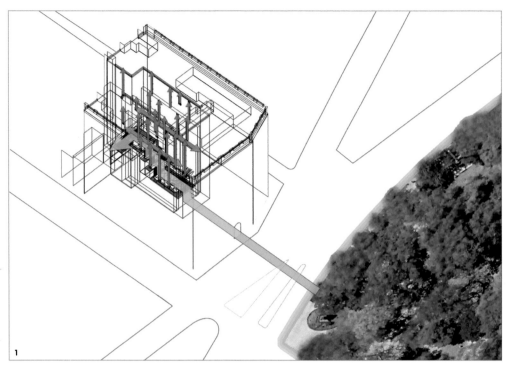

1

The designers took careful measures with this design for a courtyard in a historically sensitive site. New ecological and artistic public gathering spaces were created in this former hotel building, adjacent to Madison Square Park, as part of the remodelling project for the International Toy Center buildings, located between 23rd and 25th Streets at Fifth Avenue and Broadway.

Inserted into the space are a simple 'floating' white tray and a 'levitating' light cloud of polymer-reinforced concrete. The pair move seamlessly, transforming and adjusting to the various spaces of the building, including the lobby, courtyards and balconies, while leaving intact the historic nature of the architecture. The final design creates a variety of gathering areas, and provides both visual interest to the design and striking views for the building occupants.

Lighting, shadow effects and visual assessments were critical in the testing of the space, owing to the vertical scale, and to understand the three-dimensional spatial qualities of the courtyard. The firm used a palette of 3D modelling software, including 3D Studio MAX, Google SketchUp and AutoCAD, to generate simulated views and to develop the final design of the courtyard's vertical and horizontal design and scale.

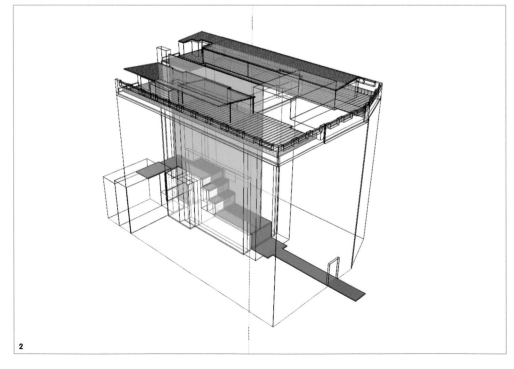

2

1. Park connector.
2. Aerial view of floating trays.
3. Platform.
4. View of 'green' ground.
5. 'Floating' white tray with planter, built form.
6. Montage of trays.

3

4

5

6

19.2
AIA Headquarters Renewal
Washington, DC

The landscape design for the headquarters of the American Institute of Architects, in Washington, DC, is reflective of an ecological and social mandate set by the AIA to achieve carbon neutrality by the year 2030. The design proposal was intended to cohesively connect the site's existing garden and building with the adjacent historic Octagon House and the nearby streets of the surrounding neighbourhood of Foggy Bottom.

Ecological performativity and sculptural form link the proposed and existing landscape systems through a newly designed bioretention system, living walls and constructed wetlands. These elements not only connect the site visually and physically, but will also treat storm water and grey water. In addition, the proposed design will help educate the public about the AIA's vision for sustainability. As part of the digital process, the design used integrated project delivery via BIM. From the schematic design phase to final production, digital applications were used and encouraged. The software Autodesk Revit was used by each consultant and member of the design team to guarantee full coordination at each stage, and to ensure a level of accuracy in the design.

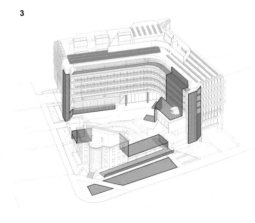

1–3. Digital model views, Google SketchUp and CAD.

19.3
Square 673
Washington, DC

1

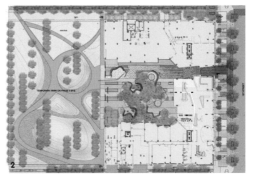

2

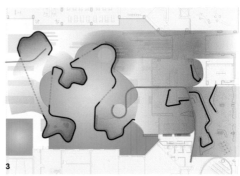

3

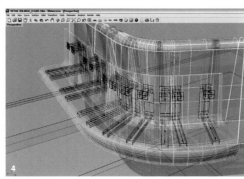

4

'Connectivity' is one of the main concepts of this design proposal for Square 673, an apartment complex in the NoMa (North of Massachusetts Avenue) neighbourhood of Washington, DC. Achieved through a careful 'weave' of sculptural expression in the form and material of the landscape, the designers created a 'stylish and playful linkage of form and surface to create a modern visual landscape identity of the space'. Together with the client, Archstone-Smith, and Studios Architecture, the team designed an interconnected space, inside and outside, with 'experiential variation and visual interest' for the residents.

The designers carefully scaled each space for particular programmes, and at the same time provided visually expressive, sculptural forms. To aid in designing and crafting a series of serpentine benches, they used Rhinoceros software at the design concept stage and

through the construction documentation processes. Using a digital 3D model, the team was able to examine the effects of lighting and test the structural framing in the complex folding forms of the benches. During the construction phase, this digital model was used for the fabrication of the custom bench forms.

1. Lighting plan of serpentine benches.
2. Plan.
3. Courtyard diagram.
4. Digital model, serpentine benches.

20
LATERAL OFFICE

Lateral Office is an experimental design-research studio, led by Lola Sheppard and Mason White, which operates at the intersection of landscape, architecture and urbanism. The studio is committed to design as a research vehicle for posing and responding to complex and urgent questions within our contemporary condition, and to seeking direct engagement with the difficult questions of contemporary urbanism, the public realm and infrastructures, demonstrated through design competitions, publications and exhibitions.

For Sheppard and White, both architecture and landscape architecture are strategic, interdisciplinary, networked, interactive and dynamic. They believe that architecture's territory has expanded, and that buildings act as surfaces, containers and conduits, which are just one part of a larger network and feedback system – an expanded urbanism. This thought is carried into their practical and research work. Recently, they have developed a blog – InfraNet Lab – as well as a research collective, which examines architecture, landscape and urbanism through the frameworks of infrastructure, networks and flows, transportation and mobility, ecology and the environment, economies and political power, energy and resource logistics to better understand architecture's wider environment.

Water Economies/Ecologies, Imperial Valley, California.

20.1
Water Economies/Ecologies
Imperial Valley, California

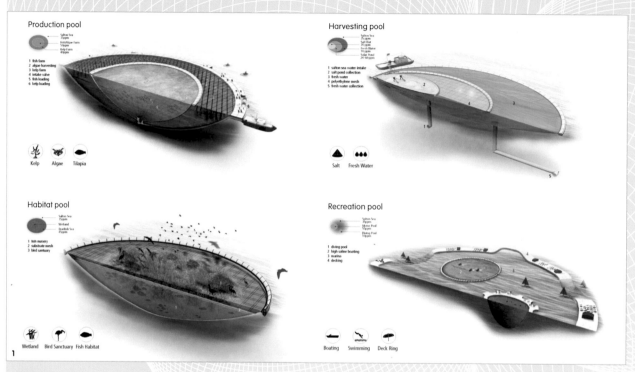

1

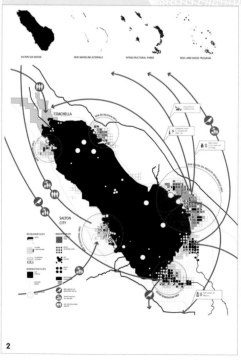

2

The Salton Sea is a hyper-saline lake, located below sea level, which was created in 1905 when one of the manmade water canals was breached and flooded the surrounding landscape. Water Economies/Ecologies proposes a flexible infrastructure that allows for production systems, various cultures and fragile ecosystems. The project examines alternative architectural infrastructure that works at a very large regional scale. The sea's shoreline will be populated by three new marina cities, which will centre around the site as productive, recreational and nature areas.

The designers have proposed four pool types – production, harvesting, recreation and habitat – with each varying in scale and complexity. These micro-ecologies will be partially settled in their area, but can also drift within a territorial range of the Salton Sea. When maintenance or substantive harvesting is necessary,

they can be drifted to the shore for collection or maintenance. The pools can merge with each other, creating new hybrid landscapes, and are designed to passively separate water and salt, generating a regional water (and salt) economy. The project envisions an infrastructure that works as an ecosystem; it can expand, shrink, change priorities, feed, protect and cultivate new species.

Water Economies/Ecologies employs adaptable, responsive interventions. Easily replaced or renewed, these infrastructures double as landscape growth, creating new sites for production or recreation.

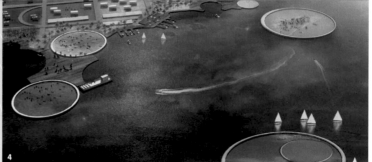

1. The four pool types.
2. Diagram showing new flows of economies, ecologies and recreation.
3, 5. Views of the industry area, for fish and algae farming, water desalination and salt harvesting.
4. View of the recreation area, with varying salinity pools for different leisure activities.
6. View of the ecology area, which supports wetlands and bird habitats.

20.2
IceLink
Bering Strait, between Russia and Alaska

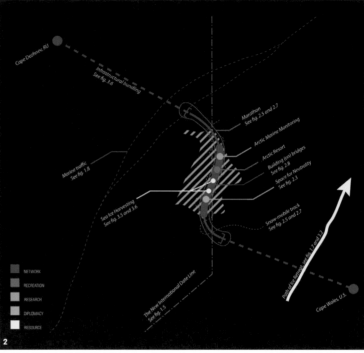

IceLink addresses the issues of connectivity with regards to the Bering Strait not only as a monumental and symbolic move, but also as a test of infrastructural links that are productive and operative. With the aim of embracing the unique geography, climate and context of the site, the scheme creates a link across the former Bering land bridge, which joined Alaska and eastern Siberia at various times during the Ice Age, while at the same time establishing a usable infrastructure.

The international date line, running between the Diomede Islands in the middle of the Bering Strait, is significant in its division. The potential of reconfiguring the date line from a line to a territory would provide a neutral space that privileges communication, community and sustainability at a local, regional and global scale. The design proposal consists of two primary infrastructural elements:

a tunnel–bridge link and an ice park. Both parts of the link – tunnel and bridge – each demonstrate potential for connection across the strait. The tunnel runs from each continent – North America and Asia – until about 2 to 3 km (1.2 to 1.9 miles) from the east and west at Little Diomede and Big Diomede islands, respectively. At this point, the enclosed tunnel emerges out of the water as a bridge, arcs around the north coast of Big Diomede and the south coast of Little Diomede, to run tangentially to and then alongside the existing date line for about 4 km (2.5 miles).

The Bering Link is composed of bundled infrastructures of road, rail, water, culture, recreation and research, among others, forming a new exchange route. It will also serve as a catalyst for cultural exchange, research and education, and other public programmes. Ice between the two islands naturally remains because of the shallow

conditions. The new ice park – with an area of 2,450 ha (6,054 acres), with a field of about 850 ice masts – seeks to enhance and highlight this phenomenon.

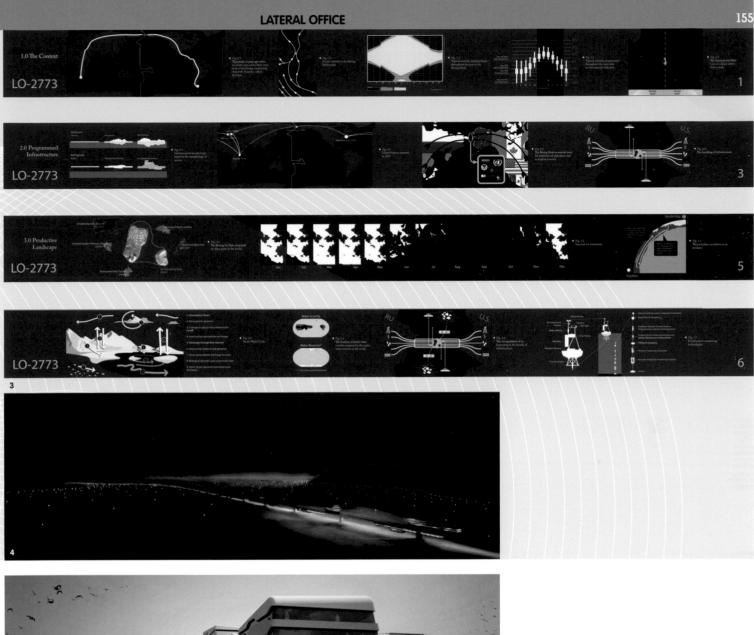

1. Site plan.
2. Concept amendment.
3. Analysis and concept development.
4. Night view.
5. Perspective view of deck.
6. Perspective view.

21
METAGARDENS

London-based Metagardens, founded by Fernando Gonzalez in 2000, is at the forefront of digital landscape experimentation, and continually pushes the envelope between the artificial and the real state of the environment. The firm's philosophy can be found in its name, with the prefix 'meta' referring to a change, or a progressive transformation. Fundamentally, Gonzalez and his team believe that 'new innovations in technology have brought on an irreversible direction towards artificial life'. This forward-thinking approach looks to new innovations in computation, biotechnology and cybernetic systems to inform the firm's design process.

Metagardens' work addresses the challenges of the modern digital age through both built and experimental projects. The firm has developed a design methodology that, through advanced digital techniques and an exploratory approach, goes beyond the ordinary and the conventional. Horticulture and vegetation is seen in a new artificial, synthetic and constructed way. The team experiments with virtual reality, CNC fabrications of the environment, parametric design and advanced digital landscape visualization, using programs such as 3D Studio MAX and Maya to achieve their unconventional, almost fantasy-like designs.

Hyde Park,
London, UK.

21.1
Hyde Park
London, UK

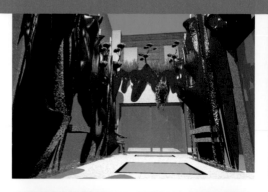

2

This project investigates surface manipulation and formal experimentation within the interior courtyard of a three-storey flat, overlooking Hyde Park, in central London. At night, this small space is transformed by dramatic lighting, produced by a light installation by American artist James Turrell. The challenge was to create an elegant, low-maintenance landscape that would complement the carefully planned interiors and glass gallery without overpowering the courtyard and Turrell's installation. Among the client's requirements were the implementation of key views outwards from inside the residence, and the design of a space for contemplation. Another challenge was to enliven an otherwise static space and 'activate' the courtyard wall.

Inspired by Chinese gardens and scroll landscape paintings, Gonzalez created an oasis landscape through the use of screening techniques and latticework windows that were reminiscent of oriental residences and courtyards. The connections between Eastern philosophies and Turrell's artwork were also important in the design, via the creation of a relationship between the self and nature through the intellectual, serene contemplative state experienced upon entering the space. Gonzalez used surface manipulation to suggest the emerging of the design from the skin of the courtyard wall. This transformation develops a new vertical surface, which is crafted through rapid prototyping.

This new wall is fabricated from an organic copper structure, with plant containers and a bench attached to the east wall. This seating structure resembles a river flowing through mountains, reinforcing the concept of a serene landscape. The curvaceous and asymmetric design offers a multitude of different effects during the day, with the reflective, warm colour of the surface lighting up the shady interior. Attention to detail and smoothness of lines are used to give the garden a sense of elegance. Three plant materials were used in the garden: bamboo, maple and fern. The feathery quality and lightness of the plants contributed to the overall sense of serenity and rest. While the bamboo and ferns provide movement and foliage throughout the year, the passage of the seasons is marked by the maple tree.

1. Digital model, perspective of courtyard.
2. Concept sketches.

21.2
Electronic Dreams

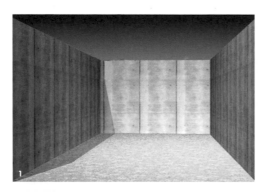

 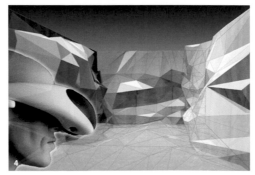

This project is not a conventional garden, but rather a new environment that creates a dynamic interaction between human behaviour and nature through virtual technology. It is inspired by a computer-aided virtual environment system, a computer-generated world that uses advanced graphics to deliver an immersive experience. Using digital means, Electronic Dreams becomes part of an augmented and reactive environment, offering a new kind of gardening that is fully programmable and flexible. The user wears special goggles (lightweight stereo glasses) and data-gloves, plugs in a computer and inserts a CD or searches online for horticultural scenes such as herbaceous borders and Japanese gardens. Alternatively, the user can grow his or her own plants, or navigate in real-time through historic gardens. These new environments then appear on the computer screen.

The digital process used to generate the tiled surface is a design tool called Genr8, a plug-in for Maya. Through the combination of surface-based L-systems and evolutionary algorithms, a generative process creates and then modifies different NURBS-surfaces, such as a model of cellular growth interacting with an environment. It is a sophisticated immersive environment, which tests the boundaries of 4D spaces in landscape architecture and the dream-like virtual landscape experience.

1. Without equipment.
2. Border.
3. Villa d'Este.
4. With equipment.

21.3
Evoterrarium

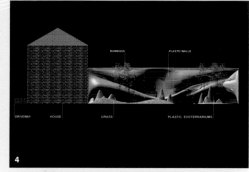

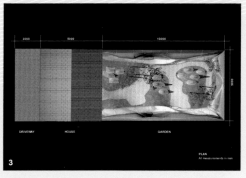

Evoterrarium is an innovative concept related to the 'evolution of gardens'. According to Gonzalez, suburban gardens have been conditioned by two constraints: the architectural framework of a box-boundary of hard, static materials, such as brick or stone; and the limitations imposed by weather, which affect the range of possible plants. To break away from those constraints, Gonzalez created a computer simulation using Maya software, which transforms the garden-box into a soft, flexible form. The space is then inserted into a virtual environment, where its geometry interacts with natural forces, including wind and rain.

The result is a smart machine that is composed of a fluid, biodegradable plastic skin, attached to a steel skeleton over the brick walls. The suburban garden is thus transformed from a simple geometry into a malleable, dynamic and highly articulated system, in which it is possible to grow all kind of unusual plants inside of the terrariums. These are also made of biodegradable plastic, and are capable of heating and cooling the space inside (like a conventional greenhouse). The brick walls are covered with biodegradable plastic sheets, laser-cut and vacuum-formed by heat over shaped foam panels. They are then attached to a skeleton made of plasma-cut stainless-steel ribs, welded on site. The forms are milled into foam moulds through CNC processes.

1. Detail view.
2. Detached house, with evoterrarium garden.
3. Plan.
4. Section.
5. Form generation.

21.4
Filigrana
London, UK

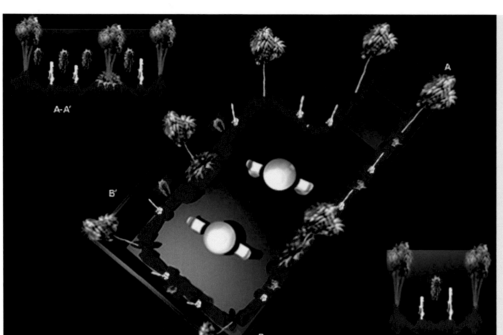

This proposal is for the creation of a stimulating office environment for a small, enclosed space in central London. The design explores the possibilities of creating an unconventional courtyard through digital explorations. The inspiration behind the scheme was Chinese gardens, and how their makers mastered the art of creating powerful spatial conditions within small external rooms, achieved by setting an ambience through overlapping layers of perforated rocks with different profiles. These stones act as a network, composed of parts that assemble as a whole to convey depth and create rhythmic patterns. At the same time, they resemble living organic systems, passing through several different forms in successive stages of development.

To achieve the complexity attained in these gardens, Gonzalez used advanced parametric software, such as Maya, to create a basic component. A NURBS-plane is transformed into a flexible surface, and changes through the interaction with physical forces. Later, various units are transformed out of that basic element by deformation procedures, and are then programmed for different functions, such as fountains, planters for ferns, or trellises for climbers. Made out of fibreglass and painted red, these surfaces are combined and multiplied by blending to resemble a dynamic organism that creates new shapes and elements in the landscape. Filigrana is a parametric landscape, always changing through computer controls.

1. Aerial view.
2. Form generation.
3. Mutations.
4, 5. Perspectives.

21.5
Monstruosa
London, UK

1–3. Form generation.
4. Plan rendering.
5. Detail.
6. Axonometric view.
7. Fabrication.

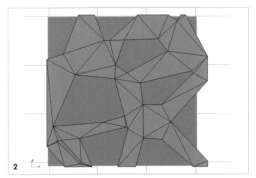

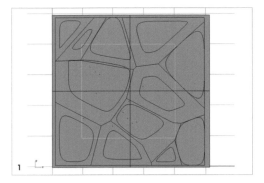

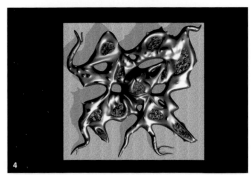

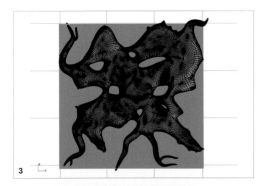

Gonzalez collaborated with fabrication specialists Metropolitan Works to produce this revolutionary, award-winning design for the 2009 Hampton Court Flower Show. Monstruosa (meaning 'monster' in Spanish) refers to an extraterrestrial visitor, a predatory creature whose primary goal is to propagate its own species. To illustrate this concept, Gonzalez uses the sophisticated biomorphology of carnivorous plants as 'living hosts'. The plants colonize, implanting their own offspring inside their tissues before evolving into more powerful 'bio-machines'.

Using parametric digital means, a series of random points were established inside a square in Rhino, and then transformed into the structure using the Voronoi algorithm. Thickness and further transformations were generated in Maya by scripting expressions. These formal expressions were crafted at a 1:1-scale using large prototyping machinery for large-scale fabrications. The plant list included *Darlingtonia californica*, *Sarracenia flava var. atropurpurea*, *Sarracenia oreophila*, *Sarracenia alata x flava maxima*, *Drosera capensis*, *Drosera binata var. multifida*, *Drosera filiformis var. filiformis*, *Dionaea muscipula* 'Spider' and *Dionaea muscipula*.

21.6
Parasitus_Imperator

The concept behind this design relates to the notion of parasites as invasive and ecosystem-controlling elements. Using this idea as a starting point, the design showcases a roof of a high-rise building, which seems to be 'bleeding' and 'flowing' over the building edges. Using parametric controls, this landscape is 'grown' in Maya software, where a NURBS-plane acting as the 'parasitus' is transformed into a soft surface. After using the space's genetic and cellular processes, the surface multiplies and invades the space.

Against the constant and motionless roof structures of modern skyscrapers, Parasitus_Imperator acts as a catalyst that feeds life, sensuality and movement into the roof surface. The rooftop is colonized through a skin made of red Corian panels and warm-coloured timber, all computer-cut. This surface provides a pathway and terrace through the movement of the grasses and water lilies. The planting plan is completed with architectural Cordyline plants, encapsulated in pods hanging outside the walls. This becomes part of a new landscape infrastructure crafted through digital means.

PARASITUS   HOST   PARASITIZING   PARASITUS_IMPERATOR

1. Concept drawing.
2. Colonization.
3. Axonometric view.

21.7
Pulsations
London, UK

This garden for the 2008 Hampton Court Flower Show demonstrated the possibilities of advanced 3D modelling tools and digital production as a means of designing and crafting the twenty-first-century urban landscape plot. The design was inspired by the rhythmic processes of natural forces, and how through their undulating movements those forces could be transformed into forms found in nature: the subtle patterns of water; the formation of mountains; the flowing of lava.

The entire surface is made of recyclable, waterproof fire-retardant expanded polystyrene, cut and carved with a CNC machine, and coated in a plastic base and sprayed with black paint. The paving is finished with a low-maintenance resin-bound surface, using a range of natural and recycled aggregates. The contractions and expansions of the material resemble that of a pulsating landscape, and behaves as a dynamic backdrop for the planting. With their spiky, dramatic shapes, the plants form bold contrasts to the smooth surface.

A single curve was created in Maya and transformed into a 'soft body', before being connected through a 'wave deformer' over a period of time. Various parameters and scripting expressions were used to drive the deformation. The plant list included *Borzicactus aureispina f. cristata*, *Echinopsis hybrid f. cristata*, *Lobivia cinnabarina f. cristata*, *Mammillaria geminispina f. cristata*, *Notocactus claviceps f. cristata*, *Opuntia cylindrica major f. cristata*, *Agave nigra*, *Oreocereus celsianus*, *Opuntia*, *Pachypodium lamerei* and *Puya serrula*.

1–3. Digital collage perspectives.
4. Fabrication, using CNC.
5, 6. Built form.

22
MEYER & SILBERBERG

Land architects Meyer & Silberberg design and build signature landscapes that are recognized for their elegance and clarity. The designers' work is based upon a foundation of creative technical proficiency, and a strong commitment to their clients and their projects, which range from small intimate gardens and mid-sized civic spaces to large-scale urban parks and masterplans. They believe that site-specificity is an important factor in the design process, and craft landscapes that celebrate the spirit and core culture of each site. Projects are built across a range of scales and typologies, and aim for coherence within local contexts, while simultaneously fulfilling the specific programmatic and functional needs.

As part of the growing trend in landscape architecture to incorporate intelligent digital applications within the design process, the architects' own design process begins with research, analysis and the conceptualization of an idea through a series of loose, freehand drawings on trace paper. As the concepts evolve in plan and section, the drawings are put into AutoCAD. The process advances digitally through the use of a variety of digital software programs. For plan and section renderings, Photoshop is the primary rendering tool, while for

perspectives, Google SketchUp and Artlantis are used to create quick, three-dimensional views, which are then brought into Photoshop to create eye-catching images.

Courthouse Square,
Santa Rosa, California.

22.1
Courthouse Square
Santa Rosa, California

1. Perspective view.
2. Market.
3. View of Third Street.

The architects' proposal for the Courthouse Square competition included the design of a civic centre that would reflect the city's unique heritage. The plan consists of three distinct zones: the Heritage Gardens, the Village Green and the Pavilion Plaza. The pathway and square are cleverly designed to follow an ecological framework to create a self-sufficient park. Lighting and jet-stream functions, together with other power required to operate the space, are generated by photovoltaic cells that are placed on the surrounding buildings. Storm water is collected into and cleansed by bio-swales that are framed by seating-walls within the gardens.

The more private space, the Heritage Gardens, celebrates Santa Rosa's famous former residents, including the cartoonist Charles Schultz and botanist Luther Burbank, while the Village Green and the Pavilion Plaza accommodate flexible civic spaces for a variety of events, from jazz festivals to farmer's markets. The architects used different software programs to help generate the design, including AutoCAD, Photoshop and Google SketchUp. Surfaces for hardscape elements were rendered with Artlantis, which crafted a more gradient spectrum of light and texture that was not achievable with Google SketchUp or Photoshop.

22.2
Daze Maze
Montreal, Quebec, Canada

Daze Maze was designed for the Jardins de Métis 2008 festival in Montreal. The architects created a space that exuded playfulness, while at the same time produced a sense of disorientation. The maze is constructed of cheerful, brightly coloured nylon lanterns that form large, vertical panels, which in turn create the maze walls. The porous openings in the walls produce a visual representation of a three-dimensional space. Unlike typical mazes, this maze does not have a start, middle or end point; there are no defined directions. It serves instead as a means of disorientating the user.

According to the designers, Daze Maze is 'a metaphor for the cacophonous and erratic movement, blur of colour and communal pleasure one experiences at a large group festivity'. The software programs used to generate this project included AutoCAD, Photoshop and Google SketchUp, which became a key design tool in the study of the project's proportions and layout.

1. Overview.
2. Perspective.
3. Plan.

23
MLZ
DESIGN

MLZ Design Studio was founded in 2007 by landscape architect Matt Zambelli, who has incorporated his research into advanced digital design and visualization in landscape while a graduate student at Penn State into his practice. Zambelli is technically proficient in a number of geographical analysis, drafting, advanced modelling, visualization and illustration software applications including Esri ArcGIS, Visual Nature Studio, Google SketchUp, 3D Studio MAX, Cinema 4D, Rhinoceros, VisualMILL, VRML Realtime Environment, and other render and modelling programs.

Armed with these digital tools and an understanding of environmental design, Zambelli explores emerging digital-design processes in landscape architecture, urban design and digital visualization. His designs often start with conceptual sketches, which eventually get digitized and combined with GIS mapping information, using GIS to SKP plug-in for SketchUp. These forms and massing models then get tested through 3D visualizations and renderings with existing contexts. Zambelli also focuses on the integration of various data formats, including CAD, GIS and BIM, in order to construct meaningful models that can solve problems and influence design decisions.

In order to enhance atmosphere, vegetation and texture visualizations, Zambelli has begun to use Vue 7 Infinite software and Cinema 4D. The practice constantly explores different methods and modes of representation to bridge the gap between proposed design illustrations and the subsequent built works. Zambelli also often collaborates with professionals in other technical fields during his design process, which provides him with valuable feedback that enhances his work and ensures both state-of-the-art and up-to-date processes.

Terra+Scapes,
Portland, Oregon.

23.1
Terra+Scapes
Portland, Oregon

An award-winning design for the Integrating Habitats 2008 competition sponsored by Oregon Metro, in Portland, Terra+Scapes is based on organic design developments that reflect the site's geographical, social, economical and environmental context. The mixed-use design fuses work, play, living and education into a small environmental footprint, which is sensitive to both the natural systems of the site and those influencing it. Zambelli has created a terracing architecture with extensive green roofs; an elaborate, intertwining system of pathways; public green space surrounding every structure, urban plazas to display storm water processes and a riparian regeneration zone.

Zambelli's digital-design process for this project started with conceptual design sketches that were digitized into CAD line work. The CAD file was then imported into Google SketchUp, and Zambelli created massing models, which were used for architectural form studies and landscape design testing. The integration of architecture and existing topography was paramount to the project. GIS-based topography was imported into Google SketchUp via the GIS to SKP plug-in; further design refinements were made in Google SketchUp, and Zambelli modelled an 'organically shaped bridge' in Cinema 4D. Once all the additions and model refinements were completed, the model was exported to Vue 6 Infinite software for the final rendering.

1. Night view of pedestrian promenade.
2. View of shared exterior open space.
3. Axonometric wire-frame model.

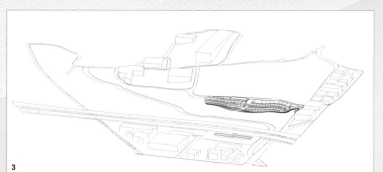

23.2
Digital Landscape
Architecture in Practice
Virtual Construction before
Physical Construction

1. Digital massing model of prominent site features.
2. Detailed digital model with triangulated irregular network surface.

For a collaboration with Toronto-based Cosburn Associates, Zambelli provided the firm with an advanced visualization of the evolving design proposal. In this case, the digital-design process was based off of existing workflows, and provided Zambelli with valuable feedback on design feasibility and aesthetics throughout the project. Through this process, he was able to tackle potential design and construction problems in a virtual environment, which resulted in a more cohesive design, and later easier construction. Zambelli was able to render convincing and high-quality imagery of the proposed design space, which was very useful in client presentations and studio discussions about design decisions and aesthetics.

The overall digital-design process was derived in CAD to allow minimal new data creation and to work seamlessly with existing design processes. CAD site, grading and planting plans were reduced to their essential line work for optimal 3D creation. The data was then imported into Google SketchUp with controlled layer management to allow for modelling of specific elements, one at a time. Once the design decisions were finalized, the model was exported into Vue 7 Infinite, in which features such as the auto-updating of linked models and the ability to replace masses with vegetation have allowed flexibility in design refinement and extreme accuracy in the visualization of planting plans.

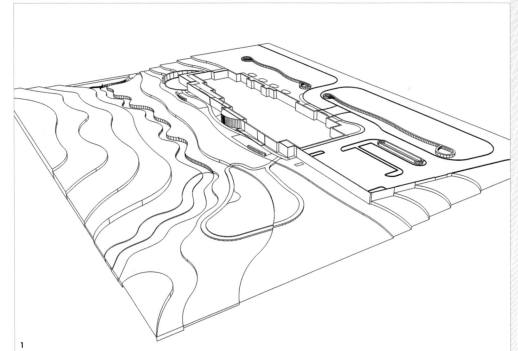

1

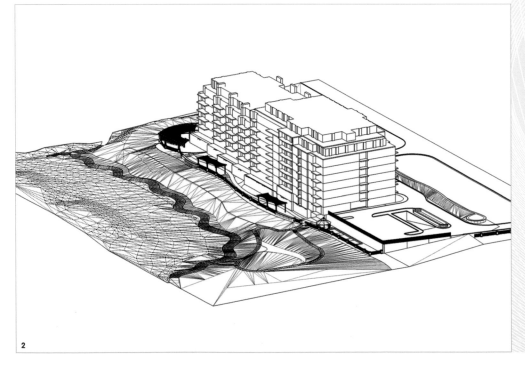

2

23.3
Porta Latina
Rome, Italy

Porta Latina stemmed from a research-based project that focused on the urban void spaces associated with the historic entry gates of the Aurelian Walls (built in Rome between AD 271 and 275, during the reigns of the emperors Aurelian and Probus). The project highlighted the history and layering of the walls' different materials by juxtaposing the brick-faced concrete with modern steel walkways and bridges that would allow visitors to intimately experience these variations. The structures also signified a new modern entrance for the Porta Latina, a single-arched gateway, while simultaneously using the wall as a guide for recreational trails and public spaces.

Zambelli's digital-design process began with the digitalization of Giambattista Nolli's 1748 map of Rome, together with maps of the city produced by S.A.R.A. Nistri, into CAD. The CAD line work was then imported into Google SketchUp for modelling. The precision needed to create the walkway that ascends along the wall and curvilinear bridges could not be achieved in Google SketchUp, so Zambelli imported his digital model into Cinema 4D, and 'lofted NURBS' was used to create the walkway geometry. Once the finished design was re-imported and completed in Google SketchUp, it was exported to Vue 6 Infinite for the addition of vegetation, atmosphere and retexturing. All final images and animations were rendered in Vue.

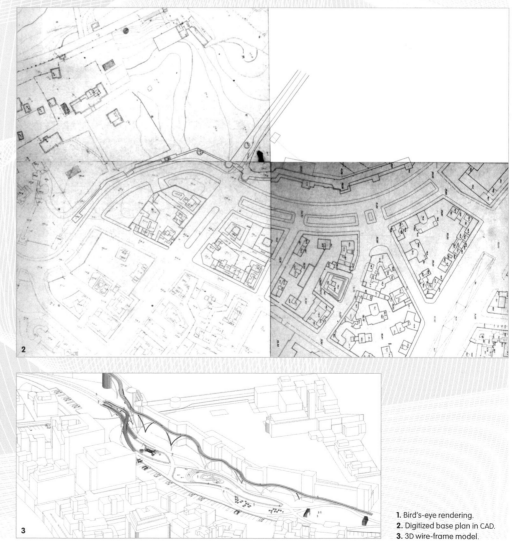

1. Bird's-eye rendering.
2. Digitized base plan in CAD.
3. 3D wire-frame model.

24
MVRDV

Based in Rotterdam, MVRDV is an innovative architecture and urban design firm, founded by Winy Maas, Jacob van Rijs and Nathalie de Vries in 1991. Since then, the firm has won many awards for design innovation and academic achievement. Their projects tend to push boundaries, using theoretical and technological approaches that focus on density and sustainability. Other recurring themes in their work have been ecology, sprawl, consumption, bio-industry, density and climate change. The significance of this research goes beyond the architectural discourse. Some of their research has opened the door to new ways of thinking, and even affecting legislation and city planning.

At the preliminary stages of the design process, MVRDV involves as many users and advisors as needed. The firm collects as much relevant information as possible, including zoning laws, the history and ecology of the site and building regulations, and the data is then used to produce designs that the architects feel will engage society, sustainability and technology equally. They also champion an interdisciplinary design approach, which includes input from a range of professions to ensure the use of the most up-to-date technologies and resources. Reactions to initial

design concepts are often implemented quickly, creating a high degree of support for the design and encouraging the sort of new insights that can lead to innovative solutions.

Among MVRDV's designs are the Dutch Pavilion for Expo 2000 in Hanover; Flight Forum, a business park in Eindhoven, Netherlands; the publication Metacity/Datatown (1999); and Gwanggyo Power Centre (p. 178), near Seoul. These and many of their other projects utilize advanced modelling programs and photorealistic collages to capture the landscape scenes. MVRDV also uses other digital-design technologies, including BIM, to ensure efficiency.

Almere 2030,
Almere Hout, Netherlands.

24.1
Gwanggyo Power Centre
Gwanggyo, South Korea

This competition-winning design for a power centre will form part of a major development for a new city for up to 77,000 inhabitants, situated 35 km (22 miles) south of Seoul. Envisioned as a verdant acropolis of organic 'hill' structures, the proposed complex is located on the southern edge of the development, surrounded by a lake and forested hills. By using advanced digital technologies, the architects will be able to test the programme requirements and phasing development, positions and sizes in the creation of the new landscape mounds.

All of the programme elements are designed as rings. By pushing these rings outwards on the lower floors, each part of the design acquires a terrace, allowing for outside usage and creating space for vegetation and waterfalls that flow from floor to floor. Housing, a museum and retail and office space will be located in a series of green hill structures. By carefully

positioning these hills, a new landscape
begins to emerge.

The rooftops of the hills and the
terraces can be planted with box hedges
and other plants, creating a valley park.
Outdoor facilities are located on the
terraces, which are connected with ramps
and hills. They form walks between the
surrounding hills, the streets and the lake.
Gwanggyo Power Centre promises to
be a signature green space and visually
powerful series of buildings, which mimics
a mountainous landscape as it emerges
from the ground.

1. Housescape.
2. Canyon.
3. Bird's-eye view.
4. Dome.
5. Nature.

24.2
Almere 2030
Almere Hout, Netherlands

Over twenty thousand plots will be up for sale for future private developments in Almere Hout, an area of fields and forest. The architects created a series of test scenarios to accommodate sustainability sound solutions for this future community, with several scenarios developed to take newly planted green areas as the starting point. By projecting a sustainable grid on the site, plots measuring 200 × 150 m (656 × 492 ft) are defined. These plots form the foundations for new developments, which are designed for flex density, ranging from low density (six houses/ha) to high density (45–60 houses/ha).

The green area will slowly evolve for new developments, while retaining a considerable amount of vegetation, trees and natural landscape. The architects set up the developmental growth slowly for future construction, adding infrastructure where needed. As a result, the city has the possibility to develop the plots one at a time, gradually replacing the green area. With this project, MVRDV established the rules for density and programme for specific plots, influencing positive and progressive development.

1. Masterplan.
2. Fields and forest density.
3. Plot development.

24.3
Eco City Montecorvo
Logroño, Spain

1. Overview.
2, 3. Perspectives.

In 2007 MVRDV, together with the Spanish architectural office GRAS, entered a competition for a sustainable urban extension area of Logroño, a city of approximately 130,000 inhabitants located in the wine region of La Rioja, in the north of Spain. The scheme consisted of approximately three thousand units for social housing, along with the associated programmes: schools, community buildings and sports facilities – all developed in a sustainable way. By producing all the energy required on site, the new neighbourhood will achieve a carbon-neutral footprint.

The 56-ha (138-acre) site is situated on the two small hills of Montecorvo and La Fonsalada, which provide beautiful views over the city, as well as solar-energy generation from its southern slopes. To achieve this, a tapestry of PV cells clad the ground, as if it is covered in gold. On top of the hills, windmills generate part of the energy needed for the houses and buildings, while at the same time functioning as iconic landmarks in the countryside. One hundred per cent of the energy needed by the new community will be generated on site by a combination of solar and wind energy. The development is designed in a compact way – only 10 per cent of the site is occupied by buildings – to minimize its impact on the landscape. The remaining space becomes a magnificent eco-park, a mix of landscape and energy production. Like a ribbon, the dense urban development meanders through the landscape.

24.4
Floriade 2012
Rotterdam, Netherlands

This design for the World Horticultural Expo in the Netherlands is a modern twist on Noah's Ark. The structure was designed to be as compact as possible, and densely planted, to become a research platform for agricultural innovation and addressing themes of growing food-production demands and an ever-increasing global population. Food production, plant refinement, ecology, forestry and the preservation of nature are no longer confined to the country, and are becoming part of the typical city experience.

This concept for a vertical structure demonstrates how issues of plants and horticulture can be addressed strategically in a world that is becoming ever denser. For Floriade 2012, the architects proposed three different concepts, each showing various ways to build up the exhibition, but all relating to the need for densification.

1. Bird's-eye view.
2. Digital model of the green building structure.
3–6. Concepts, various 'greening' densifications.

25
NOX

Founded and now directed by Dutch architect Lars Spuybroek, Nox is fundamentally concerned with the production of creative architectural and landscape works, using digital applications as a means to help foster the artistic outcome. Spuybroek believes that architecture should, above all, exude a sense of 'beauty, feelings and moods'.

Nox has been at the forefront of the development of digital design in architecture and landscape since its beginnings in the early 1990s. The firm's conceptual philosophy equates art and architecture, maintaining that architecture should be a reflection of people's feelings and moods. The use of digital technology is critical to the design process. For Spuybroek, digital applications produce a 'method that augments even human experience',

and he believes that digital technology allows the creation of designs that could have never been crafted by hand. The company's design strategy attempts to avoid the use of lines, and instead digitally analyses curves and irregular forms. Through the aid of software such as AutoCAD, 3D Studio MAX, Rhinoceros and Photoshop, the designers create 'machines' that follow particular geometric systems of intertwined parts.

The company's work has been exhibited at many museums around the world, including the Centre Pompidou in Paris, the Victoria & Albert in London and the Museum of Modern Art in New York, and has been featured at the Venice Biennale on several occasions. In 1997, Nox built the first fully interactive building with a digitally generated geometry, the

HtwoOexpo water pavilion, on Neeltje Jans Island, in the Netherlands. At the time, this project set the bar for the critical examination of spatially augmented and reactive environments.

Whispering Garden, Rotterdam, Netherlands.

25.1
Eye Bridge
Aachen, Germany

This competition-winning proposal was for an artistically designed pedestrian bridge, which intertwines river and forest. The bridge structure is elegantly designed, resembling an allée of trees that appear to move in the wind and reflecting the river that flows beneath it.

The tight spacing of wooden elements creates a striking perspective view towards the forest, while creating a fully open view in the other direction, towards the river. To strengthen this intermingling of river and forest, the designers have widened the bridge slightly at midpoint, which transforms the passage into a stop point for users and directs their attention to the river below.

1, 3. Details of the bridge structure.
2. One-point perspective.
4. Overview.

25.2
Seoul Opera House
Seoul, South Korea

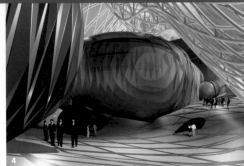

The Seoul Opera House is situated on
an island in the middle of the Han River,
connected by two bridges to the city.
The designers' concept for the building is
symbolic, based on the so-called 'viewing
stone', or *yunsanseok*, a multi-peaked
mountain-range stone. The shape of
the building resembles a mountainous
landscape, which Nox relates to the ideas
of John Ruskin and the alpine architecture
of Bruno Taut.

The structural skin is composed of a
series of valleys and peaks that perform
as columns and domes, creating a striking
silhouette for the building. This structure
accommodates an opera house and
a concert hall, together with a number
of supporting programmes. The skin
changes from opaque to fully transparent,
depending on programmatic needs.
The skin is 'closed' when covering the
backstage areas, and 'opened' when
wrapping foyers and platforms, including
the restaurant on top of the opera tower
with its stunning views over Seoul.

1, 2. Overview.
3. Night view.
4. Interior.
5. Plateau.

25.3
Whispering Garden
Rotterdam, Netherlands

Whispering Garden, another competition-winning design by the architects, is an interactive public artwork, located along the River Meuse in Rotterdam. The concept took its inspiration from the legends of sirens, who would lure passing ships onto the rocks. For this project, advanced wind studies and properties, including direction, force and duration, were interpreted by the sound artist Edwin van der Heide to create computer-generated female voices, which would continuously sing vowels that separated into other vowels, making overtones that were reproduced to create a polyphonic forest of sound.

The anthropomorphic form of the mesh-and-steel structure is reminiscent of the paintings of Art Nouveau artist Alphonse Mucha, which featured beautiful women with locks of sensuously streaming hair. According to Spuybroek, Whispering Garden is a 'synaesthetic node' ('synaesthesia' meaning a merging of the senses), connecting the elements of the space: 'wind to light, light to structure, structure to sound, sound to architecture, architecture to bodies, looping all the loops, making everything sensing everything, and making everything sensuous.'

1. Inside the garden.
2. Overview perspective of structure.

25.4
Silk Road
Xi'an, China

For this project proposal, yet another competition-winning design, the architects designed a real and virtual road. According to Spuybroek, 'the space of the building is directly related to a virtual space on the Internet, which organizes a unique form of exchange between the people of Western Europe and China'. The interior of the building delivers digital photographs of Western Europe to Xi'an, both still images and pictures that showcase feelings and thoughts.

The building has a large, unfolding roof that can alter between transparent and opaque, varying spatial forms to accommodate the different educational and cultural programmes, seminar classrooms, a 'Silk Road history' area and theatre spaces.

1. Winter scene.
2. Spring scene.
3. Night.
4. Approach to structure.
5. Interior.
6. Interior view.

26
O2 PLANNING
& DESIGN

O2 Planning & Design is a Canadian-based landscape architectural firm that specializes in the planning, geo-spatial analysis and design of large-scale landscapes. The firm's philosophy is based on a synthesis of design with a specific environmental sensibility, and their projects are driven by creativity, environmental knowledge, site analysis and sustainable outlooks for development.

Through the extensive analysis of vast territories, the designers produce practical strategies to meet specific design needs that simultaneously align with existing contexts, natural systems and ecological processes. The firm provides planning and design solutions in the areas of productive landscapes, large parks, contested areas, reclaimed sites, brownfields, regional planning, urban and town planning, and educational landscapes.

The design process is sustained by the use of various digital-design technologies that are frequently updated through rigorous continuous research. The application of landscape modelling enables the incorporation of ecological processes, such as habitat suitability and species enrichment, in planning at regional scales. The firm also uses advanced technologies, including GIS, remote sensing, digital modelling, 3D visualization and virtual-environment simulation, to assist in their design development, with the ultimate goal of visually communicating convincing images to users.

Corporate Campus
Urban Design.

26.1
Corporate Campus Urban Design

For this design of an urban corporate campus, the design team used 3D modelling tools to express both architectural and landscape solutions.

A complete 3D model of the campus was created to compare existing conditions for visualizing future design alternatives. The firm integrated several software platforms in the development of the project.

1. Rendering of the central campus building and courtyard during the day.
2. Night rendering of the same space, illustrating a special event.

26.2
Landscape Planning
for Agroforestry
Embu, Mt Kenya

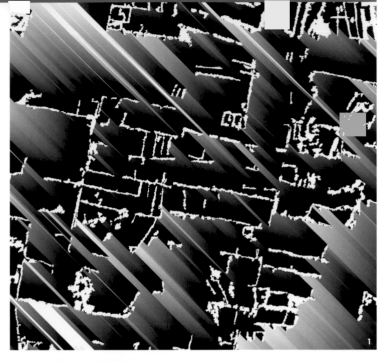

Douglas Olson, the firm's president, developed a digital model of an agroforestry landscape near the town of Embu, located on the lower slopes of Mt Kenya, about 120 km (75 miles) northeast of Nairobi, to analyse the impact of alternative arrangements of trees on the area's crop production.

A compact airborne spectrographic imager was used to create a land-cover classification and detect crop vigour and photosynthetic activity, while a series of GIS landscape pattern analyses mapped current crop production. The results were used to identify changes in the spatial arrangement of trees and distances from hedgerows, which could positively influence corn and wood production. Through this visualization process and analysis, Olson discovered an optimal hedgerow density that could maximize crop production for the area.

1. GIS landscape-pattern analysis.
2, 3. Land-cover classifications.

26.3
Petro-Canada Sullivan Gas Field Development
Alberta, Canada

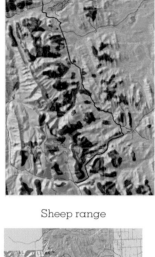

Elk habitat

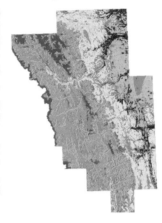

Ecological classification

Impacts on vegetation

Sheep range

Fragmentation

Site diversity

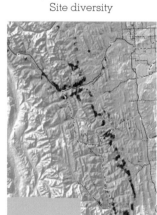

As part of a project to minimize the impact of a large natural gas field development in southwestern Alberta, the designers developed a virtual 3D model of the regional landscape. Constructed using high-resolution imagery and LIDAR, an airborne optical remote-sensing technology, this virtual model helped to obtain an understanding of the site, and to help plan access to the remote location. The highly detailed digital model includes trees and vegetation, with heights accurate to within 15 cm (6 in).

Following the development of the digital model, the architects created a series of landscape ecological GIS models to further aid the development of facilities. Landscape, wildlife and visual-impact patterns, together with other GIS analyses, were used to locate the required infrastructure during the planning phase of the project. During the detail design process, road designs were developed using LIDAR and AutoCAD Civil 3D, and integrated into landscape visualization software. Using soil data, water flow analysis and vegetation surveys, the corridor alignments were further refined. Existing surface corridors, together with proposed roadway and pipeline alignments, were also created, and alternative location and cut/fill scenarios were modelled to reduce the extent of the required clearing.

The final road-surface design is merged into existing ground LIDAR surfaces and imported into the landscape visualization software so that vegetation and ground textures are applied. The resulting visualization provides an accurate depiction of precisely how a newly designed road corridor will look in the wider landscape.

1, 2. The final design, after importation into visualization software.
3. Ecological GIS models.

26.4
TELUS Spark
Calgary, Alberta, Canada

1

This concept for TELUS Spark, a new science centre for the TELUS World of Science, located on a 6-ha (15-acre) site in the Nose Creek Valley, north of the Calgary Zoo, will incorporate, say the architects, 'excitement, playfulness, education and sustainability'. It will feature four permanent exhibition spaces, a children's museum, a learning centre, a touring exhibition gallery and a discovery theatre.

An outdoor Science Amazement Park will be organized into outdoor exhibit rooms, cut into landforms and inspired by tipped geologic fault structures. As an LEED Gold facility, the design also provides storm-water management elements to minimize the impact on a nearby stream.

1. Aerial view, with the science park in the foreground.
2. Plan of the Amazement Park.

27
PHILIP PAAR & JÖRG REKITTKE

Landscape planner and 3D-modelling and visualization expert Philip Paar, together with landscape architect Jörg Rekittke, are the co-developers of the innovative digital tools Biosphere3D and Lenné3D, which produce sophisticated image rendering and landscape modelling. Paar and his team, including computer scientists Malte Clasen and Steffen Ernet, were able to successfully turn their research into landscape visualization, and data analysis into marketable software for the masses.

Biosphere3D and Lenné3D are GIS-based, and can create sophisticated real-time 3D visualizations of landscapes and vegetation. Lenné3D was named for the German landscape architect Peter Joseph Lenné (1789–1866), who believed that the only way landscapes obtain their completion is through their relationship to humans.

Two hundred years on, Paar and Rekittke attempt to strengthen this relationship through their own complex landscape visualizations.

In 2010 Paar, together with software developer Timm Dapper and computer-graphics scientist Jalda Schaback, co-founded the Berlin-based software development company Laubwerk, which has established a new principle of digital botany in its creations of hyper-real vegetation and landscapes. Biosphere3D, Lenné3D and Laubwerk are all at the cutting edge of computer-graphics technology in terms of landscape planning and design. Paar and Rekittke continually develop new digital tools that are able to accurately – and beautifully – visualize landscape elements and scenarios.

Parametric Geotypical Landscapes.

27.1 Parametric Geotypical Landscapes

How will the landscape look in the future under different policy scenarios? According to Paar and his team, answering this question, as it relates to scenery, is difficult when communicating such abstract information using maps. One of their objectives is the development of accurate and appealing geo-visualizations for these kinds of projects.

In order to model vegetation cover for European-wide landscape visualization, the team creates a 3D landscape generator, in which land-use classifications can be matched with regionalized vegetation patterns. For thirty sections of thirty cluster regions, the Laubwerk tool generates 5 × 5-km (3 × 3- mile) virtual maps of a representative yet synthetic landscape by using a rectangular grid, composed of cells that simulate an area of 20 × 20 m (66 × 66 ft) each. This was a challenge, but the team of landscape architects, GIS specialists and computer technologists were able to develop this new program. The 3D landscape generator is able to synthesize numerical values related to the topography and land use of a region, and transform them into a generated landscape that reflects the land-use situation. It is a spatial-simulation software that is designed to visualize landscapes, based either on regional information of land use, or to use the information from other landscape dynamics spatial models as a modelling system.

The program is able to define characteristic plant communities of the thirty spatial regional reference framework clusters. GIS coverage of the cluster regions are overlaid with the GIS coverage of the potential native vegetation of Europe. For each species, one or more virtual trees, shrubs, grasses and large perennials are assigned from a 3D plant model library. One plant distribution file is calculated for each scenario in each cluster region. On average, a 1-km² (0.6-sq mile) tile of a plant distribution includes about five million occurrences.

One example of a landscape scenario.

27.2
Digital Botany

Paar's company Laubwerk develops new software programs for the depiction of landscape representation. According to the designer, plant expertise is one of the few features that is particularly unique to landscape architecture. Because too many current digital software programs render vegetation poorly, the team's goal is to develop better rendering tools for the visualization of the beauty and character of plants in digital landscape architecture.

In practice, 2D billboards and photomontages of plants are still the most common techniques, because 3D plants tend to be either rendered beautifully but slowly, or quickly and inaccurately. Laubwerk is a new means of rendering landscapes, developed by plant lovers and computer nerds, including Paar. The team believe that the digital representation of vegetation requires special attention and ingenuity, and are continually developing new approaches to create visually appealing plants that are both quick and easy to render.

1. Micro-landscape:
a large piece of turf.
2. Prototype of a European
White Birch.

27.3
Biosphere3D
The Free Landscape
Scenery Globe

Biosphere3D is an open-source landscape visualization tool that supports multiple scales and focuses on the real-time rendering of landscape scenery, providing convincing visualization of vegetation cover. The main objective of its academic predecessor, Lenné3D-Player, was to create and visualize landscape from an eye-level perspective to enable the user to wander through the planned or predicted landscape.

In 2005 numerous computational constraints, including limited size of terrain and deficient scalability, motivated the developers to fix this problem. Now satellite images and raster digital-elevation models can be combined with 3D plants models, Shapefiles and KMZ/Collada files to create photorealistic views of planned or past landscape scenarios, virtually reconstructed sites, and so on. The modelling of landscape features occurs in external applications, such as GIS, simulation models with GIS data output and 3D CAD tools, including Google SketchUp. The system offers interactive shadow mapping, scientifically accurate atmospheric rendering, and many other valuable computational features.

The open-source project was initially developed and applied within the research project Silvisio, which was funded by the German Federal Ministry of Education and Research. Currently, lead development is organized by Zuse-

Institut Berlin, and at Lenné3D, the visualization and software company co-founded by Paar. Since Biosphere3D is free and open, it can be extended by C++ software developers to meet specific processing and user-interface requirements.

1. Virtual view of Kimberley Climate Change Adaptation project, from Taylor's Mill.
2. Virtual reconstruction of King Herod's third winter palace and oasis, near Jericho.

27.4
Gleisdreieck Berlin
Berlin, Germany

This research project focuses on experimentation with digital techniques and methods. In 2006 the City of Berlin sponsored a landscape architecture competition to elicit a park concept for a former railway site in the city centre. The design team used different digital tools and techniques to produce the submitted competition entry plans and illustrations. These included both commonly used tools in landscape-design practice, such as CAD and image-editing tools, as well as those that are less well used, such as GIS and real-time landscape visualization systems.

The techniques employed included CAD drafting, 3D sketching, GIS editing, vegetation modelling, geo-referenced 3D visualization and compositing, and collage. Part of the competition requirement included the production and submission of an illustrating perspective. The team's goal was to transfer the site context model from CAD into a 3D real-time model, which served as a digital content creation tool to generate montage layers for the required perspectives.

1. The interactive, geovirtual 3D model at an early stage in the design process.
2. Final montage of the illustrating perspective, using 3D visualization, background photo and sketching layers.

27.5
Future Energy Landscapes
Welzow, Germany

This project is located in the town of Welzow, in southeastern Brandenburg, Germany, on a former open-cast brownfield coal mining site. Instead of depicting the recently implemented large biomass plantation of black locust (*Robinia pseudoacacia*), the visual simulation demonstrates an alternative cultural landscape.

New landscape scenery patterns and views arise from the implementation of linear agricultural structures, such as alley-cropping systems and time-shifted harvesting.

1. Landscape growth, 2008.
2. Landscape growth, 2015.
3. Landscape harvest.

28
PAISAJES EMERGENTES

Based in Medellín, Colombia, Paisajes Emergentes was founded in 2007 by three young architects: Luis Callejas, Sebastián Mejia and Edgar Mazo. The practice attempts to establish a continual dialogue between art, landscape and architecture, mostly through environmental operations and crossed operations between architecture and landscape design.

The trio's philosophy is reflected in their name, 'emerging landscapes'. They believe that an important factor in constructing the built environment is how a design responds, evolves and adapts itself to the invisible forces of its natural context and surroundings slowly over time. Borrowing theories from geology, biology and meteorology, they understand the landscape as a place of distinct sensibility, character and meaning, which any proposal must answer to. Through their unique representational techniques and visual style, the team experiments with the possible relationships of their designs within their context.

The firm uses various digital representational technologies in their design process. One of their main strategies in making photorealistic perspective collages, however, is their use of montage overlays of already existing real-life photographic images of a site with renders of their proposals. The designers' young and energetic vibe carries through into their projects, pushing the boundaries of novel landscapes, through the use of sophisticated image modification and renderings to envision new ideas.

Clouds,
Ituango, Colombia.

28.1
Clouds
Ituango, Colombia

For this project, the designers proposed five installations, located in every town affected by the construction of the new Ituango Dam in Colombia, which will serve as a hydroelectric power generator. Each 'cloud' of the design will serve as a communication device; every object will float to a distance of 150 m (492 ft) above ground to maintain radio communication with each other, allowing a constant exchange of information between towns separated by both distance and a complex topography. The new radio station and weather-prediction system will also be located on the installations.

1. Profile view.
2. Aerial view of the town of San Andrés de Cuerquia.

28.2
Parque del Lago
Quito, Ecuador

This project focuses on the transformation of an old airport runway into a hydrological park to generate a productive and recreational landscape. The strip is approximately 3 km (1.9 miles) long, and is divided into six zones that configure six stages of a closed cycle of water events:

— Bio-remediation wetlands, composed of nine lakes that alternate to biologically treat the residual water of the park and nearby buildings.

— An open-air excavated aquarium, filled with semi-clean water that comes from the wetlands, which will contain equatorial fauna from fluvial ecosystems around the world.

— An aquatic flora botanical garden with tropical species from all over the world. (At this stage, water from the aquarium would contain only organic material, ideal for maintaining the fertility of the botanical garden.)

— A conventional treatment plant, in which water is oxygenated and filtrated, and the organic material from the botanical garden is removed from the water. Visitors will be able to observe this process by walking along a pedestrian walkway.

— Pools and thermal baths, in which the treated water is used to fill the public pools and thermal baths. Solar energy is used to heat the aquatic complex.

— A recreational lake, which is part of the recollection zone, where water with chlorine and other contaminants is treated simply by exposing it to the sun. Water is then collected in subterranean tanks that satisfy the needs of irrigation systems and general maintenance of the park. All of the sediments in the water are taken back to the bio-remediation wetlands.

1. Aerial view.
2. Approach to site.
3. Aquarium.
4. Sunken garden.

28.3
Aquatic Complex
Medellín, Colombia

This competition-winning design was for a water complex with creative 'productive uses', in which the programme is part of a new ecosystem. The landscape and its architecture are constructed as an infrastructure that will support the complex in the current flooded landscape ecosystem. The aquatic gardens surrounding the competition areas allow a constant relationship between swimmers and a living ecosystem.

These areas are planted with species that are capable of bio-remediating the water, providing a natural cleaning agent similar to native wetlands. The service areas, including the bathrooms and dressing rooms, are located below the aquatic garden level, and are articulated by open-air courtyards, which are the only apertures in the flooded zones.

1. Large pool.
2. Aerial view.
3. Synchro-swim window.
4. Patio.
5. Entrance.
6. Concept rendering.

29
PEG OFFICE OF LANDSCAPE & ARCHITECTURE

Ripple Effect,
Manhattan and the Bronx,
New York.

PEG is a design and research think tank and practice based in Philadelphia, Pennsylvania. Founded by Karen M'Closkey and Keith VanDerSys, who also both teach in the landscape architecture department at the University of Pennsylvania, it is an interdisciplinary firm that engages in various types of projects in terms of content, scale and medium, ranging from immersive interior environments to large public spaces.

As part of their philosophy, an understanding of scale through the use of digital applications is critical in the design. The designers' operative approach aims to perceive different design elements, whether aesthetic, formal, social or programmatic, at appropriate scales, and to use these understandings to maintain variation. Larger projects allow for variations that operate on regional scales and with systems of regional circulation, and ecological and urban networks, while smaller projects allow for intimate designs that incorporate geometric and material variations that operate on a human scale.

PEG's work explores the relationship among digital media, fabrication technology and construction. New media enables innovative directions in the visualization and construction of dynamic landscapes. Their projects experiment with modular patterns, others with modular material units, and some with both; in all cases, these methods are used to craft variations in surface appearance, as well as participate in site functions, such as water collection, plant growth and maintenance zones. These incremental infrastructures have implications for more integrative thinking about natural systems in relatively dense urban environments, and offer expressive potentials for landscape via new combinations of organic and inorganic materials.

Their work is often augmented by parametric modelling practices, and incorporates ideas of materiality and fabrication in the design process. To do this, the designers use a variety of advanced digital modelling and image-modification software including Rhinoceros for modelling, Grasshopper for parametric and pattern versioning, V-Ray and the Adobe Suite for rendering, and LaserCam and CNC machining for prototype component cutting and fabrication. The use of these tools and techniques has created a signature aesthetic, establishing PEG as part of the next generation in the field of landscape design.

29.1
Ripple Effect
Manhattan and the Bronx, New York

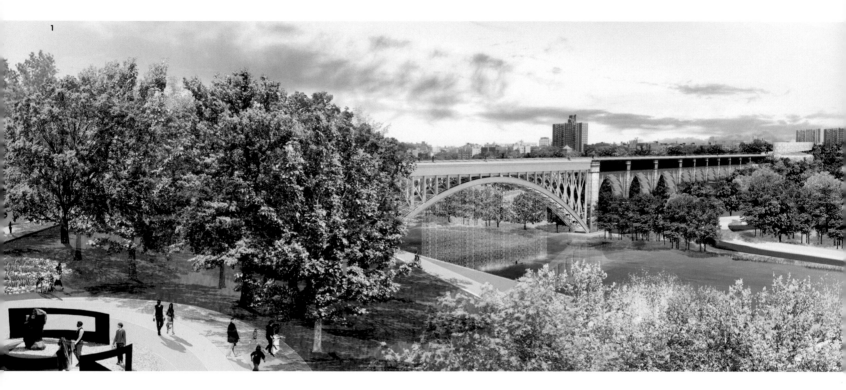

Ripple Effect is a network of social spaces, organized to merge the cultural, environmental and historical contexts that make the High Bridge, which spans the Harlem River and connects Manhattan and the Bronx, unique. PEG's proposal repurposes the aqueduct and its surroundings into a connected infrastructure for the treatment and display of hydrological resources, exploring landscape infrastructural innovations.

The concept is a circuit of displays, interweaving the programmes of art, recreation and landscape to create unique or unexpected adjacencies among them. The circuit is a distributed system, inspired by the line-arc configuration that forms both the steel and masonry structures of the bridge, as well as the complex of transport infrastructure below. The line-arc geometry loops onto itself to create a series of clusters, called infra-blooms, which function as collectors for artistic and environmental performances, and hold users, events and water.

The system of infra-blooms has three distinct areas: intermittent (landscape), interstitial (bridge) and internal (building). The 'intermittent display' is a network of paths, pools, puddles and ponds, located on the Manhattan side of the aqueduct, where the landscape is restructured to support various activities. The infra-blooms serve as a water-cleansing system that collects and filters rainfall, and then channels it back to the bridge, where it falls, days later, into the river. By reversing the flow, the structure is transformed from a distribution pipe, which transports water from distant sources, to a collecting reservoir that delivers clean water back to the Harlem River. The intermittent curtain of water falling from the bridge can be engaged by visitors and artists in a variety of ways.

The 'internal display' is housed in a building on the Bronx side of the High Bridge, creating a gateway to the aqueduct. The building and landscape is configured as a loop that intertwines street access, bridge access and courtyards, and continues as a pathway that leads down to the existing river access. PEG used Rhinoceros for advanced modelling and V-Ray and Photoshop for image modification and rendering.

1. Perspective view.
2. Section.

2

29.2
Not Garden, Not Again
Philadelphia, Pennsylvania

For their projects, the designers at PEG use the untapped design potential of low-cost engineering substrates as a means of developing new techniques of surface control and display, as well as abandoned vacant lands as a testing ground for new greening strategies. Playing off the traditional knot-garden's intertwining geometric patterns, their Not Garden prototypes are made using parametric software and laser-cutting fabrication to pre-cut customized patterns out of geo-textile (weed-control fabric), which is then laid on site and seeded.

This method produces diverse configurations with very low investment, effort, installation expertise or long-term care. The project involved two test plots: Not Garden and Not Again. The first version tested the basic carrying capacity of geo-textile, while the latter, larger version experimented with a more intricate pattern and expanded the planting to include flowering, drought-tolerant groundcover. The designers used a vast selection of software and hardware to achieve this low-cost garden, including Rhinoceros for modelling, V-Ray and Photoshop for rendering, Grasshopper for parametric and pattern versioning, and LaserCAM for the final fabrication.

1, 3, 4. Not Garden.
2. Not Again.
5. Not Again pattern.

29.3
Joie de Vie(w)
Montreal, Quebec, Canada

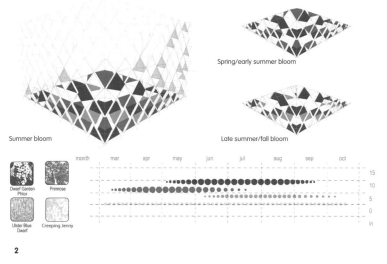

Spring/early summer bloom

Summer bloom

Late summer/fall bloom

Dwarf Garden Phlox | Primrose

Ulster Blue Dwarf | Creeping Jenny

2

1

3

The designers's proposal for the Jardins de Métis 2008 international garden festival is an exploration into some of the fundamentals of garden design: the relationship between interior and exterior, and the unfolding of space through the control of viewpoint. In order to explore these themes in a contemporary context, the firm applied new technology, in the materiality and visual representational aspects, to investigate the boundaries between the organic and the inorganic, the static and the dynamic, within the garden tradition.

Their approach is one that looks to landscape architect Gabriel Guévrékian's Garden of Water and Light (1925), in that the designers explored the relationship between surface and depth, while challenging the static nature of Guévrékian's composition. They used current visualization tools to study how to create a two-dimensional visual effect by

using three-dimensional composition, and vice versa. All of the landscape elements, including pools, walls and planting, are organized in a triangular motif. The effect was an interesting visual study that flattened the space of the garden in order to imitate the cubist principles of simultaneous composition. The layout of the landscape is organized with two walls so that, from a particular viewpoint outside the garden, a 'flattened' triangle is perceptible.

The firm used a palette of advanced modelling and image-modification software to develop the complexity of the design, including Rhinoceros for modelling, V-Ray and the Adobe Suite for rendering, and LaserCAM for prototype component cutting and fabrication. The walls of the garden are composed of a three-dimensional plastic tile, fabricated from flat sheet stock using a CNC laser-cutter. The tile is altered and used in

different orientations to control views within the garden, and to create pockets of planting in the wall, while the selective application of colour to the interior of the tiles introduced directionality to the experience of the garden.

1, 3. Perspective views.
2. Planting diagram.

30
PYO ARQUITECTOS

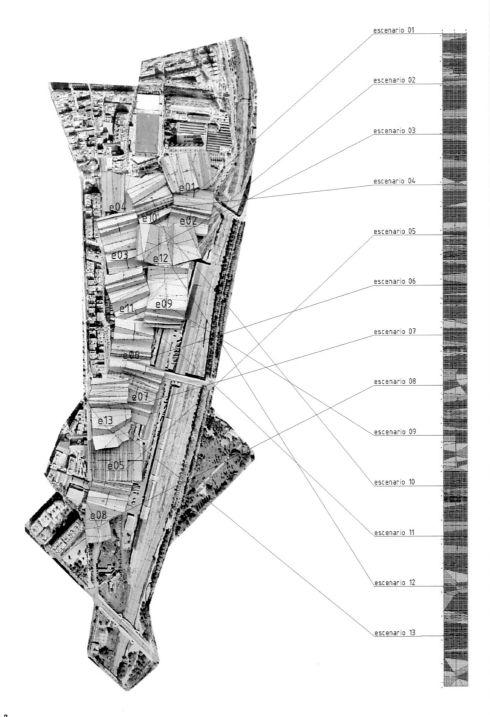

escenario 01
escenario 02
escenario 03
escenario 04
escenario 05
escenario 06
escenario 07
escenario 08
escenario 09
escenario 10
escenario 11
escenario 12
escenario 13

Paul Galindo Pastre and Ophélie Herranz Lespagnol founded PYO Arquitectos in 2007. Their ambitions regarding new media, merging digital applications and design complexity has made their company one of the most successful young architecture firms in Spain. Part of their success can be attributed to their forward-thinking approach in utilizing digital applications to test new concepts in form and space-making – an approach that is also carried through in their PhD studies and teaching. Since 2002, the pair have collaborated on a series of academic projects, competitions and professional work.

To aid their design process, the duo use digital-design technologies, including AutoCAD for creating plans and linework, Maya for construction drawings, Form z for modelling and advanced rendering visuals, and Rhinoceros for dynamic and performance-based spaces. In some of their design processes, they have also incorporated parametric scripting, using Rhino, through a collaboration with Andrew Kudless. Their academic research is clearly applied in their professional practice, pushing the envelope in both surface modification and advanced rendering processes. The work of the firm is widely published and recognized.

Urban Procedures,
Barcelona, Spain.

2

30.1
Urban Procedures
Barcelona, Spain

This design, undertaken when the pair were undergraduate students, consists of an intermodal station in the La Sagrera neighbourhood of Barcelona, and the creations of interconnections to the city. The landscape surface situated over the existing railway creates a 4-km (2.5-mile) linear-park system that will improve the green linkages to Barcelona, and revitalize two neighbourhoods that are currently disconnected. These new green public spaces are supported by mixed-use housing, along with commercial and other programmes.

The project is developed by a series of 'urban procedures', which affect every scale and connect the disparate fragments of the city. It trials multiple and ever-changing scenarios to test new forms of growth and future typology.

1

1. Concept strategies.
2. Conceptual masterplan.

2

30.2
Dynamic Transformations
in Border Conditions
Rijnhaven, Netherlands

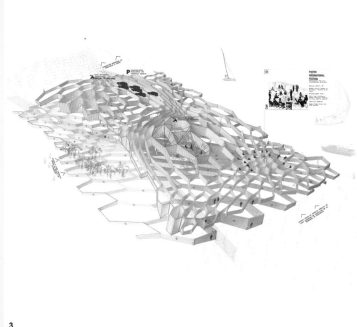

For this project, the designers developed an innovative pier structure to replace Rijnhaven's outdated port and dock facilities by 'pulling and raising' pieces of the surface to create both space and ground. The design attempts to reactivate this underused edge with the creation of new infrastructure, which is designed to organize and operate complex systems of flow, access and overall connection, and is flexible and adaptable to changing events and occupancy.

The proposal was designed as a framework with an adaptable spatial envelope and surface platform, allowing for future changes and to encourage public use along the 2 km (1.2 mile)-long border. The overall idea was 'to turn inside-out the intervention area by building the harbour perimeter: the border is an opportunity field'. Some interchange infrastructures, including an international ferry terminal, will enhance daily activity.

In addition to organizing flows, the different levels within the infrastructure reduce the distances between the areas as they allow a simultaneous use of the boarding and landing ways. The 'waiting gardens' work as temporary waiting areas for passengers, who travel with their own vehicles. A wide range of events may also occur over this structure.

The project starts from a generative design process of a deep honeycomb structure, which evolves in its flexibility and robustness by means of repetition, differentiation and continuity, remaining within the limits of available production technologies. The project explores advanced areas of form-making and surface manipulation using digital means. It should not be read as a megastructure, designed to be implemented as a total piece of architecture, but rather as a set of instructions that specify a typological performance in an urban plan.

1. Ferry.
2. Water taxi.
3. Spatial framework.

31
R&SIE(N)

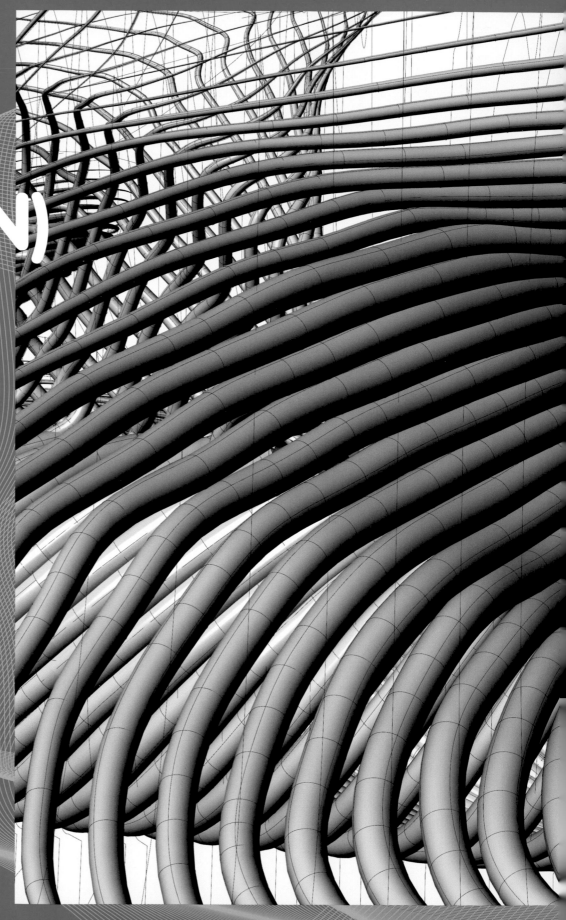

He Shot Me Down,
Heyri, South Korea

Architectural practice R&Sie(n) was founded in 1989 by François Roche and Stéphanie Lavaux, and is now based in Paris. The duo's architectural and landscape works are organic, experimental, biological and critical, often crafted using the latest digital methods and software programs in the field. They claim to use technology through 'mixing alchemically Eros (the god of love in Greek mythology) and Thanatos (the god of death) to develop consciously ambiguous scenarios that fuse realities that would seem immiscible'.

The firm seeks to articulate the real and/or fictional geographic situations, and the narrative structures that can transform them. The designers engage in various types of contemporary relationships, including those that are aesthetic, machinist, computational, natural, even artificial. They employ speculations and fictions as operative strategies to 'disalienate' operative modes, and to infiltrate media culture in order to subvert its conventions.

31.1
He Shot Me Down
Heyri, South Korea

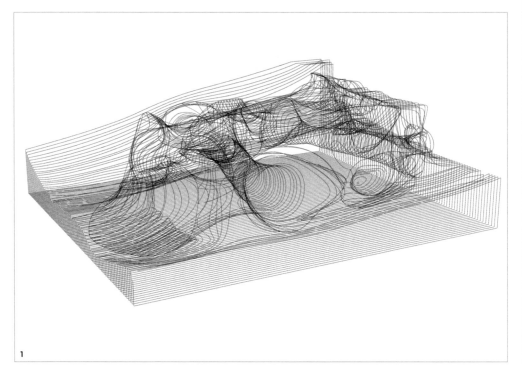

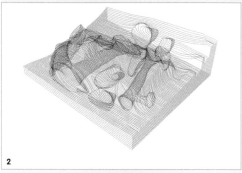

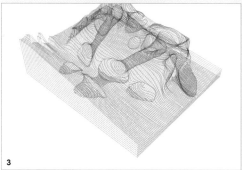

This creative digital design pushes the boundary of hybrid growth landscapes, including robotic mechanism movement and bio-mechanical surface (such as grass and groundcover) growth. The landscape accommodates a multiuse structure, including a private residence, dance centre, shop, restaurant, children's museum and retail venues, and the design, according to Roche and his team, takes into consideration the following conditions:

— Recognition of the location in the north of South Korea – the demilitarized zone – where the real danger is interweaved with the paranoia of danger and its own 'theatralization';

— Recognition of the specificities of the 'urbanism of Heyri, in which domesticity is fully embedded in the public area', where the client becomes the support of public services;

— 'Erotization of the paranoia, by "ballistic impacts" (inventions) in the extended volume' of the mountain-absorbing the programme;

— 'Trajectories of shooting as walkway access and light providers (stainless steel and glass as an homage to T1000)';

— Development of a robot, 'running (on a specific track) in the forest to bring back the biomass on its back, smearing the biograss and bioleaves in decomposition on all external surfaces to maintain the insulation of the building'.

1–3. Landscape form.
4. Robot fur.
5. Spiral.
6. Map.
7, 8. Perspectives.

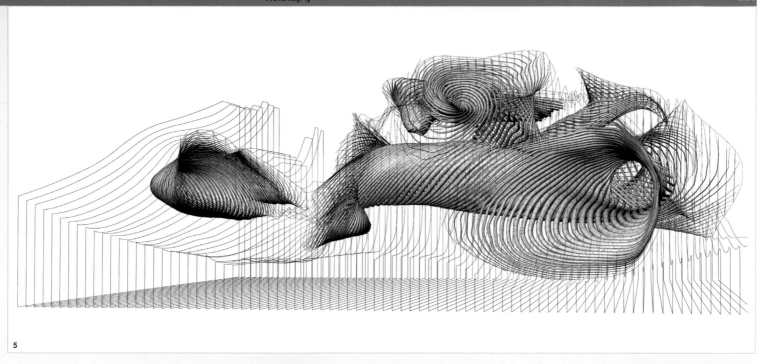

5

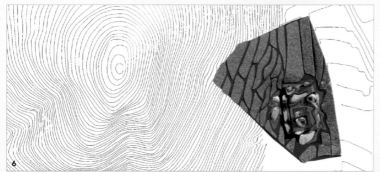

6

7

8

31.2
Green Gorgon
Lausanne, Switzerland

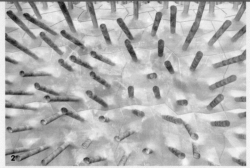

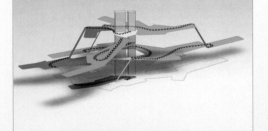

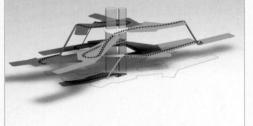

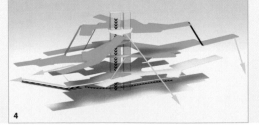

For this project, the designers have playfully combined nature and the digital in the landscape. According to Roche, 'weeds' that become part of the local woods are populated with animals – an amphibian world that has been emancipated from water, having appeared freely and spontaneously. The 'urban nature' of alignments, squares, parks and gardens, as applied to a living organism, have been subjugated to an urban system's various compositions.

The 'artificial nature' of the green skin of the landscape becomes the envelope of the building, a sort of biodynamic skin (vertical vegetal partitions on an independently micro-irrigated substrate). 'Beyond the fusion and confusion that it (the new landscape) generates with the natural environment,' he continues, 'it offers the advantage of filtering city dust and purifying the atmosphere like a new architectural material.'

1. Site overview.
2. Green skin detail.
3. Site, close-up view.
4. 'Green' surface concepts.

31.3
Olzweg
Orléans, France

1. Structure.
2. Courtyard entrance.
3. Access.
4. Courtyard from street.

The designers developed a series of conditions to craft radical 'green courtyards', using advanced modelling software and CNC fabrication to achieve this vision. The conditions were:

— The courtyard of the FRAC Centre is a composition or aggregation of glass sticks attached to the existing building, and is perceived as a 'Body Without Organ' (a 'going-to-be-done', or unachieved, process of construction). The interior becomes a labyrinthine walkway and access point. A scattering program script was written to develop the aggregation.

— Procedures of constructions and cleanings are assisted by robots, with or without automatism, to introduce randomization and uncertainty to the final shape and to be able to reprogram the labyrinth during construction.

— The elements of glass are sourced from a local glass-recycling and processing plant to reduce the raw material costs and involve the inhabitants of the agglomeration in the 'work-to-be-done' story.

— The construction schedule extends beyond ten years for the same reason: construction became a factor of desire with a desirable machine (a reference to Marcel Duchamp).

— Using individual RIFD pads (tracking devices), users can wend their way through the glass maze and redefine their XYZ coordinates, according to the specificities of an exhibition.

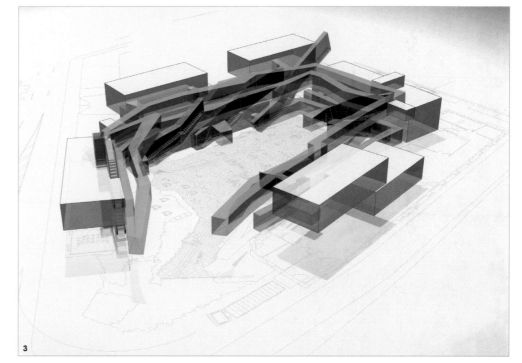

31.4
Symbiosis Hood
Seoul, South Korea

This project deals with blurring the boundaries between two properties along the North and South Korean border, a site that is 'infected' by land mines and has been abandoned since the end of the Korean War. With vegetation overtaking the site, the architects played off the concept of uncontrolled nature and the invasiveness of this 'diseased' site.

The project is supported by two clients on two separate but neighbouring lands. According to the designers, 'the twisted boundaries helped to negotiate their Siamese friendliness, and to fuzz the notion of property'. They positioned the building both in the 'interior edge' of a forest and cliff, and on the borders of the two properties, and created a 'termite' morphology, between a fungus cavern (exhibition space) in the valley of the hill and an extrusion of the ground, which becomes the domestic space.

1. Model: top angle.
2. Model: approach from the front.
3, 4. Computer rendering, digital experiment.
5–8. 'Green' growth.

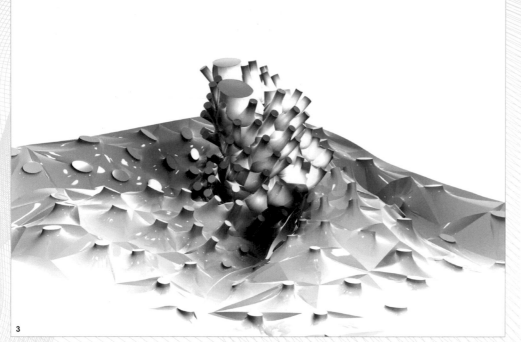

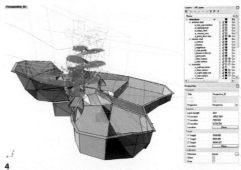

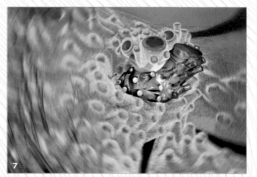

32
CHRIS
SPEED

Chris Speed teaches at the Edinburgh School of Architecture and Landscape Architecture, including the MArch programme on disruptive technologies. His research focuses on how digital technology can engage with the field of architecture through the development of new forms of spatial practice, which transform our experience of the built environment. This theme was echoed in his PhD dissertation, 'A Social Dimension to Digital Architectural Practice', which addressed developing opportunities for digital architecture that engage in the mediation of the built environment and landscape through technology by integrating social computing principles with dynamic geographical mapping techniques.

Speed's teaching incorporates the mapping of landscapes using various digital-systems hardware, including electron microscopes and mobile devices such as GPS, iPods and smartphones, and digital-media software such as TrackStick GPS tracker, Processing, Rhinoceros, SketchUp, Photoshop and his own CoMob app (p. 234), developed in collaboration with Jen Southern. More recently, Speed has been working with collaborative GPS technologies and the streaming of social and environmental data.

Digital Explorations in Architectural Urban Analysis

32.1
Digital Explorations in Architectural Urban Analysis
Dundee, UK

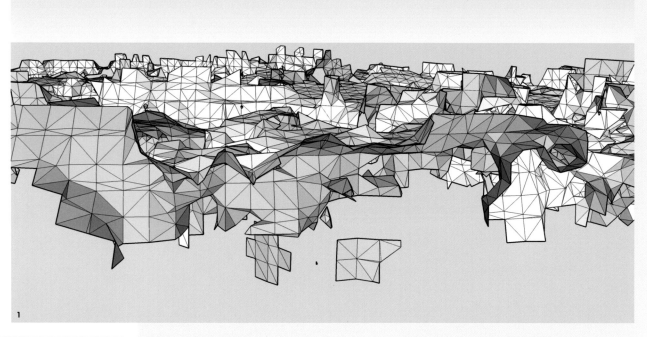

1

Working with architectural students from the Edinburgh College of Art, Speed and Chris Lowry, a lecturer in architecture, established a way of networking mobile GPS devices that would create maps that are constructed through the people's body movement within an urban context. During a site visit to the city of Dundee, on the east coast of Scotland, a group of students were equipped with GPS devices and asked to explore an area specific to an architectural brief. The GPS devices offered the students an additional method of exploration that had the potential for informing the entire navigation of the context to form a more considered and intimate design strategy than traditional recording media.

Upon returning to the studio, the team 'synthesized' all of the waypoints, data and tracks recorded by each device. From this task, over ten thousand geographic points were covered and recorded for the area of 'downtown' Dundee. A series of three-dimensional software packages was used to create a 'mesh' landscape, which would describe a social topology of the students' movements across the city. Accurate in longitude and latitude, but inaccurate in elevation due to the difficulty of the GPS devices in ascertaining specific height information, the study demonstrated the potential for collaborative and creative mapping.

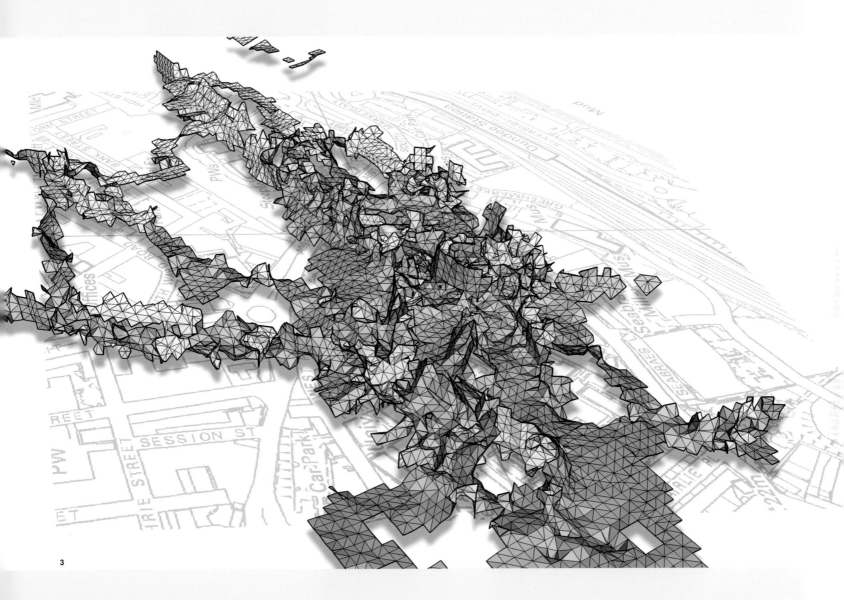

3

1, 3. Collective spatial activity.
2. GPS trails.

32.2
CoMob

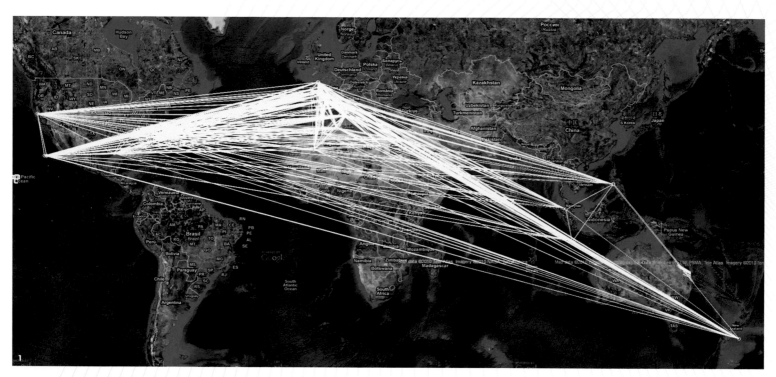

1

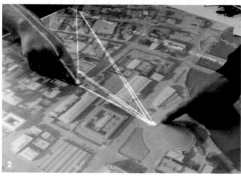

2

1. Map showing usage of the app over twenty four hours.
2. Workshop participants replay their GPS walk using visualization software.

Designed with Jen Southern, an artist and PhD student at Lancaster University, the smartphone app CoMob is a method of social and spatial mapping, which allows groups of people to see each other's movements, represented on-screen as circular nodes, with lines linking their individual positions. This data is also sent live to visualization software that allows observers to see their movements at a distance.

Previous GPS projects from Speed's research have mapped and tracked individuals, but CoMob proposes that those individual tracks are only part of how we move through space. The app allows for observation of how movement through space is a social activity, and proposes that those movements can be used to map these relationships to space. CoMob has been used at a series of international digital-art festivals in a workshop context to map pollution,

and as a catalyst for discussion of how pollution is experienced and perceived on the ground. The app has had international appeal, and has been downloaded by members of the public across the globe. Speed and Southern's project database of activities indicates that many of these worldwide users use CoMob as a way of binding social movements in space.

32.3
Yamaguchi Valley Section
Yamaguchi, Japan

1

2

Traditionally, maps of landscapes have been constructed via the measurement of physical geographical features across mathematical grids, using carefully controlled land-surveying equipment. Today's digital technologies, however, allow us to use instruments that integrate a social dimension to mapping; portable hand-held GPS devices, for example, can be used to record new boundaries that describe a landscape. Speed's work uses new social and geographical technologies to visually describe a section of the Yamaguchi Valley, and to develop a map that depicts a human perspective of the place.

This dynamic mapping process manifests an unusual topology. While not being as accurate as the common staking process used by civil engineers, the resulting three-dimensional forms offer an extra, 'fuzzy' social dimension. The project provides an opportunity to engage social networks as frameworks for better spatial mapping. Though somewhat inaccurate, the work provides a socially rich topological map of Yamaguchi.

1, 2. Three-dimensional models, generated from GPS data of residents' movements over two days.

33

STOSS LU

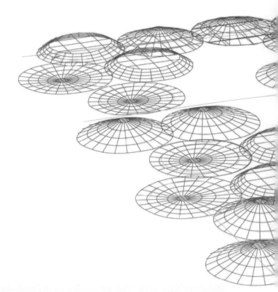

Founded in 2000, StossLU is a Boston-based landscape architectural firm that focuses on innovative design and landscape urbanism, including large-scale planning, brownfield redevelopment, storm-water management, and ecological and environmental design. As reflected in their name, the emerging concept of landscape urbanism is central to the firm's philosophy. This idea emphasizes the cross-disciplinary nature of landscape within the broader fields of engineering, ecology, environment and infrastructure, and echoes the designers' focus on three main objectives in their designs: scale, time and flexibility.

The firm incorporates time and phasing into their design process as much as any other factor, as they believe landscape solutions to be both responsive and catalytic networked systems that intervene on the land. According to the designers, landscapes need to flourish into 'evolving dynamics of ecological and civic or social systems in order to remain healthy and resilient', and must be designed to adapt to various conditions to handle a variety of functions, events and future developments. Many of their designs are adaptable and performance-based, thus able to generate performative landscapes.

To aid in this time-based methodology, the designers rely on digital technologies such as Rhinoceros, Flamingo, Illustrator, Photoshop and AutoCAD, as well as exploring dynamic parametric scripting processes, including the Grasshopper plug-in for Rhino.

Bass River Park,
West Dennis, Massachusetts.

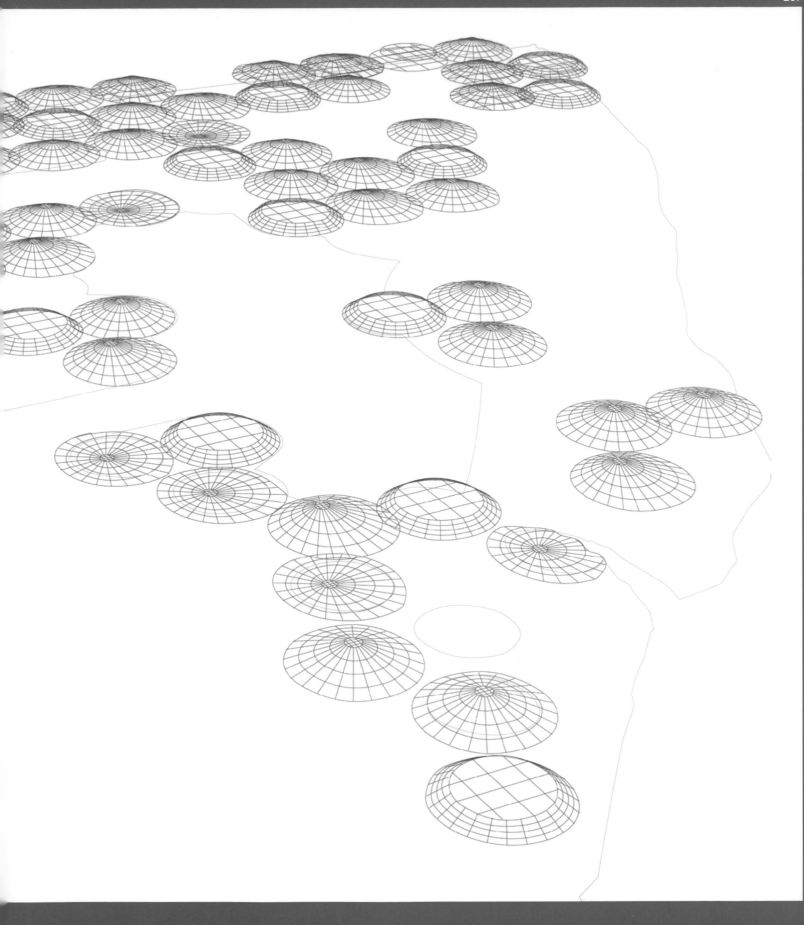

33.1
Bass River Park
West Dennis, Massachusetts

This landscape design is performative-based, and able to adapt to changing environmental conditions. The platform has been cleverly comprised of a green 'carpet' of hillocks, which accommodate ecological progression and succession for various regional vegetal communities, including a red-cedar meadow, sand plain, wet meadow and salt marsh. A series of circular landforms, dotted about the site, forms a continuous landscape carpet. The physical variations formed accommodate an array of changing conditions, upon which vegetation can, according to the designers, 'grow, adapt, and compete'. The design also accommodates events, programmes, maintenance and other human activities.

The designers created a 5.5 m- (18 ft-) wide arcing boardwalk, which runs along the river, reflecting the outline of the constructed and ecologically fragile shoreline. The shoreline consists of

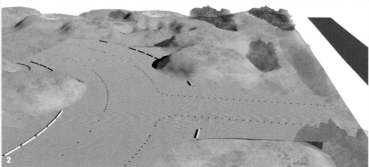

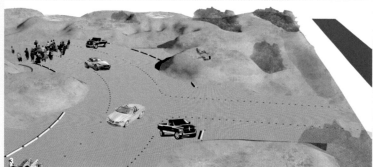

1–4. Overview, adaptive landscapes.
5, 6. Perspectives.

existing natural features, including an isolated dune and cedar grove, and hillocks that seem to emerge from the ground plane. The promenade consists of a wooden ribbon, which contracts and expands to encompass these design elements. The software used includes Rhinoceros, Grasshopper, Flamingo, Illustrator, Photoshop and AutoCAD. The digital-landscape design process explored parametric measures and augmented spaces, creating dynamic, performative-based design options.

According to company principal Chris Reed, 'the hillocks . . . were generated by draping a surface over a field of piston-like forms of varying height. As iterative generations are performed, the surface is refined and a specific mound form emerged. From this three-dimensional mound, a matrix of variations, including convex–concave, conical–offset and whole–severed were generated to create differences in elevation, slope and aspect. The mounds are arrayed on site in a grid aligned to the dominant access points and ecological features (the tidal river, access points, as well as the internal parameters of patch ecology); then they are modified to admit exception moments in the system (boardwalks, shelters and the paving field).' Serial iterations were tested in Rhino, with final construction documents then developed in AutoCAD.

The firm continually pushes the design boundaries of augmented environments, challenging the idea of twenty-first-century dynamic landscape design. Its innovative designs are aided by a collection of advanced digital tools to help develop and explore the next generation of landscape-designed spaces, which adhere to issues of sustainability, culture, ecology, creativity, artistry, indeterminacy, beauty, and overall adaptability and resilience.

33.2
Erie Plaza
Milwaukee, Wisconsin

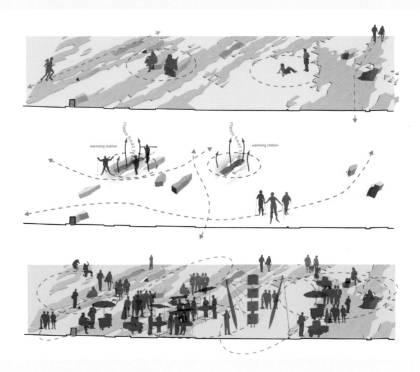

1

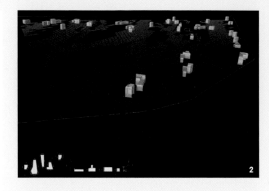

This design for a public plaza, situated along the Milwaukee Riverwalk, a 4.8-km (3-mile) pedestrian strip that links downtown Milwaukee to the Third Ward and Beerline districts, is based on the firm's core philosophy about flexibility, adaptability, sustainability and ecological parameters, while also making the space an experiential and harmonious civic place for users. In keeping with the designers' performative-based guidelines, the site is an activator, responding to human movement and other site conditions.

The plaza is a flexible platform that encourages cultural and environmental activity and uses. This flexible field activates and registers environmental cycles of storm water by collecting run-off, which is then used to nourish wetlands, marsh areas and a bamboo garden. In the winter, the water is frozen and used for other recreational activities. The yellow benches dotted throughout the space allow for flexible seating; at night, they emit a playful glow. A sophisticated digital design process was used to achieve the overall landscape design, including an array of software programs such as Rhinoceros, Grasshopper, Flamingo, AutoCAD, Illustrator and Photoshop. To achieve the performative design, the flexible field was produced through a series of mixed components and definitions in Rhinoceros and Grasshopper. By adding, subtracting and modifying components, the team was able to test dynamic surface conditions and to integrate the changing properties of water as an 'urban catalyst'.

The interlocking paving pattern outlined a clever medium through which a collection of various materials, vegetation, integrated illumination/fog features, and permeable surfaces were placed. The firm used clustered variations, arrayed to take advantage of such connective elements as river, storm water and access points. Serial iterations of the space were explored in Rhinoceros, with the final construction drawings created in AutoCAD.

1. Conceptual development.
2. Glowing siting structures in the landscape, night scene.
3. Overview.
4. Perspective.
5. Event space, changes in the landscape.

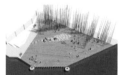

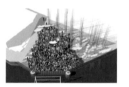

3

5

4

34
TERREFORM ONE

Based in New York, TerreformONE is a research-based urban design, landscape and architectural firm, which explores new technologies in search of solutions for the development of ever-greener and more successful cities. The ecological cities concept and sci-fi models for reversing climate change are the work of Mitchell Joachim and Maria Aiolova, the creative masterminds of the company. They address pressing issues at the intersection of design sustainability and technology, raising questions about how urban design and landscape can best embrace the new technologies.

The designers advocate such bold ideas as cloud-like mini-cars that fold and store easily for parking, or floating gym pods. Through testing design ideas and exploring the impact new technologies will have on urban space, they embrace positive change, rather than responding to perceived constraints. Joachim and Aiolova believe that foresight can take many forms, and, fundamentally, that the future promises a better world. When exploring the possibilities inherent in digital-design tools and software programs including 3D Studio MAX, Rhinoceros, Grasshopper and Photoshop, the focus is on platforms in which creative scenarios are visualized.

Growing habitats, including sophisticated tree-fabricated houses (see Fab Tree Hab; **pp. 244–45**) and plug-in landscapes, in which people 'grow' their own landscapes and homes, living from the food the systems produce through the home, are among the innovative visions proposed by this forward-thinking company.

Fab Tree Hab:
Living Graft Dwellings.

35
TOPOTEK1

Founded in 1996 by Martin Rein-Cano and based in Germany, Topotek1 is a landscape architecture studio that specializes in the design and construction of artistic and creative urban open spaces. The firm's designs vary in scale, from the masterplan to the private garden, and produce compelling concepts that respond to site conditions and programmatic needs. Important to its philosophy is the maintaining of variability, while simultaneously communicating and expressing a unique and distinctive artistic sensibility through its projects.

The designers begin their design process with a deeply rooted critical understanding of the site context, and by focusing on the inherent qualities of the site. Through a process of filtering, their projects aim to fulfil the specific design requirements via the development of conceptual ideas that deliberately highlight and emphasize certain site conditions, while at the same time diminishing others. With the aid of various digital-design tools, the firm tests and revises their concepts and ideas through drawings, models and perspectives, and uses advanced digital experimentation to help test alternative designs for these unique, open urban spaces.

The designers also collaborate with professionals in other creative fields, such as art, video and lighting, as well as in technical fields, including civil engineering and construction, to ensure the coherency and continuity of a design concept within a project.

Superkilen,
Copenhagen, Denmark.

35.1
Superkilen
Copenhagen, Denmark

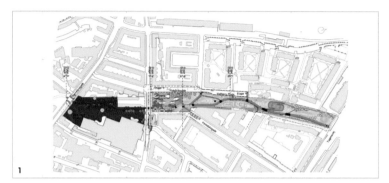

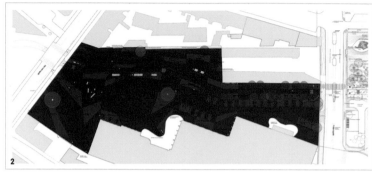

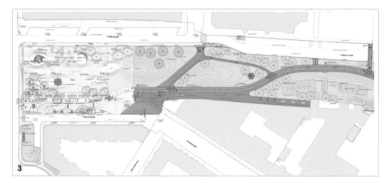

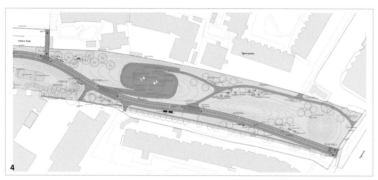

This competition-winning design for the urban revitalization of Superkilen, a multicultural neighbourhood in Copenhagen, uses open space as a physical framework for the transformation of the site from a mono-functional transit hub into an innovative, dynamic space with 'synchronicities'. The design enhances the diverse characters of users within the site.

A black square, a red square and a green park are all part of Superkilen's urban quilt. The design celebrates the concept of the contemporary and universal garden, and includes key elements from international places and cultures, reflecting the multi-ethnic dynamics of the neighbourhood and the people who live there. The furnishings for the site were derived from an international catalogue of urban-design elements, and public consultation and participation has been a significant component in the design process. Round benches, fountains, lamps, fitness equipment and other landscape furniture showcases the area's diversity and multicultural flavour. In the red square, media boards sporting international advertisements are further visual markers of this international scene. The imported advertisements also illuminate the space in a theatrical way, providing information and communication.

1–4. Plans.
5. Perspective, black square.
6. Perspective, green park.
7, 8. Perspectives, red square.
9. Model, green park.
10. Model, black park.

35.2
Broderie Urbaine
Berlin, Germany

For a small courtyard at the Bayer pension plan headquarters on Unter den Linden ('under the lime trees', a boulevard in the Mitte district of Berlin), the designers created a playful floral pattern reminiscent of a Baroque embroidery pattern. When viewed from the upper floors, the design below appears to visually dissolve from the courtyard space, extending beyond its structural boundaries.

The courtyard functions as both a public space and an intimate, private 'living room', an illusion reinforced by the painted ground, which has the appearance of an interior space with a carpet, tapestry or brocade material laid out on the floor. The playful gestures and swirls that dance upon the surface are rendered in yellow paint on asphalt, providing a strong contrast to the architectural forms that rise above.

1, 2. Floral pattern, viewed from the upper levels.
3. Pattern reflection on the interior facade.

35.3
KAiAK MarktParkPlatz
Köpenick, Germany

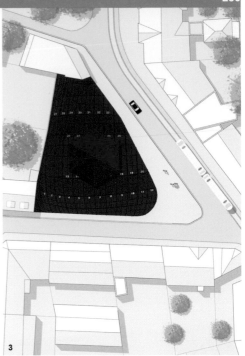

The historic town of Köpenick, located to the southeast of Berlin, is undergoing a transformation. While the streets and squares of the town centre have been renovated, the brownfields and vacant lots of its interstitial spaces await positive future interventions. The designers' proposal for the KAiAK (Kunst & Architektur in Alt Köpenick) art project tests temporary and adaptable uses for these spaces, generating creative concepts for the town's urban redevelopment. A series of design interventions within the interstitial spaces is intended to support positive and progressive change in the area.

An informal parking lot at the corner of the site is currently used as a venue for the local farmer's market and other events. The existing asphalt surface has been transformed into an urban parquet for cars and market stalls, which will use the space at different times. The vivid red surface and a grid of lines define areas for various uses. An oversized sunshade, in shiny, polished red, resembling a fresh bell pepper, signals the type of event or activity that is currently occupying the space. On market days, the sunshade is unfurled, and folded away again when the site is used as a car park.

1. Open sunshade on market day.
2. The site as a car park.
3. Market plan.
4. Parking plan.
5. View of the site.

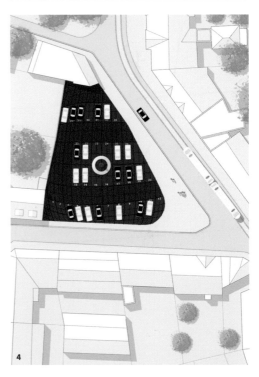

36
TURENSCAPE

Based in China, Turenscape is an interdisciplinary design firm, founded by Kongjian Yu, now a visiting professor at Harvard's Graduate School of Design, which employs over six hundred design professionals. The company focuses on architecture, landscape architecture, urban planning and design, environmental design, and landscape urbanism projects. The firm's philosophy is inherent in its name. The designers believe that nature, man and spirit are one, with the Earth (tu) at the centre of the universe and the base of all living things, and man (ren) the superior living creature that cultivated the planet. This philosophy is a recognition of the landscape as a symbolic place, in which all living creatures and spirits dwell.

With the aid of modern digital design and site-analysis technologies, the designers study the sky and earth in relation to the natural and social processes of man, in an attempt to rekindle their existence as one. The innovative firm also pursues new digital approaches to help solve and craft complex landscape designs, housing its own media studio for the development of advanced digital models and renderings.

Chicago Art Field,
Chicago, Illinois.

36.1
Chicago Art Field
Chicago, Illinois

This design for an 'art field' integrates art, culture, nature, the notion of a productive landscape and ecological urbanism into a creative form, creating a platform in which the natural cycles of the metropolitan landscape can succeed. The team used the cornfield, a symbol of the city's agrarian heritage and a continually regenerating agricultural process, as the inspiration behind the scheme.

Productive landscapes, such as crops, are connected and integrated with the various activities and interventions, including art installation, performance, children's playground, ice skating and landscape progression throughout the seasons. The vegetation and produce grown in the field will be used for events on the site, such as markets, with the art field becoming a place to showcase the landscape changes. The architects used multiple digital techniques, including animation and image modification via Photoshop, to render eye-catching landscape images. The studio extruded and illuminated specific areas to convey the layering of the design, the growing of the cornfield, and the change of seasons.

36.2
Shanghai Expo-Park
Shanghai, China

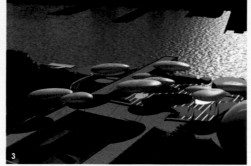

The architects' design proposal for Shanghai Expo 2010 was the creation of a kind of 'Central Park' – referencing Central Park in Manhattan – for the city. The team explored a series of schemes and methods for placing a large park in such a complex urban area, which was part of the ecological restoration and regeneration of the historic industrial site along the Huangpu Jiang River.

The designers proposed a sustainable park for a central green area, one that would be adaptable and become part of the city after the Expo ended. This landscape would be comprised of an ecological matrix, drawn from the industrial brownfield, and a network of paths and media boards that would allow visitors to experience and explore the cultural spirit of the site.

1. Computer rendering, aerial view of the site.
2, 3. Aerial view, floating canopies above the central square.
4. Perspective, floating canopies above the central square.
5. Perspective, view under the floating canopies.
6. Site plan, emphasizing the pedestrian network.
7. Digital rendering of reused industrial structure.

色彩规划分析图 1：2000

图例
生态透水地砖铺装
玻璃铺装
透水环保生态砖铺装
竹铺装
木铺装
沥青混凝土铺装
钢板铺装
沥青铺装
砾石铺装
粗砂铺装

6

7

37 URBANARBOLISMO

Urbanarbolismo is a young firm that specializes in the integration of architecture and nature. With a philosophy rooted in the idea that space has no distinction between urban and natural, projects are undertaken with a focus on the 'symbiosis between architecture and climatic and ecological conditions of the place'. The designers' aim is to integrate energy efficiency, heating, ventilation, construction, water management, vegetation and landscaping, and to minimize impervious surfaces and offset CO_2 emissions in order to make issues of sustainability more visible in urban settings.

The firm began as a research project at architecture school in Alicante, Spain. The project, which is still evolving, started as a collection of documentation relating to their thesis; given its success, the designers decided to make specialized studies in vegetation and architecture. They share their knowledge on their blog, which features projects in architecture, urban design and landscape urbanism. Many of their creative forms and space-making are driven by digital processes and complex modelling tools to help make their visions manifest.

Reforesting Tower, Benidorm, Spain.

37.1
Reforesting Tower
Benidorm, Spain

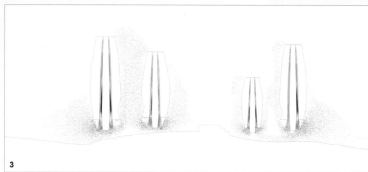

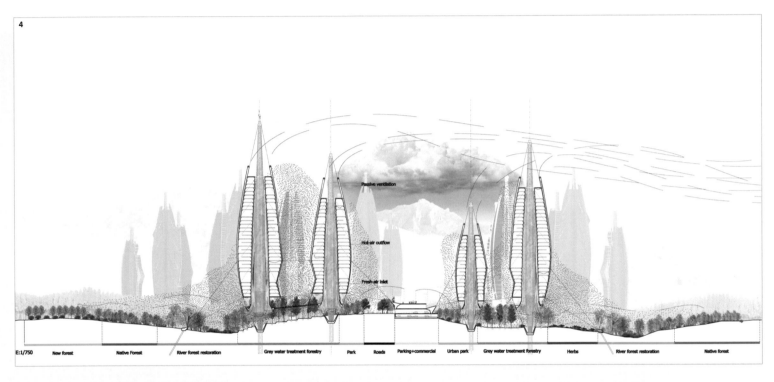

4

E:1/750 | New forest | Native Forest | River forest restoration | Grey water treatment forestry | Park | Roads | Parking+commercial | Urban park | Grey water treatment forestry | Herbs | River forest restoration | Native forest

This proposal for a skyscraper represents the firm's strategy of minimizing impact on the land, and establishing a symbolic connection between landscape and building, water, vegetation, air and climate. The project examines augmented and reactive environments, while the use of software such as Rhinoceros and Grasshopper enable the visualization of various landscape and climatic conditions. The tower's vegetated skin is irrigated with grey water from housing, and evapotranspirates to cool the immediate area. Changes in temperature are achieved in the following ways:

— Vegetation towards the bottom of the towers is used for grey-water treatment. Poplar trees absorb water and nutrients from grey water, and evapotranspirate at a high rate. This evapotranspiration is enough to change the ambient environment from 35° c (95° F) and 38 per cent relative humidity to 26° c (79° F) and 82 per cent relative humidity in summer. Trees were selected according to their evapotranspiration and waste-water treatment capacities.

— The architectural design takes advantage of the cooling strategy, and helps to restore the surrounding natural systems. The air-pressure difference between the top and the bottom parts of the towers induces vegetation-cooled air to move into the tower housing. In addition, there is a relationship between the height and the cooling capacity of the vegetation on its suction range.

— The main elements for air intake were designed in a fluid-simulator program to optimize its operation. The election of the vegetation also takes into account its own characteristics as an aromatherapy tool.

— Certain plants have the ability to clean pollutants from the air and absorb harmful substances.

1. Skyscrapers overview.
2. Airflow entering the skyscraper.
3. Diagram of airflow simulation of the building set.
4. Relationship between urban and natural area.

37.2
Eco.Acequia
Elche, Spain

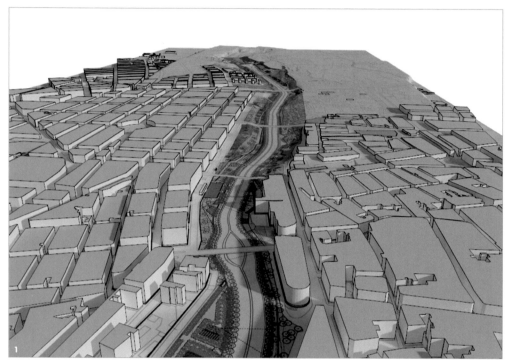

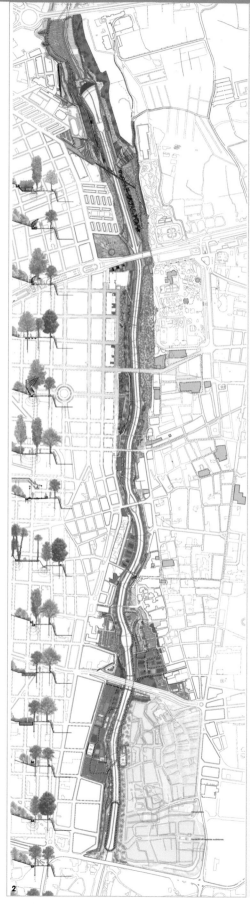

Eco.Acequia ('eco-canal') is a proposal to restore the relationship between the Vinalopó River and the canals with the palm groves in the city of Elche, Spain. The eco-canal has different elements and connected furniture that enhance the relationship between users and water, while the moisture produced allows riparian vegetation to grow. Along its route, the eco-canal provides a variable park programme. As it descends, it evolves into lighting fixtures, benches and markers to amplify the sound of water and trees, creating 'acoustic' environments. Along the 'water ribbon', newly created ponds encourage the development of species of native fauna and flora, and the creation of shallow pools of water that offer areas for play and cooling off.

The primary goal of the project is to restore the water quality of the river, which reaches Elche only after passing through several industrial cities. At the beginning of the park, the firm created a water-treatment system by using macrophytes, aquatic plants that grow in or near water. The system is comprised of water-treatment ponds, populated with native vegetation, and is arranged along the promenade. At the final stage of the treatment process, water passes through a UV light. This antibiotic filter also provides night lighting along the promenade.

1. 3D model with eco-canal proposal.
2. Plan.
3. Night view of the illumination.
4. Open-air auditorium.
5. Natural waste-water treatment zone.

38
VISIONDIVISION

VisionDivision, founded by architects Anders Berensson and Ulf Mejergren and based in Sweden, has developed a reputation for envisioning innovative projects with fantasy-like concepts that reinvestigate the notion of landscape architecture. Fundamental to the firm's philosophy is the absence of one fixed design idea, and each project is treated with a different approach. The firm embraces avant-garde, often surreal thinking in the design process by setting new territories in design through experimentation and inventiveness.

The designers believe in an interdisciplinary approach that reaches far beyond the traditional role of architecture and landscape design. The firm has developed its practice with the inclusion of detailed drawing, construction work and fabrication within the design process, while social aspects and cultural context are leading factors in their digital-design methodology. Digital technologies such as 3D Studio MAX (for modelling complex spaces and rendering lighting effects) and Photoshop are used to visualize and experiment with various possible design solutions.

Eden Falls,
Buenos Aires, Argentina.

38.3
Rapid Palace
Gothenburg, Sweden

Rapid Palace was the result of a commission to redesign a school yard, located outside Gothenburg, Sweden. As the school already had a budget for asphalt maintenance, the designers decided to use this as their main tool for the improvement of the yard. The design is a socially and environmentally responsive project, concerned with landscape infrastructural explorations. Using software programs including 3D Studio MAX and Photoshop, the team was able to test the green-edge conditions and create an imaginative landscape proposal on a limited budget.

A pattern was devised by combining plans of palaces from all over the world, and tearing away parts of the existing asphalt (the costs of laying new asphalt and ripping up the old one are similar). In the new voids, fast-growing and bushy Salix shrubs were planted. As the children begin a new school year, they will have a 'palace' made from walls of Salix plants, which have already reached half of their eventual height of 4 m (13 ft). The sculpted forest creates little niches for play areas, and larger areas for outdoor teaching when weather permits. When the plants reach their full height, they can be harvested and used as eco-fuel at the nearby heating plant, or fashioned into furniture for the new castle that will rise for the next generation of school children.

1. Spaces for play.
2. Phase 1.
3. Phase 2.
4. Phase 3.
5. Play area, close-up view.

39 WEST 8

Founded by Adriaan Geuze in 1987, West 8 is an award-winning landscape architecture firm, with its main office based in Rotterdam, and three branch offices in New York, Toronto and Opwijk, Belgium. Having won the Prix-de-Rome in 1990, Geuze, who received his MA in Landscape Architecture from the Agricultural University of Wageningen, and his team have since achieved international recognition for their creative and multidisciplinary approach to landscape planning and design.

According to the designers, landscapes cover vast territories that require involvement from a range of professions. Their philosophy encompasses an artificial 'second nature' that is highly engineered to meet specific practical needs, while being simultaneously symbolic and representational. Responding to these two landscape approaches, designs tend to be functional and formalistic. The firm has a distinct visual representational style, and is known for its elaborate imagery and realistic rendering. To achieve this, the firm uses 3D Studio MAX, along with advanced image-modification parameters in Photoshop and LightRoom to create a variety of landscape surface formations and atmospheric and lighting conditions.

The company has won many global design competitions for large-scale urban masterplanning, landscape interventions, waterfront projects, parks, squares and gardens.

Botanic Bridge Gwangju,
Gwangju, South Korea.

1

39.3
Jubilee Gardens
London, UK

Situated on the city's South Bank, beneath the London Eye, this project showcased the objectives of the mayor's 'London's Great Outdoors' scheme for improving the capital's public spaces, including high streets, town centres, parks, rivers and pathways, as well as Transport for London's Better Streets initiative.

Using 3D Studio MAX and advanced image-modification parameters in Photoshop, the designers were able to test a variety of landscape surface formations and to render different atmospheric lighting conditions.

1. Overview of garden with site context.
2. Digital model of garden.

2

39.4
Puentes Cascara
Madrid, Spain

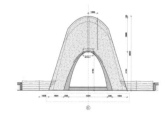

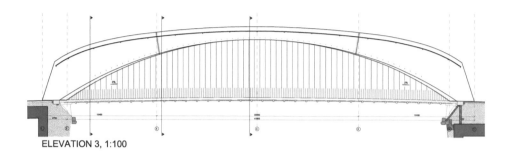

ELEVATION 3, 1:100   ELEVATION 4, 1:100

1

The designers, working together with Spanish architectural firm MRIO, designed the masterplan for the reclaimed riverbanks and the new urban area above the tunnels of the M30 highway in Madrid. The different parks of the plan are connected by pedestrian bridges, which are designed as heavy concrete domes with a rough structure. One hundred cables connect to the steel deck, resembling a 'whale-bone' structure. Upon entering the space, the fine details of the bridge become clear.

The spatial qualities of the tunnel are beautifully highlighted through the use of advanced lighting techniques via Photoshop and LightRoom. Using image-modification tools, the firm was able to render a fresco painting onto the domed ceiling, and illuminate the artwork using special lighting techniques.

1. Sections.
2. Built form.
3. Digital model, bridge concept.

39.5
City on Fire/City in Bloom
Rotterdam, Netherlands

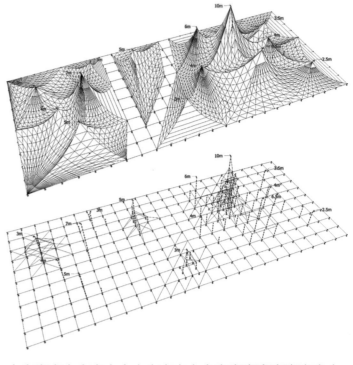

On 14 May 2007, exactly sixty-seven years after the city of Rotterdam was destroyed by bombs during the Second World War, City on Fire/City in Bloom was unveiled – one of the projects for Rotterdam 2007 City of Architecture. For it, the firm designed a flower sculpture, consisting of 64,000 red and purple flowers, to fit within the Schouwburgplein, a public square originally designed by West 8 in 1996. The project's title makes reference to the burning city and the blossoming of Rotterdam in the aftermath of the war. This temporary installation was designed to bloom during a six-week period, until the end of June that year.

Notes Geuze: 'Is it possible for a blaze of flowers to explain what happened on 14 May 1940, without being instantly a historic monument. The Schouwburgplein is an open space from where you can enjoy the skyline. It is the place to get together during the day. Flowers are hereby the finishing touch, the smile.' The design team used digital-modelling software to help pin-point the 'pulling' of the mounds, and to render the effects of the blooming process.

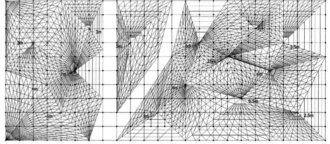

1

2

1. Formal experimentation, digital model.
2. Project installation, Schouwburgplein.

AFTERWORD
A REFLECTION ON DIGITAL LANDSCAPE ARCHITECTURE, TODAY AND IN THE FUTURE

With the rise of ever-more sophisticated digital tools, we are training our students to become digitally savvy in the creation of the perfect landscape scene, by teaching them to craft new landscape forms using a palette of software. These young innovators are the future of the profession's digital-design practice, and continually seek out new ways to reinvent design and representation to better develop solutions for the built environment. Photoshop has become the predominant tool in the design process, and is often employed to compose the 'eye-candy' perspective images of landscape, as seen in the renderings of the Horseshoe Cove project (p. 60), in California (fig. 1), by Fletcher Studio (pp. 58–63).

As landscape architects, academics and designers of the built environment, we strive towards creative design solutions, while still maintaining a level of accuracy. We strive to design innovative outdoor spaces and visualize our concepts in striking ways, as demonstrated by many of the projects presented in *Digital Landscape Architecture Now*. Three landscape representations, developed by students, serve to illustrate the innovative ways in which a younger generation of landscape artists are utilizing digital technologies in their work. A skilful hand-sketch by Starling Childs (fig. 2), a former student of the author at Cornell University, was created using graphite to depict

a petroleum industrial landscape. Chaotic yet purposeful, twisted and brightly rendered tube-like forms were modelled in 3D Studio MAX and then carefully collaged to create a seamless composition. By superimposing these rendered atomic-like forms, the landscape describes a scene of potential danger, a pseudo-nuclear environment that is all too relevant in our modern age.

Shelter Array by Joaquin Martinez (fig. 3), a former student of Bradley Cantrell (pp. 38–43) at Louisiana State University, explores the composite of object and surface. This project required the development of a sheltering device, which, notes Cantrell, was then sited within a specific context that acted as a cue for landscape phenomena, such as light, wind and texture. The digital model/object was then sited, and the final illustration used to explore the interactions between the two systems. A third image (fig. 4), by William Jeffrey Cock, a former student of the author at the University of Toronto, details the changing terrain surfaces that come with augmented environments. Using effects such as lighting, atmospheric rendering and texturing, the drawing successfully captures the media-saturated landscape that is the ever-changing urban square. Using a selection of these visual effects, Cock depicted a night scene, while illuminating the centre of the square. This allowed him to critically

showcase the atmosphere of this media-driven, commercial environment.

Testing creative and futuristic landscapes are a large part of the work of TerreformONE (pp. 242–47), whose forward-thinking staff of architects, landscape architects, researchers and scientists rely heavily on digital applications to develop their 'sci-fi'-based solutions. At a public lecture in 2010, co-founder Mitchell Joachim posed the question of how urban design should foresee new instrumentalist technologies for cities, continuing:

For 150 years the innovation of the elevator has done more to influence urban design than most urban designers ... As a wide-ranging discipline, it can effortlessly illuminate the technological potentials for cities. Urban design will successfully situate itself by the production of future macro-scaled scenarios, predicated on innovative devices. One of the main directives at TerreformONE is the shrewd intersection between technology and urbanism, especially under the rubric of ecology. Our projects range from highlighting the possible effects of self-sufficient cities to studying flocks of jet-packs (figs. 5, 6). These ideations keep us thriving as urban-design researchers. It is our supposition that the prospective ecological city is about extreme

5

6

7

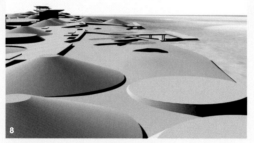

8

solutions to an extreme predicament. Our future fundamentally depends on the immensity our solutions envision. 'Envisioning' is by definition a view or concept, which evolves beyond existing boundaries. This notion of foresight may be interpreted in many different ways, each foregrounding particular ideations and processes describing the next event ... Current research attempts to establish new forms of design knowledge and new processes of practice at the interface of design, computer science, structural engineering and biology.

Through digital means, the designers at TerreformONE construct the futuristic urban environments critical to sustainable development. The firm's MATscape project (fig. 7) is a beautifully crafted landscape composed of a mosaic of materials, components and spaces. Its three-dimensional form is derived from both landscape and climatic vectors. The grid is encoded as an interpretation of climatic inputs, including solar directions, wind forces, rainfall and ambient temperature, in reference to human desires for comfort, light, air, water and electricity. Soil pockets serve as gardens that accommodate native species and capture moisture from the water cycle. Minute channels within the grid framework collect and direct rainfall.

Performative landscapes and adaptive environments are part of present and future landscape designs. Our designed environments must be able to adapt to positive and negative changes, according to a variety of external inputs. Many landscape architects are now experimenting with performative landscapes and parametric designs, including StossLU (pp. 236–41), whose innovative Bass River Park (pp. 238–39), in Massachusetts, responds to human activity with a carpet of green hillocks that adapt to environmental changes (fig. 8). For their University College Dublin project (p. 33; fig. 9), Balmori (pp. 26–37) has also tested performative environments. In their design, the landscape and built form unite to form continuous, multilayered public surfaces and green building façades. Pathways bind the landscape topography, and openings in the ground surface are layered with plantings and materials, so that they become usable and inhabitable spaces that extend the landscape to roof gardens and terraces.

We are more compelled to use, modify and reclaim software tools to suit our needs. François Roche at R&Sie(n) (pp. 222–29) experiments with augmenting terrain through Rhino-scripting, while Chilean firm GT2P (pp. 80–87) utilizes parametric software, such as Grasshopper, to address geo- and terra-morphic environments. Students, too, desire to

develop and explore digital projects as precedents for design solutions. The innovation of architectural landscape design will increasingly focus on a continuum of technological advances to address complex forms, performative and adaptive environments, virtual geographies, sustainable experimentation and visual stimulation. A series of student projects, illustrated here and conducted in association for MA studies in landscape architecture each relies upon digital design applications for exploration.

A project by Nadia D'Agnone, another former student of the author, revisits the role of landscape art in modern society by using ecological and digital applications to derive expressive and strong design solutions. The Isole delle Tresse, on the coast of the Porto Marghera, an industrial zone in a lagoon near Venice, is a completely artificial landfill island, approximately 1.5 km (0.9 miles) long and 0.5 km (0.3 miles) wide (fig. 10). The project investigates a dynamic dredge dumping system as a means of enhancing the biological diversity of the area, while creating expressive landforms that expose the dredging process and provide deeper insights into the landscape. Through a carefully phased formal dumping system, as well as natural succession and a specialized planting scheme, the project establishes a framework through which constant and undetermined change,

9

10

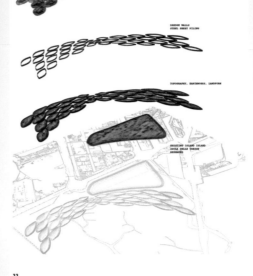

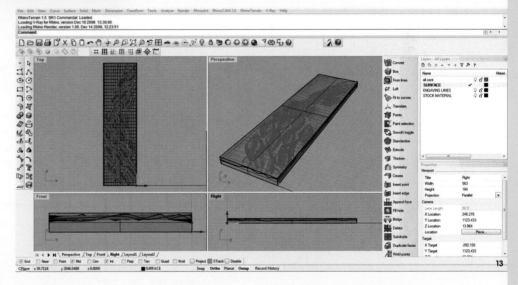

11

13

5, 6. TerreformONE, S.O.F.T. (Sustainable Omni Flow Transport).
7. TerreformONE, MATscape.
8. StossLU, Bass River Park, Massachusetts.
9. Balmori, University College Dublin.
10. Nadia D'Agnone, formal expressions, views from air and boat.
11. Nadia D'Agnone, autonomy and formal expression.
12. Nadia D'Agnone, digital applications in Rhino.

formed by and subject to the ephemeral hydrodynamic processes of the lagoon (wind direction, water currents, varying tides), creates a performative landscape and a new way of looking at eco-land art (fig. 11). D'Agnone used advanced digital tools, including Rhino, Grasshopper, 3D scanning and CNC modelling outputs, to explore many facets of the project (fig. 12).

William Jeffrey Cock investigated augmented and reactive landscapes, which examine the relationships between cognitive geomatics and the perception of spatial contexts through the senses, as shaped by human–computer interactions. The transformation of the urban square is related to several factors: the agent/user, the environment and the event. This data is gathered, synthesized and later entered through a device that encodes these variables and transforms the landscape into a new form. Some of the factors pertain to contextual (light, temperature, climate, colour), tactile (touch, pressure), biometric (user behaviours, body temperatures, moods) or spatial elements that represent specific points on site (figs 13–15). Cock devised a weather-shield algorithm, in which the canopy structure at the site opened or closed depending on the rainfall or sun/shade inputs (fig. 16). A surface algorithm, in which transformations in vertical and horizontal surfaces occurred according to these input variables, was also utilized.

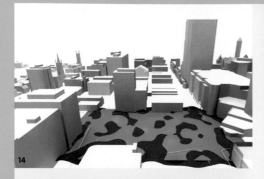

14

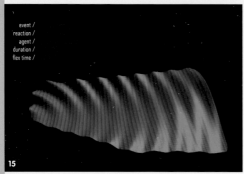

event /
reaction /
agent /
duration /
flex time /

15

16

Our students are thirsting for more knowledge within the digital-design realm of landscape architecture. These future landscape architects are setting the standards of innovative and radical design for the environments of tomorrow. Jorge Ayala, co-founder of [Ay]A, an international design studio based in Paris and a former student at the Architectural Association, notes:

As a young graduate from the AA, I benefited thoroughly from the palette of alternative paths that I was proposed. My priority was to pursue my landscape research via digital tooling within the professional realm. At that time, I was spotted by Plasma Studio Architects [see Groundlab; pp. 74–79], a firm that is continually developing visionary projects, which are all by now under construction. Plasma, among a shortlist of practices in Europe, is the manifestation of how experimental theories are brought to reality, embodied within avant-garde forms (fig. 17).

Ayala's studies and his related studio projects helped to prepare him with the technical skill sets and digital-research expertise that enabled him to materialize this digital-design trend in the field of landscape architecture. Such knowledge allowed him to test various landscape moves, including such projects as Paris Agenda (fig. 18) and the Artificial Topography investigation. According to Ayala, a shift from virtual to physical models has helped him to understand how landscape urbanism relates to the crafting of physical conditions that are engaged with the dynamics of contemporary cities. He was able to test Artificial Topography, which allowed the production of new spatial configurations, which emerge from the existing conditions of a chosen site (fig. 19). Programmatically, surfaces not only provide greenery, but also become specific features that are embedded within larger systems. The parallelism between the research and technical applications of digital exploration has helped to explore ground conditions to a higher degree.

In closing, *Digital Landscape Architecture Now* profiles a series of projects that examine an array of digital landscape-design positions, ranging from 3D optional scanning and advanced digital drawings of experiential landscapes, to new ways of approaching and developing terrain models, geo-mapping, masterplanning and large-scale park developments. The projects presented here provide a snapshot of the ways in which digital tools and media are utilized in landscape design practices, research and landscape visualization. By providing a survey of modern landscape architecture and a critical overview of its future, *Digital Landscape Architecture Now* demonstrates the crucial role of digital technology in expanding the boundaries of the field, while providing landscape architects with the tools necessary to create virtual landscape scenarios and complex surfaces. Increasingly, the designer also assumes the role of the cyborgian landscape architect, who evaluates and designs nature with new digital and adaptive ways of thinking and production. If we are to become design leaders in this ever-expanding, tech-saturated profession, our skill sets must be in a state of continuous development, growing and expanding as fast as our imagination allows.

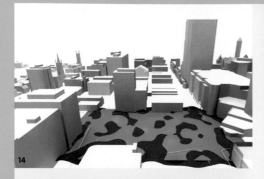

17

18

19

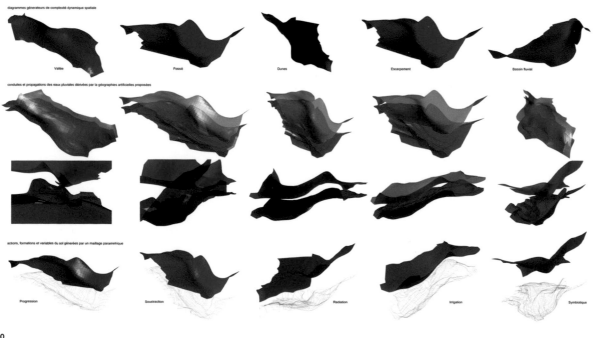

20

Mike Silver
Experimenting with Space and Shape through Advanced Digital Mapping

1

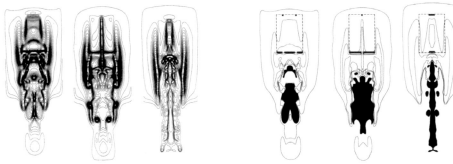

2

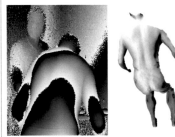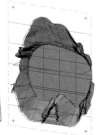

3

1. 3D optical scans of the human form.
2. A 3D optical scanner was used to build customized furniture suited to the body of a specific user.
3. Three sediment transport models of the baptistery at Mont St Michel, produced on a Beowulf cluster supercomputer.

Mike Silver has explored digital mapping and landscape since the early 1990s, using advanced 3D scanning machines, LIDAR technologies, CNC fabrication, coordinate measuring machines (CMM), and other more advanced machinery. Through a digital and artistic process, he takes the resultant outcome and distorts and reconfigures new surfaces and forms.

More recently, faster and higher-resolution optical scanners that record objects with lasers, or by mathematically interpreting the distortion of flat lines, projected onto a 3D surface such as moiré contour mapping, are taking over CMM technology. These machines provide quick measures through a safe process, a technology that Silver employs in scanning people for his experiments. According to the designer, the digital scans register 'complex shapes in a multi-perspectival data space that exceeds the functional constraints of conventional drawings and photographs'. He then produces a series of scans taken from different individuals at different moments. Through the use of digital mapping, data architectural components, furnishings and landscape surfaces can take 'an unprecedented degree of dimensional specificity', and transform into new surfaces and spaces.

Silver is at the forefront of innovative research, design technology and software and digital mapping, and helped to develop AutomasonMP3, an open-source software, developed 'by architects and programmers for architects and masons'.

Karres en Brands
A New Plan for De Draai

The masterplan by landscape architects Karres en Brands for De Draai, a new development in Heerhugowaard, Netherlands, was influenced and defined by elements such as power lines, gas mains, existing private residences and a windmill, as well as the site's landscape characteristics, including roadways and water canals. The team used a multilayered system that allowed for a gradual and flexible mixed-housing scheme. To help solve and produce the flexible programme structure, the team used parcellation software developed by ETH Zürich (p. 296), which reacts to the framework and develops unexpected housing layouts, while maintaining 'efficiency and programmatic parameters'.

The parameters of the plots are based on size and proportion, and further site parameters such as soil and water conditions and commercial growth. According to the architects, these parameters 'relate with the layout of the streets in a dynamic fashion – a recursive, circular optimization algorithm'. 'It is important', they continue, 'to understand that the solutions the software generates are not ready-made urban designs. The computer does not replace a creative process, but rather organizes complex interdependencies that can help to develop scenarios, which cannot be made manually.' By using this software, the architects were able to obtain spatially efficient layouts quickly and effectively through digital means.

1. Neighbourhood collage.
2–7. Masterplan, programme changes.

2

3

4

5

6

7

FreelandBuck
Detroit Super Division

This project is an examination of the large amounts of vacant land in Detroit's urban centre, and how the 'vacant' can be repurposed in a meaningful way. The architects note that the design offers an 'inverse strategy of "Superdivision": a scaling up of occupied territory and repurposing of unused infrastructure'. They continue: 'Given that an infrastructure built for over 1.5 million people will soon serve less than half that many, the project proposes a strategy of reterritorialization, rather than of construction.'

The architects saw hedgerows as means of landscape division, which would offer strips of urban renewal by defining new, super-scaled, occupied territories. The team proposed an algorithmic and interactive tree-planting in publicly owned parcels to create a connective network of trails and a set of preliminary boundaries, which would scale up the existing pattern of property ownership to adapt to the declining population. The Superdivision conforms and 'manages that depopulation, eventually stabilizing home ownership as an archipelago of dense neighbourhoods'.

As an algorithm, the proposal is both geometric and social, involving homeowners, stakeholders, banks, local government and emerging rural populations. Based on year-by-year patterns of demolition and overall density, the design allocates a series of hedgerows to be planted annually at specific locations, allowing for areas to be repurposed for community gardens, commercial agriculture or forest growth. Initially a set of ecological nodes, the hedgerows will eventually grow together into an interconnected network that collects the remaining houses as a set of revitalized neighbourhoods.

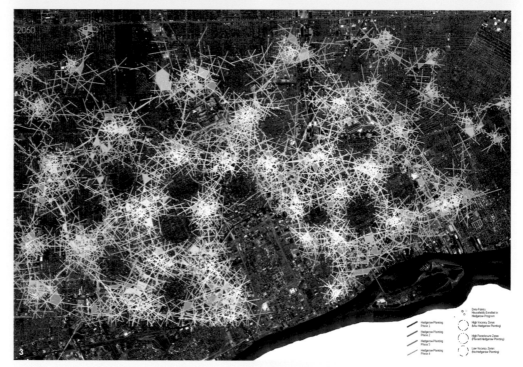

1. Neighbourhood superdivision 2020.
2. Neighbourhood superdivision 2040.
3. City superdivision 2060.

David Lieberman
The Alchemist's Garden

Toronto-based architect David Lieberman is passionate about landscape and drawings. Using traditional drawing and hand-rendered methods, he applies digital techniques that poetically alter his animated painted landscapes, which shift temporally, topographically and geographically to offer newfound experiences of site that enhance the 'experience of time of day, seasonal difference, climatic shifts, and the fictive archaeologies of histories past and of futures'. The intention is that the viewer reflects on each space, before moving on to the next.

The Alchemist's Garden is part of a larger body of work, in which, as Lieberman notes, he fuses 'architecture as a performing art, not a fine art, in that the understanding of its composition and intent is a continually evolving and eroding condition'. His digital paintings are constructed through the multiple overlays of manipulated images of selected landscapes, sourced by Lieberman and his team from all over the world employing Photoshop to its maximum capacity. Inserted into the 'experiential section' (a phrase, according to Lieberman, of 'extraordinary meaning', first used by architectural colleague Geoffrey Thun) are perspective renderings of sixteen sculptural installations, developed as two-dimensional AutoCAD drawings, distorted to specific spatial and temporal conditions, and then painted as the background in Photoshop. The twelve panels are further enhanced by insertions of small-scale plans to 'choreograph the journey' through the landscapes. The panels are framed or cut at various sizes to articulate the rhythms subject to the limitations of the digital software. The scroll was printed as a 19.5 m- (64 ft)-long drawing, and also forms the background of a continuous 64-minute cinematic pan, in which the detailed renderings appear as variations on a theme.

The drawings are part of a much larger project, which encompasses 1:50 physical models, digitally generated perspectives, hand-rendered graphite and hand-rubbed acetone transfers, the scroll and the film.

1. The Edge of the World.
2. The Alchemist's Compass to Navigate the River Styx.
3. Prometheus + The Furrow.

José Lameiras, Ian Jørgensen and Paulo Farinha Marques
Landform Design Systems

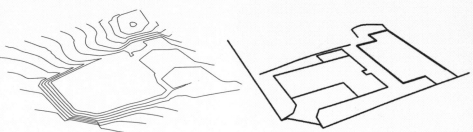

Landscape architecture projects often concentrate on issues regarding the terrain surface. A new, designed landform incorporates scientific knowledge, engineering skills and artistic creativity, making it one of the most complex tasks for a landscape architect to achieve. Three-dimensional geometry requires a high level of abstraction in order to make it feasible, work with existing contexts, and reveal a certain degree of artistry.

For years, landscape architects have adopted contours, spot elevation, different media, and physical and digital models, which have allowed them to visualize, design and test their intentions before the real terrain was built. Even today, many designers believe that current landscape-design methods do not reflect the potential achieved by computational 3D modelling technologies. Research undertaken by José Lameiras, Ian Jørgensen and Paulo Farinha Marques focused on improving the landscape-design process by bridging the gap between the creative and built stages, through the integration of state-of-the-art 3D modelling tools and a new design method that required less abstraction. The result of this research is Land 3D, based at the University of Copenhagen, a new system of terrain modelling for digital landscape design that allows architects to create and understand landforms more intuitively. A landscape can be described by its

elements: a hill, a mound, ridge, path, wall, ramps, an s-shaped slope, a flat area. Supported by this, the three designers developed a working method that allows users to model any landscape element by describing it as a shape, which is typically modelled by three-dimensional lines and profile lines, but can also be modelled through several other surface-modelling methods.

As the final terrain is a single surface on which all of the elements are incorporated, the shape of each of these elements will influence and be influenced by other, surrounding elements. This new tool enables landscape architects to have better control over their designs, and allows them to edit the surface's shape either by free-form manipulation, or according to parameters such as slope, profile and elevation. Any changes to the element's boundaries will force the surrounding elements to adapt to the new modifications. This happens in a language that reflects the design intentions by previewing the design's visual results, spatial quality and analysis. Design performance feedback is given throughout the process, as a way of enabling the landscape architect to make better design decisions. This feedback also includes accessibility, water drainage, slope stability and earthworks calculation, among several user-defined, site-specific restrictions.

Proposed landform; the landform designed through elevated contours; designed through landscape elements.

Nicholas de Monchaux
Local Code: Real Estates

This project by Nicholas de Monchaux, an architect and urbanist based at the University of California, Berkeley, applies geospatial analysis to showcase thousands of publicly owned, abandoned sites in major us cities, including New York, Los Angeles, Chicago and Washington, DC, and explore how these vacant landscapes can be visualized into a new urban system. These neglected spaces are then analysed in an attempt to provide design solutions for the betterment and health of the social and physical and environment.

Using parametric design, a landscape proposal for each site is customized to local conditions, optimizing thermal and hydrological performance to enhance the city's ecology, thus relieving the burden on the existing infrastructure, and offering maximum ecological benefits to the area. The project's quantifiable effects on energy usage and storm-water remediation reveals other means for storm-water management and energy uses, rather than employing costly infrastructural upgrades. In addition, Local Code uses public participation to develop a new, more public infrastructure with a network of urban greenways.

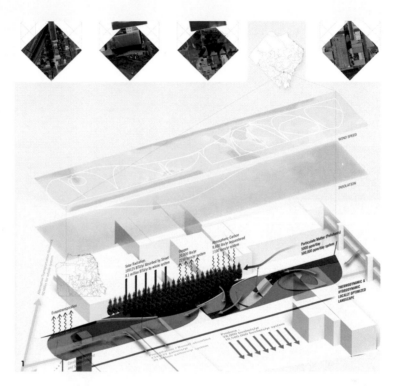

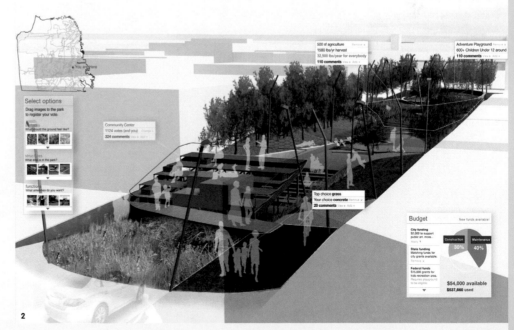

1. Parametric tools maximize the site's ecological performance.
2. The platform allows collaborative editing of shared programme and surfaces.

Architectural Association
Landscape Urbanism

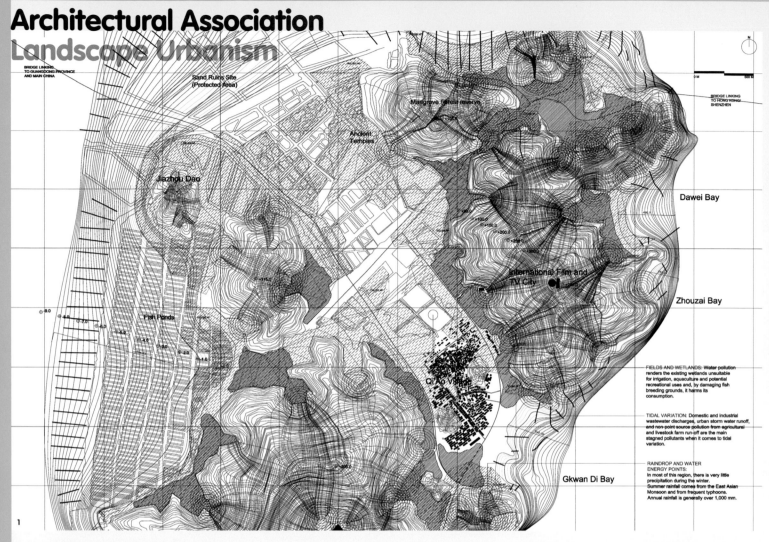

Labels on the plan (figure 1):

BRIDGE LINKING TO GUANGDONG PROVINCE AND MAIN CHINA

Sand Ruins Site (Protected Area)

Mangrove Forest reserve

Ancient Temples

Jiazhou Dao

Dawei Bay

BRIDGE LINKING TO HONG KONG, SHENZHEN

International Film and TV City

Zhouzai Bay

Fish Ponds

Qi'Ao Village

FIELDS AND WETLANDS: Water pollution renders the existing wetlands unsuitable for irrigation, aquaculture and potential recreational uses and, by damaging fish breeding grounds, it harms its consumption.

TIDAL VARIATION: Domestic and industrial wastewater discharges, urban storm water runoff, and non-point-source pollution from agricultural and livestock farm run-off are the main stagned pollutants when it comes to tidal variation.

RAINDROP AND WATER ENERGY POINTS:
In most of this region, there is very little precipitation during the winter.
Summer rainfall comes from the East Asian Monsoon and from frequent typhoons.
Annual rainfall is generally over 1,000 mm.

Gkwan Di Bay

1

2

Eva Castro, co-founder of Groundlab (pp. 74–79), is also the director of the landscape urbanism programme at the Architectural Association in London. Under her direction, together with colleagues Alfredo Ramirez and Eduardo Rico, the programme encourages an interdisciplinary approach that addresses and integrates knowledge frameworks from a variety of disciplines, including urbanism, environmental engineering and landscape ecology. Basing its premise on the emerging theory of landscape urbanism, Castro and her team adopt systemic thinking that incorporates natural processes and networks in the design process.

Digital-design technologies are at the forefront of the programme's adopted design methodologies, as they allow for fluidity, flexibility and indeterminacy. Software programs and processes such as Scripting, Maya, Autodesk, Rhino, Land Desktop, Space Syntax and Grasshopper, as well more common digital-design tools, including AutoCAD, Photoshop and Illustrator, are emphasized through workshops and tutorial sessions. Indexing, advanced diagramming, parametric modelling, rapid prototyping and fabrication are all part of the applied research in landscape urbanism. The digital landscape designed projects illustrated here represent a selection of research and design projects by students in the programme.

1, 2. Masterplan development, systems and networks, CAD framework.

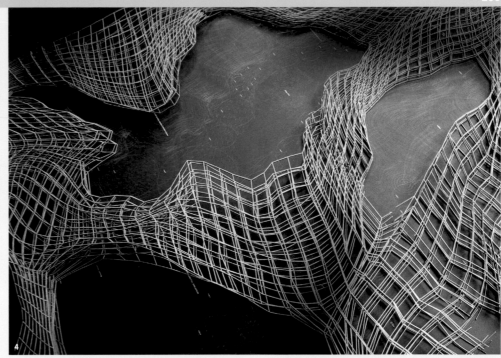

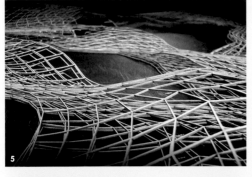

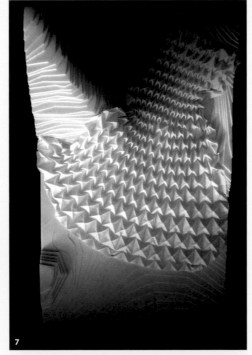

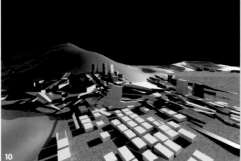

3. Road infrastructure proposal.
4, 5. Artificial topography.
6. Density scenario.
7, 8. Folded surface scenario.
9. Ecotransitional urbanism.
10. Massing model.

ETH Zürich
Waterscapes

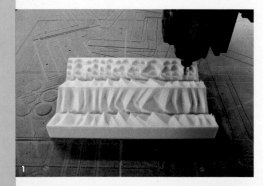

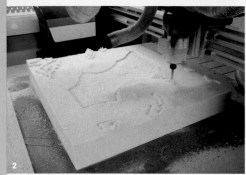

The focus of this research project was the development of new solutions for tackling extreme fluctuations in water levels of Switzerland's lakes and rivers, as well as to introduce students to the problems of large-scale topographical interventions.

The students produce a number of CNC models, starting with a topographical concept modelled in Rhinoceros. Milled into a foam block, the prototypes evolve in a constant exchange between scales and iterations, becoming more detailed and refined. Because formal concepts such as oscillating, folding and compression are easier to represent three-dimensionally than on paper, the resulting models are often closer to the initial idea than the drawings. Students also experiment with different materials and modes of expression, working with plaster and wood through section and plan. The result is a series of model developments that document the project's evolving concept.

1, 2. Model fabrication process, CNC.
3, 4. Final model output, CNC processed.

Centre for Landscape Research
Capital Views

The work of the Centre for Landscape Research at the University of Toronto focuses on issues of landscape design, technology and sustainability. Co-founder and director John Danahy's particular interest lies in exploring how visual-spatial human intelligence and perception can be extended through digital prostheses. Part of his area of research is computational perspectival projection as a means of representing the 'optic array' described by psychologist J. J. Gibson in his theory of ecological perception.

The Capital Views project addressed the search for and capture of key vistas and images of a symbolic landscape, composed of cultural and natural vocabularies. These extensive visual dialogues, using millions of images linked systematically to simulations of meaning and economy, resulted in a zoning law designed to constrain the negative impacts of development height and a guideline document, *National Capital Views Protection*. The dynamic model linked economic capacity analysis with the 'ray tracing' of eye-level views from the public realm of the capital landscape and its approaches to Parliament Hill.

Images from the project show a set of key controlling view planes that were negotiated with each stakeholder in the project to balance the need for economic development in the downtown area with the visual symbolic primacy of the capital.

1. Various eye-level views, simple computer-generated perspectives.
2. Panoramic view.

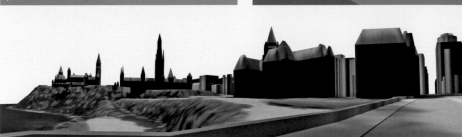

RESOURCES

DIRECTORY OF ARCHITECTS

Nadia Amoroso
University of Guelph, 50 Stone Road East, Guelph, Ontario, N1G 2W1
nadiaamoroso.com / dataappeal.com

Architectural Association [294]
School of Architecture, 36 Bedford Square, London WC1B 3ES
aaschool.ac.uk

Ballistic Architecture Machine [20]
22 International Art Plaza, Building 1-005
No. 32 Baiziwan Road, Chaoyang District, Beijing 100022
bam-usa.com

Balmori [26]
833 Washington Street, 2nd floor, New York, New York 10014
balmori.com

Bradley Cantrell [38]
Louisiana State University
311 Design Building, Baton Rouge, Louisiana 70808
reactscape.visual-logic.com

Centre for Landscape Research [297]
John Danahy
University of Toronto, 230 College Street, Toronto, Ontario M5T 1R2
clr.utoronto.ca

Nicholas de Monchaux [293]
nicholas.demonchaux.com

EcoLogicStudio [44]
6 Westgate Street, London E8 3RN
ecologicstudio.com

Emergent [50]
2404 Wilshire Boulevard, Suite 8D, Los Angeles, California 90057

Fletcher Studio [58]
2339 3rd Street, Suite 43R, San Francisco, California 94107
fletcherstudio.com

Freise Brothers [64]
freisebrothers.com / freisebros.blogspot.com

Groundlab [74]
Unit 51, Regents Studios, 8 Andrews Road, London E8 4QN
groundlab.org

GT2P [80]
gt2p.com

Paulo Guerreiro [88]
genscapes.blogspot.com

Kathryn Gustafson [94]
Linton House, 39-51 Highgate Road, London NW5 1RS
gustafson-porter.com
Pier 55, 1101 Alaskan Way, Floor 3, Seattle, Washington 98101
ggnltd.com
www.kathryngustafson.com

Zaha Hadid Architects [100]
10 Bowling Green Lane, London EC1R 0BQ
zaha-hadid.com

Hargreaves Associates [108]
398 Kansas Street, San Francisco, California 94103
hargreaves.com

Hood Design [116]
3016 Filbert Street, #2, Oakland, California 94608
wjhooddesign.com

Institute of Landscape Architecture [296]
ETH Zürich, Wolfgang-Pauli-Straße 15, 8093 Zürich Hönggerberg
girot.arch.ethz.ch

Andrés Jaque Arquitectos [122]
Calle de Otero, 3, 28028 Madrid
andresjaque.net / oficinadeinnovacionpolitica.blogspot.com

Laboratory for Visionary Architecture [126]
72 Campbell Street, Sydney, New South Wales 2010
l-a-v-a.net / l-a-v-a.blogspot.com

LAND [132]
Via Varese, 16A, Milan 20121
landsrl.com

Land-I Archicolture [138]
archicolture.com

Landworks Studio [144]
112 Shawmut Avenue, #6B, Boston, Massachusetts 02118
landworks-studio.com

Lateral Office [150]
242 Concord Avenue, Toronto, Ontario M6H 2P5
lateraloffice.com

David Lieberman [291]
University of Toronto, 230 College Street, Toronto, Ontario M5T 1R2

Metagardens [156]
69 Shalimar Gardens, London W3 9JG
metagardens.co.uk

Meyer & Silberberg [166]
1443 Cornell Avenue, Berkeley, California 94702
mslandarchitects.com

MLZ Design [170]
mlzdesign.com

MVRDV [176]
Dunantstraat 10, 3024 BC Rotterdam, Netherlands
mvrdv.nl

Nox [184]
nox-art-architecture.com

O2 Planning & Design [192]
255 17th Avenue SW, Suite 510, Calgary, Alberta T2S 2T8
o2design.com

Philip Paar [198]
Laubwerk, Kurfürstenstraße 141, 10785 Berlin
laubwerk.com

Paisajes Emergentes [206]
Cr33 n 5g 13 Edificio el Atajo, int 402, Medellín, Colombia
paisajesemergentes.com

PEG Office of Landscape & Architecture [212]
614 South Taney Street, Philadelphia, Pennsylvania
peg-ola.com

PYO Arquitectos [218]
Calle San Vicente Ferrer 20, 3° Izquierda Exterior, 28004 Madrid
pyoarquitectos.com

R&Sie(n) [222]
24 rue des Maronites, 75020 Paris
new-territories.com

Jörg Rekittke [198]
National University of Singapore, 4 Architecture Drive
Singapore 117566

Chris Speed [230]
Edinburgh College of Art, Lauriston Place, Edinburgh EH3 9DF
fields.eca.ac.uk

StossLU [236]
423 West Broadway, #304, Boston, Massachusetts 02127
stoss.net

TerreformONE [242]
33 Flatbush Avenue, 7th Floor, Brooklyn, New York 11217
terreform.org

Topotek1 [248]
Sophienstraße 18, 10178 Berlin
topotek1.de

Turenscape [254]
Innovation Centre, Room 401, Peking University Science Park
127–1, Zhongguancun North Street, Haidian District, Beijing 100080
turenscape.com

Urbanarbolismo [260]
C/ Gabriel Miró n°18, 03001 Alicante, Spain
urbanarbolismo.es

VisionDivision [268]
Granits väg 2, 171 65 Solna, Sweden
visiondivision.com

West 8 [274]
Schiehaven 13M, 3024 EC Rotterdam, Netherlands
west8.nl

PROJECT CREDITS

1.1 Velopark, London 2012 [22]
London, UK
Client: London 2012 Olympic committee
Design: Ballistic Architecture Machine, in the office of Martha Schwartz
Architectural design: Heatherwick Studio
Stadium consultant: FaulknerBrowns Architects
Structural engineer: Structural: Adams Kara Taylor

1.2 22 Art Plaza [23]
Beijing, China, 2011
Design: Ballistic Architecture Machine

1.3 Biornis-Aesthetope [24]
Manhattan, New York, 2009
Design: Ballistic Architecture Machine, in the office of Martha Schwartz
Structural engineer: Büro Happold
Ornithology consultant: Scott Edwards, Harvard University; Viviana
Ruiz-Gutierez, Cornell University
Green-roof technology: Christian Werthmann, Harvard University

2.1 Shenzhen Cultural Park [28]
Shenzhen, China, 2003–7
Client: Shenzhen Municipal Planning and Land Information Centre
Design: Balmori Associates
Design team: MAD Office

2.2 Puerto de la Luz [30]
Gran Canaria, Spain, 2005
Client: Ayuntamiento de Las Palmas de Gran Canaria
Design: Balmori Associates
Design team: Cesar Pelli & Associates

2.3 Equestrian venue, NYC 2012 [31]
Staten Island, New York, 2004
Client: NYC 2012
Design: Balmori Associates
Design team: Mark Thomann, Karen Tamir, Kathleen Bakewell,
Adrienne Cortez, Cecilia B. Martinic, Sangmok Kim, Jason Holtzman

2.4 Amman Performing Arts Centre [32]
Amman, Jordan
Client: Darat King Abdullah II
Landscape design: Balmori Associates
Lead architect: Zaha Hadid

2.5 University College Dublin [33]
Dublin, Ireland, 2007
Client: UCD Gateway Project
Landscape design: Balmori Associates
Architect: Zaha Hadid

2.6 Governors Island [34]
New York, New York
Design: Balmori Associates, with studioMDA

2.7 Water (Works) [36]
Seoul, South Korea
Design: Balmori Associates, with studioMDA

3.1 Abstraction Language: Digital/Analogue Dialogues [40]
2009
Design: Bradley Cantrell, with Natalie Yates, Washington University in
St Louis, Missouri

3.2 Ambient Space [42]
Manhattan, New York, 2007
Design: Bradley Cantrell

3.3 Thresholds [43]
Baton Rouge, Louisiana, 2008
Design: Bradley Cantrell

4.1 Tropical Playgrounds [46]
Linz, Austria
Design: EcoLogicStudio
Design team: Claudia Pasquero; Oliver Bertram, Different Futures,
University of Applied Arts Vienna
Curator: Sandrine von Klot
Assistant: Ebru Kurbak
Workshop participants: Nizar Aguir, Florian Aistleinter, Nina Bammer,
Miha Cojhter, Ramona Ehrle, Gita Ferlin, Vytautas nGecas, Mignon
grube, Christine Gunzer, Desiree Hailzl, Dominique Holzl, Thomas
Huemer, Daniel Mandel, Wolfgang Novotny, Anna Pech, elisabeth
Pfeffer, Sonja Pizka, Sarmite Polakova, Eva-Maria Pribyl, Marija
Puipaite, Tatjana Schinko, Elena Silaeva, Felix Vierlinger, Stephanie Wolf

4.2 EcoMachines [47]
Venice, Italy, 2008
Design: EcoLogicStudio
Design team: Claudia Pasquero, Marco Poletto

4.3 CyberGardens [48]
London, UK
Design: EcoLogicStudio
Workshop tutors: Claudia Pasquero, Marco Poletto
Workshop technical assistants: Neil Grant, Manuele Gaioni, Justin Iszatt
Jurors: Brett Steele, Giorgio Jeronimidis, Maria Arcero
AAInter10 students: (CyBraille) Alessandro Bava, Leila, Michalis, Noam,
Lola; (Photosythesis-Sense) Wesley, Katie, Zach Fluker, LiWei, YuWon;
(Fish and Chips) Simon, Wei, LiWei, Masaki

5.1 Garak Fish Market [52]
Seoul, South Korea, 2009
Client: Oh Se Hoon, Mayor of Seoul
Design: Emergent/Tom Wiscombe
Executive architect: Chang-jo Architects, Seoul
Project architect: Eui Sung Yi
Design team: Chris Eskew, Bin Lu, Ryan Macyauski, Cody Derra

5.2 Prototypes I–III [56]
Los Angeles, California, 2009
Design: Emergent/Tom Wiscombe

5.3 Perth Photobioreactor [57]
Perth, Australia, 2009
Client: Department of Culture and the Arts, Perth
Design: Emergent/Tom Wiscombe
Design team: Bin Lu, Chris Eskew, Gabriel Huerta, L. J. Roxas, Ryan
Macyauski

6.1 Horseshoe Cove [60]
Marin Headlands, California, 2009
Design: Fletcher Studio, with Matsys
Design team: Andrew Kuddless, Haley Waterson, Lora Martens,
Eustacia Brossart, Sarah Donato, Nenad Katic

6.2 Polish History Museum [62]
Warsaw, Poland, 2009
Design: Fletcher Studio, with WROAD Architects
Design team: Haley Waterson, Sarah Donato, Lora Martens, Eustacia
Brossart

7.1 Unseen Realities [66]
2006
Design: Nathan Freise, Adam Freise

7.2 Fallen Silo [67]
2009
Design: Nathan Freise, Adam Freise
Design team: Shiouwen Hong

7.3 Virtual Reality Topology [68]
Design: Nathan Freise, Adam Freise
Design team: Rebecca Nordmann

7.4 Megatourism [70]
Saemangeum, South Korea
Design: Nathan Freise, Adam Freise

Design team: Dwayne Dancy, George Quavier, John Cerone,
Matthew Pauly, Jeffrey Inaba, Darien Williams, Andrew Kovaks, Glenn
Cummings, Tatiana von Preussen, Junhong Choi

7.5 Scapegote [72]
Design: Nathan Freise, Adam Freise

8.1 Flowing Gardens [76]
Xi'an, China, 2009–11
Client: Chan Ba Ecological District
Design: Groundlab, with Plasma Studio
Design team: Eva Castro, Holger Kehne, Sarah Majid, Alfredo Ramirez,
Eduardo Rico, Jorge Ayala, Hossein Kachabi, with Nadia Kloster, Steve
De Micoli, Elisa Kim, Filipo Nassetti, Rui Liu, Kezhou Chan, Clara Oloriz
Architecture design team: Eva Castro, Holger Kehne, Ulla Hell, Mehran
Gharleghi, Evan Greenberg, Xiaowei Tong, with Tom Lee, Ying Wang,
Nicoletta Gerevini, Peter Pichler, Benedikt Schleicher, Katy Barkan,
Danai Sage
Structural engineering: Arup; John A. Martin & Associates

8.2 Deep Ground: Longgan Masterplan [78]
Shenzhen, China, 2009
Design: Groundlab
Design team: Eva Castro, Eduardo Rico, Alfredo Ramirez, Holger Kehne,
Sarah Majid
Competition team: Alejandra Bosch, Maria Paez, Brendon Carlin
Collaborators: Clara Oloriz, Arturo Lyon, Enriqueta Llabres
Consultants: Arup ILG; InGame

9.1 Furrow Fields [82]
2009
Design: GT2P
CNC machining: Benjamin Leyton, LabFAU
Thermoforming: SYP Ltd

9.2 Wave Interference [84]
2009
Design: GT2P

9.3 Velo Catalyst [85]
Santiago, Chile, 2007
Design: GT2P
Design team: Juan Cristobal Caceres, Jaime Baeza

9.4 Grapevine Vibrational [86]
Rancagua, Chile, 2009
Client: Nemesio Antúnez Commission
Design: GT2P
Design team: Guillermo Parada, Sebastián Rozas, with Tamara Pérez.
Structural engineer: Jorge Tobar.
Construction: Héctor Díaz Montajes
Hilam specialist: Héctor Jofré
Governmental inspection: Carolina Pelegri, Alicia Alarcón
Local clinic assistance: Roberto Mayorga

10.1 Biotope [90]
Design: Paulo Guerreiro

10.2 Fractal Grid [91]
Design: Paulo Guerreiro

10.3 Skinning Steel [92]
Design: Paulo Guerreiro

10.4 Digital Waterfront [93]
Design: Paulo Guerreiro

11.1 Gardens by the Bay [96]
Marina East, Singapore
Client: National Parks Board
Design: Gustafson Porter
Design team project manager: Confluencepcm
Client project manager: PM Link
Engineer: Arup
Architect: Hamiltons
Quantity surveyor: Davis Langdon
Local engineer: CPA

11.2 Lurie Garden [97]
Chicago, Illinios, 2004
Client: Millennium Park
Design: Gustafson Guthrie Nichol
Plantsman: Piet Oudolf
Theatre set designer: Robert Israel

Structural and civil engineers: KPFF
Fountain consultants: CMS Collaborative
Plant sourcing, construction observation: Terry Guen Design Associates

11.3 Diana, Princess of Wales Memorial Fountain [98]
London, UK, 2004
Client: Department of Culture, Media and Sport
Design: Gustafson Porter
Sponsor: The Royal Parks
Engineers: Arup
Surface design consultant: SDE
Surface texture consultant: Texxus
Water feature specialist: OCMIS

12.1 Abu Dhabi Performing Arts Centre [102]
Abu Dhabi, United Arab Emirates, 2007–
Design: Zaha Hadid with Patrik Schumacher
Project director: Nils-Peter Fischer
Project architects: Britta Knobel, Daniel Widrig
Project team: Jeandonne Schijlen, Melike Altisinik, Arnoldo Rabago,
Zhi Wang, Rojia Forouhar, Jaime Serra Avila, Diego Rosales, Erhan
Patat, Samer Chamoun, Philipp Vogt, Rafael Portillo
Structural, fire, traffic and building services consultant: WSP Group,
with WSP (Middle East): Bill Price, Ron Slade
Acoustics consultant: Sound Space Design: Bob Essert
Façade sample construction: King Glass Engineering Group
Theatre consultant: Anne Minors Performance Consultants
Cost / QS: Gardiner & Theobald: Gary Faulkner

12.2 Dubai Opera House [104]
Dubai, United Arab Emirates, 2006–
Design: Zaha Hadid with Patrik Schumacher
Project director: Charles Walker
Project architect: Nils-Peter Fischer
Project team: Melike Altinisik, Alexia Anastasopoulou, Dylan
Baker-Rice, Domen Bergoc, Shajay Bhooshan, Monika Bilska, Alex
Bilton, Elizabeth Bishop, Torsten Broeder, Cristiano Ceccato, Alessio
Constantino, Mario Coppola, Brian Dale, Ana Valeria Emiliano, Elif
Erdine, Camilla Galli, Brandon Gehrke, Aris Georgiadis, Pia Habekost,
Francis Michael Hill, Shao-Wei Huang, Chikara Inamura, Alexander
Janowsky, DaeWha Kang, Tariq Khayyat, Maren Klasing, Britta Knobel,
Martin Krcha, Effi e Kuan, Mariagrazia Lanza, Tyen Masten, Jwalant
Mahadevwala, Rashiq Muhamadali, Monica Noguero, Diogo Brito
Pereira, Rafael Portillo, Michael Powers, Rolando Rodriguez-Leal,
Federico Rossi, Mireia Sala Font, Elke Scheier, Rooshad Shroff, William
Tan, Michal Treder, Daniel Widrig, Fulvio Wirz, Susu Xu, Ting Ting Zhang
Project director (competition): Graham Modlen
Project architect (competition): Dillon Lin
Competition team: Christine Chow, Daniel Dendra, Yiching Liu, Simone
Fuchs, Larissa Henke, Tyen Masten, Lourdes Sanchez, Johannes
Schafelner, Swati Sharma, Hooman Talebi, Komal Talreja, Claudia Wulf,
Simon Yu
Engineering consultant: Ove Arup & Partners: Steve Roberts
Acoustics consultant: Arup Acoustics: Neill Woodger
Theatre consultant: Anne Minors Performance Consultants
Lighting consultant: Office for Visual Interaction

12.3 Olabeaga and San Mamés Masterplans [106]
Bilbao, Spain, 2005–
Client: Bilbao City Council
Design: Zaha Hadid with Patrik Schumacher
Project architect: Manuela Gatto
Project team: Atrey Chhaya, Fabian Hecker, Dipal Kotari, Fernando
Perez, Diego Rosales
Engineer: Ove Arup & Partners
Urban strategy: Larry Barth

13.1 Governors Island [110]
New York, New York
Design: Hargreaves Associates
Design team: George Hargreaves, Mary Margaret Jones, Glenn Allen,
Gavin McMillan, Kirt Rieder, Catherine Miller, Ken Haines, Jacob
Petersen, Brian Jencek, Alan Lewis, Matthew J. Tucker, Bernward
Engelke, Andy Harris, Misty March, Lara Rose

13.2 One Island East [111]
Hong Kong, China
Design: Hargreaves Associates
Design team: George Hargreaves, Mary Margaret Jones, Glenn Allen,
Gavin McMillan, Kirt Rieder, Catherine Miller, Ken Haines, Jacob
Petersen, Brian Jencek, Alan Lewis, Matthew J. Tucker, Bernward
Engelke, Andy Harris, Misty March, Lara Rose

13.3 Allergan Headquarters [112]
Irvine, California
Design: Hargreaves Associates
Design team: George Hargreaves, Mary Margaret Jones, Glenn Allen, Gavin McMillan, Kirt Rieder, Catherine Miller, Ken Haines, Jacob Petersen, Brian Jencek, Alan Lewis, Matthew J. Tucker, Bernward Engelke, Andy Harris, Misty March, Lara Rose

13.4 American Indian Cultural Center [113]
Oklahoma City, Oklahoma
Design: Hargreaves Associates
Design team: George Hargreaves, Mary Margaret Jones, Glenn Allen, Gavin McMillan, Kirt Rieder, Catherine Miller, Ken Haines, Jacob Petersen, Brian Jencek, Alan Lewis, Matthew J. Tucker, Bernward Engelke, Andy Harris, Misty March, Lara Rose

13.5 Olympic Park, London 2012 [114]
London, UK
Design: Hargreaves Associates
Design team: George Hargreaves, Mary Margaret Jones, Glenn Allen, Gavin McMillan, Kirt Rieder, Catherine Miller, Ken Haines, Jacob Petersen, Brian Jencek, Alan Lewis, Matthew J. Tucker, Bernward Engelke, Andy Harris, Misty March, Lara Rose

13.6 Mission Rock Seawall 337 [115]
San Francisco, California
Design: Hargreaves Associates
Design team: George Hargreaves, Mary Margaret Jones, Glenn Allen, Gavin McMillan, Kirt Rieder, Catherine Miller, Ken Haines, Jacob Petersen, Brian Jencek, Alan Lewis, Matthew J. Tucker, Bernward Engelke, Andy Harris, Misty March, Lara Rose

14.1 Garden Passage [118]
District Hill, Pittsburgh, Pennsylvania, 2009
Design: Walter Hood, Hood Design Studio
Project manager: Kelley Lemon
Collaborator: The Hill House Association
Consultant: Arup

14.2 Timber Crossing: Damming I-5 [119]
Vancouver, Washington, 2008
Client: Vancouver Community Connector
Design: Walter Hood, Hood Design Studio, with Diller, Scofidio + Renfro
Project manager: Chelsea Johnson
Consultant: Buro Happold; Atelier Ten

14.3 Airport Gateway [120]
San Jose, California, 2007
Design: Walter Hood, Hood Design Studio
San Jose Public Art Program coordinator: Mary Rubin

15.1 Landscape Condenser [124]
Yecla, Spain, 2010
Design: Andrés Jaque Arquitectos
Design team: Ondrej Laciga, Alejandro Martín, David Segura, Juliana Gutierrez

16.1 Municipal Office District [128]
Hanoi, Vietnam, 2007
Client: People's Committee of Hanoi
Design: Laboratory for Visionary Architecture
Design team: Chris Bosse, with PTW Architects

16.2 Oasis of the Future [130]
Masdar, United Arab Emirates, 2008
Client: Abu Dhabi Future Energy Company
Design: Laboratory for Visionary Architecture
Design team: Chris Bosse, Tobias Wallisser, Alexander Rieck
Partners: Kann Finch Group: Bob Nation; Arup Sydney; SL Rasch; Transsolar; EDAW

17.1 Duisburg Bahnhofsvorplatz [134]
Duisburg, Germany, 2009
Client: Innenstadt Duisburg Entwicklungsgesellschaft
Design: LAND
Design team: Andreas Kipar, Kornelia Keil, Laura Pigozzi, Susanne Günther, Melanie Müller, Roberta Filippini, Erika Cormio, Piera Chiuppani, Caterina Gerolimetto, Sebastian Rübenacker
Architects: Kiparlandschaftsarchitekten

17.2 Econovello Cesena [136]
Cesena, Italy, 2007
Client: Municipality of Cesena
Design: LAND

Design team: Andreas Kipar, Giovanni Sala, Mauro Panigo, Dong Sub Bertin, Laura Pigozzi, Giuseppe Anastasi, Erica Cormio, Piera Chiuppani, Andrea Jungers, José Acosta, Lorenza Crotti, Ugo Perillo, Anna Bocchietti, Simone Marelli, Matteo Pedaso
Collaborators: Studio GAP Associati (team leader), Bruno Gabrielli, Benedetto Camerana, Hermann Kohlloffel

18.1 Ombre [140]
Montreal, Quebec, Canada, 2002
Design: Land-I Archicolture

18.2 Orange Power [141]
Ponte de Lima International Garden Festival, Portugal, 2006
Design: Land-I Archicolture

18.3 Tracce [142]
Festival di Arte Topiaria, Lucca, Italy, 2001
Design: Land-I Archicolture
Organizers: Grandi Giardini Italiani
Sponsor: Martini e Rossi

19.1 200 Fifth Avenue [146]
New York, New York
Client: L&L Holding Company
Design: Landworks Studio
Project management: Gardiner & Theobald
Architect: Studios Architecture
Lighting: Johnson Light Studio
Precast concrete fabrication: Concreteworks Studio

19.2 AIA Headquarters Renewal [148]
Washington, DC
Client: American Institute of Architects
Design: Landworks Studio
Architect: Studios Architecture

19.3 Square 673 [149]
Washington, DC
Client: Archstone-Smith
Design: Landworks Studio
Architects: Studios Architecture; Davis Carter Scott

20.1 Water Economies/Ecologies [152]
Imperial Valley, California, 2009–10
Design: Lateral Office
Design team: Lola Sheppard, Mason White, Daniel Rabin, Fei-Ling Tseng, Kristin Ross, Joseph Yau

20.2 IceLink [154]
Bering Strait, between Russia and Alaska, 2009
Design: Lateral Office
Design team: Lola Sheppard, Mason White, Matthew Spremulli, Fei-Ling Tseng, Sandy Wong, Ghazal Jafari

21.1 Hyde Park [158]
London, UK, ongoing
Design: Metagardens
Fabricators: Fineline; Seamless Industries
Plants: Norfield Nurseries
Water irrigation: Watermatic

21.2 Electronic Dreams [160]
2006
Design: Metagardens

21.3 Evoterrarium [161]
2006
Design: Metagardens

21.4 Filigrana [162]
London, UK
Design: Metagardens

21.5 Monstruosa [163]
Hampton Court Flower Show, UK, 2009
Design: Metagardens
Fabricator: Metropolitan Works
Suppliers: Fineline; Isothane; CED Ltd; Colorite Paint Co
Plants: South West Carnivorous Plants

21.6 Parasitus_Imperator [164]
2006
Design: Metagardens

21.7 Pulsations [165]
Hampton Court Flower Show, UK, 2008
Design: Metagardens
Fabricator: Fineline
Suppliers: Addaqrip; PSCo Ltd; CCE Surfacing
Plants: Cactusshop; Amulree Exotics

22.1 Courthouse Square [168]
Santa Rosa, California
Client: City of Santa Rosa
Design: Meyer & Silberberg Land Architects
Architect: Jim Jennings Architecture; Brito Rodriguez Arquitectura

22.2 Daze Maze [169]
Montreal, Quebec, Canada, 2008
Design: Meyer & Silberberg Land Architects

23.1 Terra+Scapes [172]
Portland, Oregon, 2008
Design: MLZ Design
Modelling and rendering: Matt Zambelli
Studio professors: Barry Kew, Larry Gorenflo, Penn State University

23.2 Digital Landscape Architecture in Practice [174]
Design: MLZ Design
Modelling and rendering: Matt Zambelli, with Cosburn Associates
Design and facilitation: Cosburn Associates

23.3 Porta Latina [175]
Rome, Italy
Design: MLZ Design
Modelling and rendering: Matt Zambelli
Studio professors: George Dickie, Luca Peralta, Penn State University

24.1 Gwanggyo Power Centre [178]
Gwanggyo, South Korea, 2007
Client: Daewoon Consortium and DA Group
Design: MVRDV
Design team: Winy Maas, Jacob van Rijs, Nathalie de Vries, with Youngwook Joung, Wenchian Shi, Raymond van den Broek, Paul Kroese, Naiara Arregi, Wenhua Deng, Doris Strauch, Bas Kalmeijer, Simon Potier, Silke Volkert, Marta Pozo, Francesco Pasquale
Engineer: Arup
Local architect: DA Group

24.2 Almere 2030 [180]
Almere Hout, Netherlands, 2008–
Client: Municipality of Almere
Design: MVRDV
Design team: Winy Maas, Jacob van Rijs, Nathalie de Vries, with Jeroen Zuidgeest, Klaas Hofman, Martine Vledder, Sabina Favaro, Hui Hsin Liao, Francesco Pasquale, Fokke Moerel, Paul Kroese, Johannes Schele, Stefan de Koning, Oana Rades, Silke Volkert, Fabian Wagner, Wouter Oostendorp, Marta Pozo, Naiara Arregi, Jaap van Dijk, Marta Gierczynska, Daniel Marmot, Pablo Munoz Paya, Di Miao, Manuel Galipeau
Sustainability: Arup
Model: Made by Mistake
Artist's impressions, 3D modelling: MVRDV, with Luxigon
Animation: Wieland & Gouwens
Graphic design: Stout/Kramer

24.3 Eco City Montecorvo [181]
Logroño, Spain, 2008
Client: LMB Grupo
Design: MVRDV
Design team (competition phase): Winy Maas, Jacob van Rijs, Nathalie de Vries, with Martine Vledder, Raul Lazaro Santamaria, Aser Giménez Ortega, Gijs Rikken and Philipp Keiss
Design team (design phase): Winy Maas, Jacob van Rijs, Nathalie de Vries, with Fokke Moerel, Maria Lopez, Adelaida Riveira, Wouter Oosterdorp, Jose Ignacio Velasco, Marta Pozo
Co-architect: GRAS: Guillermo Reynes
Facilitary office: Why Factory
Environmental engineer: Arup

24.4 Floriade 2012 [182]
Rotterdam, Netherlands, 2004
Client: Municipality Of Rotterdam
Design: MVRDV
Design team: Winy Maas, Jacob van Rijs, Nathalie de Vries, with Marc Joubert, Jeroen Zuidgeest, Guillermo Reyes, Youngwook Joung, Martin Larsen, Kamilla Heskje, Chris Hei-shing Lai, Esther Rovira

Landscape: Tedder & Keus: Katie Tedder, Corine Keus, Nanne Verbrugen, Henkie Claassen

25.1 Eye Bridge [186]
Aachen, Germany, 2007–10
Client: City of Aachen
Design: Nox
Design team: Lars Spuybroek, Thomas Wortman, Florian Dubiel, Yang Wang
Engineer: Bollinger + Grohmann

25.2 Seoul Opera House [188]
Seoul, South Korea, 2005
Client: City of Seoul
Design: Nox
Design team: Lars Spuybroek, Marcus Leinweber, Hanna Stiller, Hartmut Flothmann, Florian Brillet, Mehdi Kebir
Engineer: Buro Happold

25.3 Whispering Garden [190]
Kop-van-Zuid, Rotterdam, Netherlands, 2005
Client: City of Rotterdam, CBK
Design: Nox
Design team: Lars Spuybroek, Hanna Stiller, Beau Trincia
Sound artist: Edwin van der Heide

25.4 Silk Road [191]
Xi'an, China, 2006
Client: City of Xi'an
Design: Nox
Design team: Lars Spuybroek, Hanna Stiller, Stephen Form, Karl Rosenvinge Kjelstrup-Johnson, Li Peng, Mehdi Kebir, with OKRA Landscape Architects

26.1 Corporate Campus Urban Design [194]
Design: O2 Planning & Design

26.2 Landscape Planning for Agroforestry [195]
Embu, Mt Kenya
Design: O2 Planning & Design
Concept: Douglas Olson, PhD thesis, Harvard University

26.3 Petro-Canada Sullivan Gas Field Development [196]
Alberta, Canada
Client: Petro-Canada
Design: O2 Planning & Design

26.4 TELUS Spark [197]
Calgary, Alberta, Canada
Client: City of Calgary, TELUS World of Science
Design: O2 Planning & Design
Architects: Cohos Evamy Integrated Design

27.1 Parametric Geotypical Landscapes [200]
2009
Design: Philip Paar

27.2 Digital Botany [201]
2006
Design: Philip Paar, Laubwerk

27.3 Biosphere3D [202]
2007
Design: Philip Paar
Design team: Malte Clasen, Steffen Ernst
Kimberley Climate Change Adaptation project:
Modelling and interactive visualization: Olaf Schroth, University of Vancouver
Virtual reconstruction of King Herod's third winter palace and oasis:
Modelling: Jochen Mülder, Agnes Kirchhoff
Interactive visualization: Philip Paar

27.4 Gleisdreieck Berlin [204]
Berlin, Germany, 2006
Client: City of Berlin
Design: Jörg Rekittke
3D modelling and visualization: Philip Paar

27.5 Future Energy Landscapes [205]
Welzow, Germany, 2006
Design: Philip Paar, Lenné3D
Recultivation design: HochC Landschaftsarchitektur, with Horst Schumacher, Büro für Gartenkunst und Kultur der Energie, on behalf of IBA-Fürst-Pückler-Land

28.1 Clouds [208]
Ituango, Colombia, 2009
Design: Paisajes Emergentes
Design team: Juan Esteban Gomez, Farid Maya, Sebastián Monsalve, Juan Carlos Aristizabal

28.2 Parque del Lago [209]
Quito, Ecuador, 2008
Design: Paisajes Emergentes
Design team: Luis Callejas, Seastian Mejia, Edgar Mazo

28.3 Aquatic Complex [210]
Medellín, Colombia, 2008
Design: Paisajes Emergentes
Design team: Luis Callejas, Edgar Mazo Sebastian Mejia
Architectural consultants: Juanita Gonzales, Andres Zapata, Sebastian Betancourt, Eliana Beltran, Clara Arango, Adriana Tamayo, Farid Maya, Sebastián Monsalve, Juan Esteban Gomez
Landscape consultant: Andres Ospina
Structural engineering consultant: Ing. Jorge Aristizabal

29.1 Ripple Effect [214]
Manhattan and the Bronx, New York, 2010
Design: PEG Office for Landscape & Architecture
Team: Karen M'Closkey, Keith VanDerSys, Marisa Bernstein, Young Joon Choi, Marguerite Graham
Competition sponsor: Emerging New York Architects Committee

29.2 Not Garden, Not Again [216]
Philadelphia, Pennsylvania, 2009
Design: PEG Office for Landscape & Architecture
Design team: Karen M'Closkey, Keith VanDerSys, Aaron Cohen, Marguerite Graham, Tiffany Marston, Sahar Moin, Elizabeth Rothwell, Steven Tucker, Jordan Gearhart, Seean Williams
Collaborators: Redevelopment Authority of the City of Philadelphia; Urban Tree Connection

29.3 Joie de Vie(w) [217]
Montreal, Quebec, Canada, 2008
Design: PEG Office for Landscape & Architecture
Design team: Karen M'Closkey, Keith VanDerSys, Elizabeth Rothwell

30.1 Urban Procedures [220]
La Sagrera, Barcelona, Spain, 2004–6
Design: PYO Arquitectos
Design team: Paul Galindo Pastre, Ophélie Herranz Lespagnol

30.2 Dynamic Transformations in Border Conditions [221]
Rijnhaven, Netherlands, 2003, 2006–7
Design: PYO Arquitectos
Design team: Paul Galindo Pastre, Ophélie Herranz Lespagnol

31.1 He Shot Me Down [224]
Heyri, South Korea, 2006–7
Client: Julieta and J. J. Lee
Design: R&Sie(n)
Design team: François Roche, Stephanie Lavaux, Jean Navarro, with Marion Gauguet, Leopold Lambert, Andrea Koning, Igor Lacroix, Daniel Fernandez Flores
Robotic design: Stephan Henrich

31.2 Green Gorgon [226]
Lausanne, Switzerland, 2005
Client: Ville de Lausanne
Design: R&Sie(n)
Design team: François Roche, Stéphanie Lavaux, Jean Navarro, with Miguel-Angel Munoz, Quck Zhong-Yi, Kika Estarellas, Maud Godard, Julien Jacquot
Artists: Philippe Parreno, Mark Dion
Engineer: Guscetti et Tournier
Façade engineer: VP & Green
Thermal engineer: Klaus Daniels, HL Technik
Landscape: Michel Boulcourt
GPS designer: Mathieu Lehanneur
Botanist: Sergio Ochatt
Museographer: Ami Barak

31.3 Olzweg [227]
Orléans, France, 2006
Client: Fonds Regional d'Art Contemporain
Design: R&Sie(n)
Design team: François Roche, Stéphanie Lavaux, Jean Navarro, with Alexander Römer, Agnes Vidal, Daniel Fernández Florez
Artist: Pierre Huyghe

Furniture design: Mathieu Lehanneur
Robotic design: Stephan Henrich
Façade engineer: Nicholas Green
Engineer: Sibat
Script programmer: Julien Blervaque

31.4 Symbiosis Hood [228]
Seoul, South Korea, 2009
Clients: Julieta and J. J. Lee, and Pablo Lee
Design: R&Sie(n)
Design team: François Roche, Stéphanie Lavaux, Toshikatsu Kiuchi, with Leopold Lambert

32.1 Digital Explorations in Architectural Urban Analysis [232]
Edinburgh, UK, 2008
Design: Chris Speed
Design team: Chris Lowry, Dermot McMeel, Mark Wright

32.2 CoMob [234]
2009
Design: Chris Speed, with Jen Southern
Software: J. Ehnes, H. Ekeus, with Chris Lowry, William Mackaness

32.3 Yamaguchi Valley Section [235]
Yamaguchi, Japan, 2009
Design: Chris Speed
GPS parsing: Dermott McMeel
3D modelling: Klas Hyllen

33.1 Bass River Park [238]
West Dennis, Massachusetts, 2006–10
Client: City of West Dennis
Design: StossLU
Design team: Chris Reed (principal), Jill Desimini (project manager), Scott Bishop, Steve Carlucci, Adrian Fehrmann, Julia Hunt, Susan Fritzgerald, Kristin Malone, Chris Muskopf
Site and civil engineering: Nitsch Engineering
Marine engineering: Childs Engineering
Cost estimate: Davis Langdon

33.2 Erie Plaza [240]
Milwaukee, Wisconsin, 2010
Client: City of Milwaukee
Design: StossLU
Design team: Chris Reed (principal), Scott Bishop (project manager), Adrian Fehrmann, Kristin Malone, Chris Muskopf, Graham Palmer, Meg Studer
Engineering and wetland ecology: GRAEF
Urban design: Vetter Denk Architects

34.1 Fab Tree Hab: Living Graft Dwellings [244]
Design: TerreformONE
Design team: Mitchell Joachim, Lara Greden, Javier Arbona

34.2 New York 2106: Self-Sufficient City [246]
Design: TerreformONE
Volunteers: Mitchell Joachim, Makoto Okazaki, Kent Hikida, Serdar Omer, Andrei Vovk, Noura Al Sayeh, Byron Stigge, Nathan Leverence, Oliver Medvedik, Lukas Lenherr, Matt Kipilman, Adam Watson, Craig Schwitter
Part-time salaried critic: Michael Sorkin

34.3 Rapid Re(f)use: Waste to Resource City 2120 [247]
Design: TerreformONE
Design team: Mitchell Joachim, Maria Aiolova, Melanie Fessel, Emily Johnson, Ian Slover, Philip Weller, Zachary Aders, Webb Allen, Niloufar Karimzadegan, Lauren Sarafan

35.1 Superkilen [250]
Copenhagen, Denmark
Client: City of Copenhagen
Design: Topotek1
Collaborators: Bjarke Ingels Group, Superflex, with Help, Lemming Eriksson

35.2 Broderie Urbaine [252]
Berlin, Germany, 2006
Client: Bayer-Pensionskasse
Design: Topotek1
Architects: NPS Tchoban Voss

35.3 KAiAK MarktParkPlatz [253]
Köpenick, Germany, 2007

Client: StadtKunstProjekte
Design: Topotek1

36.1 Chicago Art Field [256]
Chicago, Illinois, 2009
Client: Design & Construction Administration Services
Design: Turenscape, with JJR
Design team: Kongjian Yu, Deb Mitchell, Si Cun, Alex Camprubi
Animation team: Turenscape Mulimedia Studio

36.2 Shanghai Expo-Park [258]
Shanghai Expo 2010, China, 2007–10
Client: Shanghai World Expo Land Development Co
Design: Turenscape, with the Peking University Graduate School of Design
Design team: Kongjian Yu, Lin Shihong, Fang Wanli, Liu Xiangjun, Malte Selugg, Pan Yang, Niu Jing, Yuan Tianyuan
Rendering: Turenscape Multimedia Studio

37.1 Reforesting Park [262]
Benidorm, Spain
Design: Urbanarbolismo
Design team: Jordi Serramía Ruíz, Luis Alberto Hernández Calvarro

37.2 Eco.Acequia [264]
Elche, Spain
Design: Urbanarbolismo
Design team: Jordi Serramía Ruíz, Luis Alberto Hernández Calvarro, Enrique Pérez Manzano, Pedro Rodenas Caparros

37.3 Velo [266]
Alicante, Spain
Design: Urbanarbolismo
Design team: Jordi Serramía Ruíz, Luis Alberto Hernández Calvarro, Jorge Toledo García, Jose Carrasco Hortal

38.1 Eden Falls [270]
Buenos Aires, Argentina, 2009–11
Design: VisionDivision

38.2 Agua Libre [271]
Buenos Aires, Argentina, 2005–6
Design: VisionDivision

38.3 Rapid Palace [272]
near Gothenburg, Sweden, 2008
Design: VisionDivision

39.1 Botanic Bridge Gwangju [276]
Gwangju, South Korea, 2001
Client: Gwangju Biennale
Design: West 8
Design team: Adriaan Geuze, Jerry van Eyck, Pieter Rabijns, Sabine Müller, Yoon-Jin Park
Consultant: Prof. Oh Koo-Kyoon

39.2 Máximapark [277]
Utrecht, Netherlands, 1997
Client: Project Development Leidsche Rijn
Design: West 8
Design team: Adriaan Geuze, Edzo Bindels, Robert Schütte, Ard Middeldorp, Cyrus Clark, Edwin van der Hoeven, Esther Kruit, Freek Boerwinkel, Fritz Coetzee, Gaspard Estourgie, Jacco Stuy, Jeroen de Willigen, Joost Koningen, Joost Emmerik, Joris Hekkenberg, Kees Schoot, Maarten Buijs, Martin Biewenga, Nigel Sampey, Perry Maas, Pieter Hoen, Ronald van Nugteren

39.3 Jubilee Gardens [278]
London, UK, 2005
Client: South Bank Employers' Group
Design: West 8
Design team: Adriaan Geuze, Edzo Bindels, Jerry van Eyck, Alyssa Schwann, Freek Boerwinkel, Joris Weijts, Karsten Buchholz, Maarten van de Voorde, Matthew Skjonsberg, Perry Maas
Consultants: AKT engineers; BDSP Partnership (mechanical/electrical); Soil and Land Consultants, Buro Happold (security)

39.4 Puentes Cascara [280]
Madrid, Spain, 2006–11
Client: Municipality of Madrid
Design: West 8
Design team: Adriaan Geuze, Christian Dobrick, Edzo Bindels, Alexander Sverdlov, Claudia Wolsfeld, Enrique Ibáñez González, Freek Boerwinkel, Joost Koningen, Juan Figueroa Calero, Karsten Buchholz,

Lennart van Dijk, Luna Solas, Mariana Siqueira, Marta Roy, Martin Biewenga, Matthew Skjonsberg, Michael Gersbach, Perry Maas, Riccardo Minghini, Sander Lap, Shachar Zur, Silvia Lupini
Partners: MRIO arquitectos, a joint venture of three firms: Burgos & Garrido Arquitectos Asociados, Porras La Casta Arquitectos, Rubio & Álvarez-Sala

39.5 City on Fire/City in Bloom [281]
Rotterdam, Netherlands, 2007
Client: Rotterdam City of Architecture 2007
Design: West 8
Design team: Adriaan Geuze, Gaspard Estourgie, Jerry van Eyck, Gaspard Estourgie, Perry Maas

De Draai [289]
Heerhugowaard, Netherlands, 2000–11
Client: Gemeente Heerhugowaard
Design: Karres en Brands
Design team: Bart Brands, Marco Broekman, Marijke Bruinsma, Tijl Dejonckheere, Kristian van Schaik, Paul Portheine, Lucy Knox Knight, Lieneke van Campen, Marc Springer, Jan Martijn Eekhof
Software advisor: ETH Zürich

Detroit Super Division [290]
Detroit, Michigan, 2009
Design: FreelandBuck
Design team: David Freeland, Brennan Buck
Collaborator: Fletcher Studio

The Alchemist's Garden [291]
Toronto, Ontario, Canada, 2007
Design: David Lieberman
Design team: Fiona Lim Tung

Local Code: Real Estate [293]
Design: Nicholas de Monchaux
Design team: Natalia Echeverri, Benjamin Golder, Elizabeth Goodman, Sha Hwang, Sara Jensen, David Lung, Shivang Patwa, Thomas Pollman, Kimiko Ryokai, Matthew Smith, Laurie Spitler

Capital Views [297]
Ottawa, Canada, 2002
Design: Centre for Landscape Research
Design team: John Danahy, Shannon McKenzie, Rodney Hoinkes, Stephen Bohus, Robert Wright
Collaborators: DuToit Allsopp Hillier: Robert Allsopp; National Capital Commission: John Able, Renata Jentus

PHOTO CREDITS

Nathan Freise, Adam Freise 66, 68, 70, 72; Nathan Freise, Adam Freise, Shiouwen Hong 67; Sebastián Rozas, desbastando.blogspot.com 86 (photos of the construction process); Nicolas Saieh, nico-saieh.cl 86 (photos of the completed project); Paulo Guerreiro 90, 91, 92, 93; Jason Hawkes, Helene Binet 98; Mir, mir.no 130 (top and middle); Laboratory for Visual Architecture 131 (top left); CJ Williams Contemporary Photography 163; K. C. Man 165; O2 Planning & Design 194, 196, 197 (rendered images; Philip Paar, Lenné3D, 2006 204 (top); Jörg Rekittke, Philip Paar, 2006 204 (bottom); Hanns Joosten 252, 253

ACKNOWLEDGMENTS

This book would not be possible without the effort and support of key individuals. I would like to acknowledge my colleagues and friends who have immersed themselves in digital design experimentations and novitiates. I offer a special thanks to all the contributors and support staff who provided the means and material to help shape this publication, including, but not limited to: Eva Castro and the group from the Architectural Association and Groundlab; Daniel Gass/ Ballistic Architecture Machine; Diana Balmori, Monica Hernandez/ Balmori; Bradley Cantrell; John Danahy, Rob Wright, Centre for Landscape Research; Chris Reed/StossLU; Claudia Pasquero/ EcoLogicStudio; Tom Wiscombe/Emergent; Alexandre Kapellos/ ETH Zürich; David Fletcher and team/Fletcher Studio; David Freeland and Brennan Buck/FreelandBuck; Adam and Nathan Freise/Freise Brothers; Alexy Narvaez/GT2P; Paulo Guerreiro; Kathryn Gustafson and team; Davide Giordano/Zaha Hadid Architects; Hood Design and staff; Andrés Jaque; the team at Karres en Brands; Chris Bosse, Erik Escalante/Laboratory for Visionary Architecture; José Lameiras; Piera Chiuppani/LAND; Raffaella Sini/LAND-I Archicolture; Luis Callejas/Paisajes Emergentes; Michael Blier, Kris Lucius/Landworks Studio; Mason White, Lola Sheppard/Lateral Office; David Lieberman; Fernando Gonzalez/Metagardens; David Meyer and team/Meyer & Silberburg; Matt Zambelli/MLZ Design; Nicholas de Monchaux; Lars Spuybroek, Bart Lans/NOX; Douglas Olson and team/O2 Planning & Design; Karen M'Closkey, Keith VanDerSys/PEG Office for Landscape & Architecture; Philip Paar; Ophélie Herranz Lespagnol/PYO Arquitectos; François Roche/R&Sie(n); Mike Silver; Chris Speed; Mitchell Joachim/ TerreformONE; Jordi Serramia Ruiz/Urbanarbolismo; Ulf Mejergren, Anders Berensson/VisionDivision; Adriaan Geuze and team/West 8; Kongjian Yu, Yansheng Yang, Turenscape; the team at Topotek1; Charles Waldheim; Jason King from the Landscape+Urbanism blog; and to the many other friends and colleagues who have helped shape this much-needed book on the current and future research and endeavours about digital design of the environment and visual communications.

Thank you to my former students Jordan Martin and Justin Miron for their assistance and time. I would like to especially acknowledge Nadia D'Agnone for her time, dedication and efforts in producing additional research, reviewing the work and overall assistance. I am also grateful for the compelling foreword provided by George Hargreaves, which sets the tone of the overall discussion of the book, and to Alan Lewis for the continual back-and-forth discussion on the topic of digital design in the profession. I would like to thank my colleagues at the University of Guelph and the University of Toronto, my team at DataAppeal and Carlo for the ongoing discussions on the digital-design trends in landscape architectural practices. I would like to especially thank Lucas Dietrich, Elain McAlpine, Adélia Sabatini, and the team at Thames & Hudson who have made this publication a reality. And thanks to my future design innovators – Vincent, Jacob, Monica, John, Julia, Daniel, Michael, Alex, Julia, Isabella, Alyssa, Sofia, Siena, Giuliano and Serena – who are growing up in the digital world, and embrace the digital platform as a positive medium for design experimentation.

Finally, I am grateful to my parents, my family and close friends for their ongoing support, and to Haim, for his devotion and patience, which has made this publication process a rewarding experience.